taste of home
fast FIXES
WITH mixes

NEW EDITION

taste of home
BOOKS

REIMAN MEDIA GROUP, LLC • GREENDALE, WI

taste of home · Reader's Digest

A TASTE OF HOME/READER'S DIGEST BOOK
©2012 Reiman Media Group, LLC
5400 S. 60th St., Greendale WI 53129
All rights reserved.

Taste of Home and Reader's Digest are registered
trademarks of The Reader's Digest Association, Inc.

Editor-in-Chief: Catherine Cassidy

Vice President, Executive Editor/Books:
Heidi Reuter Lloyd

Creative Director: Howard Greenberg

North American Chief Marketing Officer:
Lisa Karpinski

Food Director: Diane Werner, RD

Senior Editor/Retail Books: Faithann Stoner

Editor: Sara Rae Lancaster

Associate Creative Director: Edwin Robles Jr.

Layout Designer: Catherine Fletcher

Project Art Director: Holly Patch

Content Production Manager: Julie Wagner

Copy Chief: Deb Warlaumont Mulvey

Proofreader: Victoria Soukup Jensen

Recipe Asset System Manager: Coleen Martin

Recipe Testing & Editing: Taste of Home Test Kitchen

Food Photography: Taste of Home Photo Studio

Administrative Assistant: Barb Czysz

The Reader's Digest Association, Inc.

President and Chief Executive Officer: Robert E. Guth

President, North America: Dan Lagani

President/Publisher, Trade Publishing: Harold Clarke

Associate Publisher: Rosanne McManus

Vice President, Sales & Marketing: Stacey Ashton

"Cooking, Caring, Sharing" is a registered
trademark of Reiman Media Group, LLC.

For other Taste of Home books and products,
visit us at **tasteofhome.com.**

For more Reader's Digest products and information,
visit **rd.com** (in the United States)
or see **rd.ca** (in Canada).

International Standard Book Number
(10): 0-89821-964-7
International Standard Book Number
(13): 978-0-89821-964-7
Library of Congress Control Number: 2011943074

Cover Photography

Photographer: Lori Foy
Food Stylist: Kaitlyn Besasie
Set Stylist: Melissa Haberman

Pictured on front cover:
Hot Berries 'n' Brownie Ice Cream Cake, page 186

Pictured on back cover: Lasagna in a Bun, page 94;
Holiday Brunch Casserole, page 32;
Dreamy Creamy Peanut Butter Pie, page 212.

Printed in China.
1 3 5 7 9 10 8 6 4 2

Contents

Cooking with *Mixes*

With the hectic schedules so many families have these days, it's difficult to serve a sit-down meal night after night. But with the **help of prepared mixes**, you can whip up a home-style meal in minutes. The secret is that the mixes **provide shortcuts** that reduce prep time **without sacrificing taste!**

In *Taste of Home Fast Fixes with Mixes*, you'll discover **314 time-saving recipes** created by the readers of *Taste of Home*, the #1 food and entertaining magazine in the world. You won't have to search high and low for these **flavorful mixes**...some may **already be in your kitchen**, waiting to enhance a meal. For example, savory dishes make use of taco seasoning, Italian and ranch salad dressing mixes, or pasta and potato mixes. Desserts use cake and pudding mixes as well as flavored gelatin. All you need to do is **add a few items**, and dinner is started. **You'll be out of the kitchen in no time**!

LOOK INSIDE — Here is what you'll find in the chapters that follow:

Breakfast & Brunch starts the day off with a filling meal without making you rise and shine at an earlier hour. You can serve up Eggs Benedict Cups or Bacon and Cheese Waffles.

Main Dishes provides you with family-pleasing choices for beef, pork, poultry and seafood. Choose from Slow Cooker Sloppy Joes, Chicken Marsala with Pasta or Puffed Pizza Casserole.

Salads & Side Dishes, Soups and Breads rounds out dinner with delicious extras, such as Creamy Italian Noodles, Simple Taco Soup or Zucchini Cheddar Biscuits.

Cakes, Cookies & Bars and More Sweet Treats make a delightful ending to suppertime. Satisfy your sweet tooth with such desserts as Pecan Butterscotch Cookies, Raspberry Oatmeal Bars or Candy Bar Brownie Trifle.

Snacks & Beverages are wonderful for after-school munchies, casual get-togethers or just for nighttime snacking. Ranch Pretzels, Pepperoni Pinwheels or Coconut Fruit Dip are sure to satisfy your snackin' craving.

With *Taste of Home Fast Fixes with Mixes*, you won't have to **resort to a dash through the drive-thru**. It's **never been easier** to put **fast, fabulous food** on the table **in a flash**!

Snacks & Beverages

LASAGNA PIZZA, PG. 7

TACO DIP

Prep/Total Time: 10 min.

I've made this tried-and-true recipe more times than I can count! It looks very colorful on the table and never fails to get gobbled up by guests of all ages.

Rhonda Biancardi // Blaine, Minnesota

- 1 package (8 ounces) cream cheese, softened
- 1 cup (8 ounces) sour cream
- 1 carton (8 ounces) French onion dip
- 1 envelope taco seasoning
- 4 cups shredded lettuce
- 2 cups (8 ounces) shredded cheddar cheese
- 1-1/2 cups chopped tomatoes
- Tortilla chips

1 In a large bowl, beat the cream cheese, sour cream, onion dip and taco seasoning until blended. Spread onto a 12-in. round serving platter. Top with lettuce, cheese and tomatoes. Serve with tortilla chips. **YIELD:** 10-12 servings.

SEEDING A TOMATO

To seed a tomato, cut in half horizontally and remove the stem. Holding a tomato half over a bowl or sink, scrape out seeds with a small spoon or squeeze the tomato to force out the seeds. Then slice or dice as directed in the recipe. —*Taste of Home Test Kitchen*

The tangy combination of lemonade and cranberry juice in this recipe is a real thirst-quencher on warm days. Plus, the recipe can easily be doubled or tripled if you're hosting a gathering and have to serve a larger group.

Margaret O'Bryon // Bel Air, Maryland

LEMON-BERRY PITCHER PUNCH

Prep/Total Time: 10 min.

    1/2 cup sweetened lemonade drink mix
      4 cups cold water
    2/3 cup cranberry juice, chilled
  1-1/2 cups lemon-lime soda, chilled

1 In a pitcher, combine the drink mix, water and cranberry juice. Stir in soda. Serve immediately. **YIELD:** about 6 cups.

LASAGNA PIZZA

Prep: 20 min. **Bake:** 25 min.

Do you like lasagna but not the time it takes to make? These savory squares quickly capture the fabulous flavor by relying on handy hot roll and spaghetti sauce mixes.

Angie Dierikx // Taylor Ridge, Illinois

      1 pound lean ground beef (90% lean)
      1 can (8 ounces) tomato sauce
    1/4 cup water
      1 envelope spaghetti sauce mix, *divided*
      1 package (16 ounces) hot roll mix
      1 cup warm water (120° to 130°)
  1-1/2 cups (12 ounces) 4% cottage cheese
    1/4 cup shredded Parmesan cheese
      1 cup (4 ounces) shredded part-skim
         mozzarella cheese

1 In a large skillet, cook beef over medium heat until no longer pink; drain. Stir in the tomato sauce, water and 3 tablespoons spaghetti sauce mix; heat through.

2 In a large bowl, combine contents of roll mix and yeast packets; add remaining spaghetti sauce mix. Stir in warm water until dough pulls away from sides of bowl. Turn onto a lightly floured surface; knead until smooth and elastic, about 5 minutes.

3 Roll into a 17-in. x 12-in. rectangle. Transfer to a greased 15-in. x 10-in. x 1-in. baking pan; build up edges slightly. Spread cottage cheese over dough. Top with meat mixture and Parmesan cheese.

4 Bake at 400° for 20 minutes or until bubbly. Sprinkle with mozzarella cheese. Bake 5 minutes longer or until cheese is melted. Let stand for 5 minutes before serving. **YIELD:** 12-15 servings.

If you're looking for a refreshing drink, I can guarantee that you'll find it in an orange frost. This tasty drink is so fast to whip up in the blender.

Karen Radford // Seattle, Washington

FROSTY ORANGE DRINK

Prep/Total Time: 15 min.

- 1 cup water
- 1 cup 2% milk
- 1/2 cup orange breakfast drink mix
- 1/2 cup sugar
- 1 teaspoon vanilla extract
- 10 to 12 ice cubes

1 In a blender, combine water, milk, drink mix, sugar, vanilla extract and ice. Cover and process until blended. Serve immediately. **YIELD:** 4 servings.

RANCH PRETZELS

Prep: 5 min. **Bake:** 1 hour

For a fast, fun snack, start with plain pretzels and add a new taste twist by coating them with simple seasonings and popping them into the oven to bake.

Lois Kerns // Hagerstown, Maryland

- 1 package (20 ounces) large thick pretzels
- 1 envelope ranch salad dressing mix
- 3/4 cup canola oil
- 1-1/2 teaspoons dill weed
- 1-1/2 teaspoons garlic powder

1 Break pretzels into bite-size pieces and place in a large bowl. Combine remaining ingredients; pour over pretzels. Stir to coat.

2 Pour into an ungreased 15-in. x 10-in. x 1-in. baking pan. Bake at 200° for 1 hour, stirring every 15 minutes. **YIELD:** 12 cups.

PARTY MIX MAKEOVER

I use leftover savory party mix (made with cereal, pretzels, bagel chips, etc.) in salads in place of croutons. —Bill W., McConnellsburg, Pennsylvania

BEAR'S PICNIC VEGGIE DIP

Prep: 5 min. + chilling

I served this delicious dip alongside a colorful array of vegetables at a teddy bear theme party I hosted years ago. Now it's a popular appetizer with family and friends no matter the occasion.

Susan Schuller // Brainerd, Minnesota

- 1 cup mayonnaise
- 1 cup (8 ounces) sour cream
- 1 package (1.7 ounces) vegetable soup mix
- 1 package (10 ounces) frozen chopped spinach, thawed and squeezed dry
- 1 can (8 ounces) water chestnuts, drained and chopped

Assorted fresh vegetables

1 In a large bowl, combine the mayonnaise, sour cream and soup mix. Stir in spinach and water chestnuts. Cover and refrigerate for at least 2 hours. Serve with vegetables. **YIELD:** 3 cups.

DRESSED-UP CARROTS

To dress up a tray of veggies and dip, I make holes in the stem ends of baby carrots and insert sprigs of fresh parsley. People always ask, are they really tiny carrots? —Jean C., Lago Vista, Texas

PEPPERONI PINWHEELS

Prep/Total Time: 25 min.

- 1 package (8 ounces) cream cheese, softened
- 1 package (3-1/2 ounces) sliced pepperoni, finely chopped
- 1 cup (4 ounces) shredded provolone cheese
- 2 tablespoons onion soup mix
- 2 tablespoons sour cream
- 1 teaspoon grated Romano cheese
- 2 tubes (13.8 ounces *each*) refrigerated pizza crust

1 In a small bowl, combine the first six ingredients. Unroll each tube of pizza dough into a long rectangle; spread each rectangle evenly with 1 cup pepperoni mixture.

2 Roll up jelly-roll style, starting with a short side; pinch seam to seal. Cut each roll into 16 slices; place cut side down on ungreased baking sheets.

3 Bake at 400° for 10-14 minutes or until golden brown. Serve warm. Refrigerate any leftovers.
YIELD: 32 appetizers.

LEMON ICE TEA MIX PICTURED ON RIGHT

Prep/Total Time: 5 min.

A friend who has a large family and does a lot of entertaining created this wallet-friendly mix that makes five batches of refreshing lemon-flavored tea.
Linda Fox // Soldotna, Alaska

7-1/2 cups sugar
   2 cups unsweetened instant tea
   5 envelopes (.23 ounce *each*) unsweetened lemonade soft drink mix
ADDITIONAL INGREDIENTS:
   1 cup warm water
Cold water

1 In a large bowl, combine the sugar, tea and drink mix. Divide into five equal batches; store in airtight containers in a cool dry place for up to 6 months.
YIELD: 5 batches (8-1/2 cups total).

2 TO PREPARE TEA: Dissolve about 1-2/3 cups tea mix in 1 cup warm water. Place in a gallon container. Add cold water to measure 1 gallon. Cover and refrigerate.
YIELD: about 16 (1-cup) servings per batch.

BACON CHEESEBURGER BALLS

Prep: 25 min. **Cook:** 10 min.

When I serve these, my husband and sons are often fooled into thinking we're having plain meatballs until they cut into the flavorful filling inside.

Cathy Lendvoy // Boharm, Saskatchewan

1 egg
1 envelope onion soup mix
1 pound ground beef
2 tablespoons all-purpose flour
2 tablespoons 2% milk
1 cup (4 ounces) shredded cheddar cheese
4 bacon strips, cooked and crumbled

COATING:

2 eggs
1 cup crushed saltines (about 30 crackers)
5 tablespoons canola oil

1 In a large bowl, combine egg and soup mix. Crumble beef over mixture and mix well. Divide into 36 portions; set aside. In another large bowl, combine the flour and milk until smooth. Add cheese and bacon; mix well.

2 Shape cheese mixture into 36 balls. Shape one beef portion around each cheese ball. In a shallow bowl, beat eggs. Place cracker crumbs in another bowl. Dip meatballs into egg, then coat with crumbs.

3 In a skillet, cook meatballs over medium heat in oil for 10-12 minutes or until the meat is no longer pink and coating is golden brown. **YIELD:** 3 dozen.

These jazzed-up oyster crackers have such great flavor, we bet you'll have trouble not eating them all at once! With Parmesan cheese and seasoning from a soup mix, they're a sure-fire hit.

Taste of Home Test Kitchen

FLAVORED OYSTER CRACKERS

Prep/Total Time: 25 min.

    2 packages (10 ounces *each*) oyster crackers
1/2 cup canola oil
1/4 cup grated Parmesan cheese
    1 envelope savory herb with garlic soup mix

1 Place the crackers in a large bowl. Combine the oil, cheese and soup mix; pour over crackers and toss gently. Transfer to two ungreased 15-in. x 10-in. x 1-in. baking pans.

2 Bake at 350° for 5-7 minutes, stirring once. Cool. Store in an airtight container. **YIELD:** 12 cups.

FRIENDSHIP TEA MIX

Prep/Total Time: 5 min.

I combine seven simple ingredients to make a big batch of this hot spiced drink mix. Placed in a jar and tied with pretty ribbon, it is one of my favorite gifts for neighbors.

Arma White // Golconda, Illinois

    1 jar (21.1 ounces) orange breakfast drink mix
    1 cup sugar
1/2 cup sweetened lemonade drink mix
1/2 cup unsweetened instant tea
    1 package (3 ounces) apricot gelatin
2-1/2 teaspoons ground cinnamon
    1 teaspoon ground cloves
ADDITIONAL INGREDIENTS:
    1 cup boiling water

1 In a large bowl, combine the first seven ingredients. Store in an airtight container in a cool dry place for up to 6 months. **YIELD:** 50 batches (about 5 cups total).

2 **TO PREPARE 1 CUP OF TEA:** Dissolve 4-1/2 teaspoons tea mix in boiling water; stir well. **YIELD:** 1 serving.

SUGAR SUBSTITUTES

Not only does sugar impart sweet flavor to foods, but it also plays an important role in baked goods, affecting the volume, texture and browning of foods as they bake. There are some foods in which no-calorie sweeteners (such as Equal and Sweet 'n' Low) work well. For example, they're fine for sweetening drinks, like smoothies, or other foods that contain a fair amount of liquid, like puddings and pie fillings. —Taste of Home Test Kitchen

Kids love this refreshing punch. Sweet sherbet, fruity soft drink mix and orange juice concentrate make this beverage a popular way to beat the heat on summer days.

Margaret Bossuot //
Carthage, New York

KOOL-AID FLOATS
Prep/Total Time: 30 min.

    3 envelopes unsweetened strawberry Kool-Aid
    3 cups sugar
    6 quarts cold water
    1 can (12 ounces) frozen orange juice
       concentrate, thawed
    1 liter ginger ale, chilled
    1 quart raspberry *or* orange sherbet

1 In large pitchers, prepare Kool-Aid with sugar and water according to package directions. Stir in orange juice concentrate. Just before serving, add ginger ale. Serve in chilled tall glasses. Add a scoop of sherbet to each glass. **YIELD:** 2 gallons.

NO-BAKE PARTY MIX
Prep/Total Time: 15 min.

This munchable snack is sure to disappear in a hurry at picnics and parties. A packet of ranch salad dressing mix makes it a breeze to throw together on a moment's notice.

Regina Stock // Topeka, Kansas

    8 cups Crispix
2-1/2 cups miniature pretzels *or* pretzel sticks
2-1/2 cups miniature cheese crackers
    3 tablespoons canola oil
    1 envelope ranch salad dressing mix

1 In a heavy-duty resealable 2-gal. plastic bag, combine the cereal, pretzels and crackers; drizzle with oil. Seal and toss gently to mix. Sprinkle with dressing mix; seal and toss until well-coated. Store in an airtight container. **YIELD:** about 12 cups.

COCONUT FRUIT DIP

Prep/Total Time: 10 min.

I usually serve this dip with melon slices, strawberries and grapes, but you could use whatever fruit you have on hand.

Nancy Tanguay // Lakeville, Massachusetts

- 1 can (8 ounces) crushed unsweetened pineapple, undrained
- 3/4 cup fat-free milk
- 1/2 cup (4 ounces) fat-free sour cream
- 3/4 teaspoon coconut extract
- 1 package (3.4 ounces) instant vanilla pudding mix

Fresh pineapple, grapes and strawberries *or* other fruit

1 In a blender, combine the first five ingredients; cover and process for 1 minute or until smooth. Serve dip with fresh fruit. Store in the refrigerator.
YIELD: 2 cups.

INSTANT PUDDING MIX

Our Test Kitchen has found that it can be very difficult to replace regular instant pudding mix with sugar-free instant pudding mix. The sugar-free variety does not have the same consistency nor does it set up like regular instant pudding. It also provides less bulk to a recipe. For these reasons, we don't recommend using sugar-free instant pudding as a substitute. —Taste of Home Test Kitchen

BERRY SLUSH

Prep: 10 min. + freezing

This make-ahead punch is perfect to serve when hosting a party for a crowd. For a festive touch, garnish with any fresh fruit of your choice.

Ruth Seitz // Columbus Junction, Iowa

- 1 package (3 ounces) berry blue *or* raspberry gelatin
- 2 cups boiling water
- 2 cups sugar
- 1 can (46 ounces) pineapple juice
- 2 liters ginger ale
- 4-1/2 cups cold water
- 1 cup lemon juice
- Blue *or* red liquid food coloring, optional
- Fresh raspberries, blueberries and star fruit, optional

1 In a large container, dissolve gelatin in boiling water; stir in sugar until dissolved. Add the pineapple juice, ginger ale, water and lemon juice. Add food coloring if desired. Freeze for 8 hours or overnight.

2 Remove from freezer 20 minutes before serving. Stir until mixture is slushy. Serve in a chilled glass. For garnish, thread fruit on wooden skewers if desired. Serve immediately **YIELD:** 5 quarts.

I first sampled this warming beverage on a camping trip in the mountains. It was a wonderful treat on crisp mornings.

Ruby Gibson //
Newton, North Carolina

HOT COCOA MIX
Prep/Total Time: 15 min.

6-2/3 cups nonfat dry milk powder
   1 cup instant chocolate drink mix
   1 package (5 ounces) cook-and-serve chocolate pudding mix
  1/2 cup confectioners' sugar
  1/2 cup powdered nondairy creamer
  1/2 cup baking cocoa
ADDITIONAL INGREDIENTS:
   1 cup boiling water
Miniature marshmallows, optional

1 In a large bowl, combine the first six ingredients. Store in an airtight container in a cool dry place for up to 3 months. **YIELD:** 21 batches (about 7 cups total).

2 **TO PREPARE HOT COCOA:** Be sure to stir the mix well before measuring. Dissolve 1/3 cup cocoa mix in boiling water. Top with miniature marshmallows if desired. **YIELD:** 1 serving per batch.

CUCUMBER SANDWICHES
Prep/Total Time: 15 min.

I was introduced to a similar sandwich by a friend many years ago. For a change of pace, I sometimes add thinly sliced onions on top.
Karen Schriefer // Stevensville, Maryland

   1 carton (8 ounces) spreadable cream cheese
   2 teaspoons ranch salad dressing mix
  12 slices pumpernickel rye bread
   2 to 3 medium cucumbers

1 In a large bowl, combine cream cheese and dressing mix. Spread on one side of each slice of bread. Peel cucumbers if desired; thinly slice and place on six slices of bread. Top with remaining bread. Serve immediately. **YIELD:** 6 servings.

FRESH CUCUMBERS

I've discovered a great way to keep cucumbers fresh longer. I have a plastic lettuce keeper that keeps my lettuce fresh for at least 2 weeks. So I bought another one and placed six cucumbers in it. Amazingly, they didn't get soft spots and stayed fresh and crisp for almost 2 weeks, too. I think this would work with almost any veggie.
—Noreen H., Walton, Kentucky

My husband and his friends would often buy a similar version of this creamy, vanilla-flavored beverage at a nearby coffee house. One day, I decided to make my own, and this smooth sensation was the result.

Heather Kunkel //
Wellsville, New York

CREAMY VANILLA COFFEE

Prep/Total Time: 10 min.

1/3 cup ground coffee
1 cup water
1/4 cup sugar
2 tablespoons instant vanilla pudding mix
2-1/2 cups 2% milk

1 Place ground coffee in the coffee filter of a drip coffeemaker. Add water; brew according to manufacturer's directions.

2 In a small bowl, combine sugar and dry pudding mix. Stir in milk and coffee. Chill until serving. **YIELD:** 3 servings.

Breakfast & Brunch

EGGS BENEDICT CUPS, PG. 21

TACO QUICHE

Prep: 25 min. **Bake:** 20 min.

This is the dish I take most often to potlucks, and the pan comes home empty every time. It's a stick-to-your-ribs casserole that has the taco taste everyone loves.

Kim Stoller // Smithville, Ohio

  2 pounds ground beef
  2 envelopes taco seasoning
  4 eggs
3/4 cup 2% milk
1-1/4 cups biscuit/baking mix
Dash pepper
  1/2 cup sour cream
  2 to 3 cups chopped lettuce
3/4 cup chopped tomato
1/4 cup chopped green pepper
1/4 cup chopped green onions
  2 cups (8 ounces) shredded cheddar cheese

1 In a skillet, cook beef over medium heat until no longer pink; drain. Add taco seasoning and prepare according to the package directions. Spoon meat into a greased 13-in. x 9-in. baking dish.

2 In a large bowl, beat eggs and milk. Stir in biscuit mix and pepper. Pour over meat.

3 Bake, uncovered, at 400° for 20-25 minutes or until a thermometer reads 160°. Let quiche cool 5-10 minutes.

4 Spread sour cream over the top; sprinkle with lettuce, tomato, green pepper, onions and cheese. **YIELD:** 8 servings.

Club soda gives these crisp waffles a light, fluffy texture. With only four ingredients, homemade waffles can't get much easier than this!

Taste of Home Test Kitchen

LIGHT 'N' CRISPY WAFFLES

Prep/Total Time: 20 min.

  2 cups biscuit/baking mix
  2 eggs, lightly beaten
1/2 cup canola oil
  1 cup club soda

1 In a large bowl, combine the biscuit mix, eggs and oil. Add club soda and stir until smooth.

2 Bake in a preheated waffle iron according to manufacturer's directions until golden brown. **YIELD:** 12 waffles.

EGGS BENEDICT CUPS

Prep: 15 min. **Bake:** 20 min.

Here's a scrumptious way to jump start winter mornings. I use the leftover Hollandaise sauce from this savory breakfast treat to dress up broccoli at night.

Jennifer Reisinger // Sheboygan, Wisconsin

  2 slices white bread
1/3 cup shredded cheddar cheese
  1 green onion, chopped
  2 slices Canadian bacon, finely chopped
1/4 teaspoon garlic powder
1/4 teaspoon minced fresh basil
  2 eggs, lightly beaten
  2 tablespoons butter
  2 tablespoons plus 2 teaspoons hollandaise
    sauce mix
1/2 cup water
Minced fresh parsley

1 Coat two 8-oz. ramekins or custard cups with cooking spray; line each with a slice of bread. Layer with cheese, onion, Canadian bacon, garlic powder and basil. Pour eggs into cups.

2 Place on a baking sheet. Bake at 350° for 20-25 minutes or until a thermometer reads 160°.

3 In a small saucepan, melt butter. Whisk in sauce mix; gradually stir in water. Bring to a boil; cook and stir for 1 minute or until thickened. Gently remove bread cups to serving plates; serve with hollandaise sauce and parsley. **YIELD:** 2 servings.

I serve these yummy frosted rolls warm from the oven as a Christmas morning treat at our house. Even if you are not accustomed to working with yeast dough, you'll find this dough is easy to handle.

Julie Sterchi // Harrisburg, Illinois

CINNAMON ROLLS

Prep: 30 min. + rising **Bake:** 10 min. + cooling

    5 to 6 cups all-purpose flour
    1 package (18-1/4 ounces) yellow cake mix
    2 packages (1/4 ounce *each*) quick-rise yeast
2-1/2 cups warm water (120° to 130°)
    1/4 cup butter, melted
    1/2 cup sugar
    1 teaspoon ground cinnamon
FROSTING:
    6 tablespoons butter, softened
    3 cups confectioners' sugar
1-1/2 teaspoons vanilla extract
    2 to 3 tablespoons 2% milk

YEAST BREADS

For better yeast breads use aluminum pans with a dull rather than shiny or dark finish. Glass baking dishes and dark finishes will produce darker crusts. Leave at least 1 in. of space between pans and between pans and sides of oven for air circulation.
—Taste of Home Test Kitchen

1 In a large bowl, combine 4 cups flour, cake mix, yeast and warm water until smooth. Add enough remaining flour to form a soft dough.

2 Turn onto a lightly floured surface; knead until smooth and elastic, about 5 minutes. Place in a greased bowl, turning once to grease top. Cover and let rise until doubled, about 45 minutes.

3 Punch dough down. Turn onto a lightly floured surface; divide in half. Roll each portion into a 14-in. x 10-in. rectangle. Brush with butter; sprinkle with sugar and cinnamon.

4 Roll up jelly-roll style, starting with a long side. Cut each roll into 12 slices; place cut side down in two greased 13-in. x 9-in. baking pans. Cover and let rise until almost doubled, about 20 minutes.

5 Bake at 400° for 10-15 minutes or until golden brown. Cool for 20 minutes. For frosting, in a large bowl, cream the butter, confectioners' sugar and vanilla and enough milk to achieve desired consistency. Frost warm rolls. **YIELD:** 2 dozen.

BACON AND CHEESE WAFFLES

Prep/Total Time: 20 min.

Pancake mix gives a jump-start to this hearty hurry-up breakfast. Including bacon and cheese in the waffle batter gives an all-in-one breakfast flavor. Freeze extras to reheat another day.

MarGenne Rowley // Oasis, Utah

2 cups pancake *or* biscuit/baking mix
1 egg
1 cup 2% milk
1 cup (8 ounces) sour cream
1 tablespoon butter, melted
6 to 8 bacon strips, cooked and crumbled
1 cup (4 ounces) shredded cheddar cheese

1 Place pancake mix in a large bowl. In another bowl, whisk the egg, milk, sour cream and butter. Stir into pancake mix until blended. Fold in bacon and cheese.

2 Bake in a preheated waffle iron according to manufacturer's directions until golden brown. **YIELD:** 12 waffles (4-inch square).

People are always surprised when I tell them there are only four ingredients in these tasty bite-size puffs. Cheesy and spicy, the golden morsels are a fun novelty at a breakfast or brunch, and they also make yummy party appetizers.
Della Moore // Troy, New York

SAUSAGE CHEESE PUFFS

Prep/Total Time: 25 min.

   1 pound bulk Italian sausage
   3 cups biscuit/baking mix
   4 cups (16 ounces) shredded cheddar cheese
3/4 cup water

1 In a large skillet, cook sausage over medium heat until no longer pink; drain.

2 In a large bowl, combine biscuit mix and cheese; stir in sausage. Add water and toss with a fork until moistened. Shape into 1-1/2-in. balls. Place 2 in. apart on ungreased baking sheets.

3 Bake at 400° for 12-15 minutes or until puffed and golden brown. Cool on wire racks. **YIELD:** about 4 dozen.

BANANA CHIP PANCAKES   PICTURED ON RIGHT

Prep/Total Time: 30 min.

Perfect for weekends or a birthday-morning special, these fluffy pancakes can be flavor-adjusted to your heart's content! One of my kids eats the plain banana pancakes, another likes just chocolate chips added and a third one goes for the works.
Christeen Przepioski // Newark, California

   2 cups biscuit/baking mix
   1 egg
   1 cup milk
   1 cup mashed ripe bananas
3/4 cup swirled milk chocolate and
     peanut butter chips
Maple syrup and additional swirled milk chocolate
     and peanut butter chips, optional

1 Place biscuit mix in a large bowl. Combine the egg, milk and bananas; stir into biscuit mix just until moistened. Stir in chips.

2 Pour batter by 1/4 cupfuls onto a greased hot griddle; turn when bubbles form on top. Cook until the second side is golden brown. Serve with syrup and additional chips if desired. **YIELD:** 12 pancakes.

BANANA-NUT CORN BREAD

Prep: 10 min. **Bake:** 35 min. + cooling

A boxed corn bread mix gets a fabulous treatment when it's dressed up with bananas and chopped walnuts. The moist golden loaves are a great addition to a brunch buffet or bake sale.

Janice France // Depauw, Indiana

- 2 packages (8-1/2 ounces *each*) corn bread/muffin mix
- 1 cup mashed ripe bananas (about 2 medium)
- 1 cup chopped walnuts
- 1 cup 2% milk

1 In a bowl, combine all ingredients just until blended. Spoon into two greased 8-in. x 4-in. loaf pans.

2 Bake at 350° for 35-40 minutes or until a toothpick inserted near the center comes out clean. Cool for 10 minutes before removing from pans to wire racks to cool completely. **YIELD:** 2 loaves (16 slices each).

Make a memorable morning or late-night meal with this special dish. Cool and creamy avocado tames the jalapeno perfectly.
**Laura Denney //
Redondo Beach, California**

EGGS BENEDICT WITH JALAPENO HOLLANDAISE

Prep: 20 min. **Bake:** 40 min. + cooling

- 1 tablespoon white vinegar
- 4 eggs
- 1/4 cup butter, cubed
- 1 cup milk
- 1 package hollandaise sauce mix
- 2 tablespoons chopped seeded jalapeno pepper
- 2 English muffins, split and toasted
- 4 slices Canadian bacon, warmed
- 4 slices tomato
- 1 medium ripe avocado, peeled and sliced

1 Place 2-3 in. of water in a large skillet with high sides; add vinegar. Bring to a boil. Reduce heat; simmer gently. Break cold eggs, one at a time, into a custard cup or saucer. Holding cup close to the surface, slip each egg into water. Cook, uncovered, until whites are completely set and yolks begin to thicken (but are not hard), about 4-5 minutes.

2 Meanwhile, in a small saucepan, melt butter over medium heat. Whisk in milk and sauce mix. Bring to a boil. Reduce heat; simmer, uncovered, for 1 minute or until thickened. Stir in jalapeno. Set aside and keep warm.

3 With a slotted spoon, lift each egg out of the water. On each muffin half, layer the Canadian bacon, tomato, avocado and an egg; spoon sauce over tops. Serve immediately. **YIELD:** 4 servings.

SAUSAGE BRUNCH MUFFINS

Prep: 20 min. **Bake:** 20 min.

You'll enjoy these sausage-filled muffins for both weekend brunches and breakfasts on the run.
Beverly Borges // Rockland, Massachusetts

- 1 pound bulk pork sausage
- 4 cups biscuit/baking mix
- 3/4 cup 2% milk
- 1/2 cup water
- 1 can (4 ounces) diced green chilies, undrained
- 1 egg, lightly beaten
- 1 can (11 ounces) whole kernel corn, drained

1 In a large skillet over medium heat, brown sausage until no longer pink. Drain and set aside. In a large bowl, combine the biscuit mix, milk, water, chilies and egg. Stir in the corn and sausage.

2 Fill greased or paper-lined muffin cups two-thirds full. Bake at 425° for 16-18 minutes or until a toothpick inserted near the center comes out clean. Cool for 5 minutes; remove from pan to a wire rack. Serve warm. **YIELD:** 2 dozen.

With four small children, I am always looking for simple, quick and tasty recipes that they'll enjoy. They love pancakes, and these are great with breakfast sausage. I usually double or triple the recipe, depending on how hungry they are.

Megan Schwartz // Burbank, Ohio

PUMPKIN PANCAKES

Prep: 20 min. **Bake:** 40 min. + cooling

  1 cup complete buttermilk pancake mix
1/2 teaspoon ground cinnamon
1/8 teaspoon ground ginger
2/3 cup cold water
1/3 cup canned pumpkin
  1 cup maple syrup, warmed
1/4 cup chopped pecans, toasted

1 In a large bowl, combine the pancake mix, cinnamon and ginger. In a small bowl, whisk water and pumpkin until blended; stir into dry ingredients just until moistened.

2 Pour batter by 1/4 cupfuls onto a hot griddle coated with cooking spray. Flatten with back of spoon. When underside is browned, turn pancakes and cook until second side is browned. Top with syrup and pecans. **YIELD:** 6 pancakes.

MINI HAM QUICHES

Prep: 15 min. **Bake:** 20 min.

These adorable quiches are delightful for an after-church brunch when you don't want to fuss. Replace the ham with bacon, sausage, chicken or shrimp, or substitute chopped onion, red pepper or zucchini for the olives if you like.

Marilou Robinson // Portland, Oregon

3/4 cup diced fully cooked ham
1/2 cup shredded sharp cheddar cheese
1/2 cup chopped ripe olives
  3 eggs, lightly beaten
  1 cup half-and-half cream
1/4 cup butter, melted
  3 drops hot pepper sauce
1/2 cup biscuit/baking mix
  2 tablespoons grated Parmesan cheese
1/2 teaspoon ground mustard

1 In a large bowl, combine the ham, cheddar cheese and olives; divide among 12 greased muffin cups. In another bowl, combine the remaining ingredients just until blended.

2 Pour over ham mixture. Bake at 375° for 20-25 minutes or until a knife inserted near the center comes out clean. Let stand for 5 minutes before serving. **YIELD:** 1 dozen.

USING EGG SUBSTITUTE

People who are watching their cholesterol often prefer to use egg substitute instead of whole eggs. It can be used to replace whole eggs in many recipes with good results, especially in frittatas, omelets and quiches or for coating purposes (such as breading chicken breasts).
—Taste of Home Test Kitchen

RASPBERRY COFFEE CAKE

Prep: 15 min. + cooling **Bake:** 35 min.

Raspberries are abundant at our summer home nearby Aziscohos Lake. So I developed this recipe to share the bounty with our guests. The pretty crumb-topped cake's fruity flavor really shines through.

Marian Cummings // West Paris, Maine

- 1 cup plus 3 tablespoons sugar, *divided*
- 1/4 cup cornstarch
- 3 cups fresh *or* frozen unsweetened raspberries
- 2 cups biscuit/baking mix
- 2/3 cup 2% milk
- 2 eggs
- 2 tablespoons canola oil

TOPPING:

- 1 package (3.4 ounces) instant vanilla pudding mix
- 1/2 cup sugar
- 1/4 cup cold butter, cubed

1 In a large saucepan, combine 1 cup of sugar and cornstarch. Add raspberries; bring to a boil over medium heat. Boil for 2 minutes, stirring constantly. Remove from the heat; allow to cool.

2 Meanwhile, in a large bowl, combine the biscuit mix, milk, eggs, oil and remaining sugar. Spread two-thirds of the batter into a greased 13-in. x 9-in. baking pan. Spread with raspberry mixture. Spoon remaining batter over top.

3 For topping, combine pudding mix and sugar. Cut in butter until crumbly; sprinkle over batter. Bake at 350° for 35-40 minutes. **YIELD:** 12 servings.

PEANUT BUTTER PANCAKES

Prep/Total Time: 15 min.

*Pancakes are one of my husband's specialties.
So it's not unusual for him to wake me with those
hot-from-the griddle cakes that get their delicious
difference from peanut butter.*

Dorothy Pritchett // Wills Point, Texas

- 1 cup pancake mix
- 2 tablespoons sugar
- 1 egg
- 1/3 cup peanut butter
- 1 can (5 ounces) evaporated milk
- 1/3 cup water

HONEY BUTTER:
- 1/4 cup butter, softened
- 2 tablespoons honey

1 In a large bowl, combine pancake mix and sugar. In a small bowl, beat egg and peanut butter; add milk and water. Stir into dry ingredients just until moistened.

2 Pour batter by 1/4 cupfuls onto a lightly greased medium-hot griddle. Turn when bubbles form on top of pancakes; cook until second side is golden brown. In a small bowl, combine honey butter ingredients. Serve honey butter with pancakes.
YIELD: 10 pancakes.

EDITOR'S NOTE: Reduced-fat or generic brands of peanut butter are not recommended for this recipe.

I like to linger over a cup of coffee and a warm sweet treat on weekend mornings. These moist muffins are perfect because making them ties up so little time in the kitchen. I also serve them with holiday meals for something different.

Teresa Raab // Tustin, Michigan

SWEET RASPBERRY MUFFINS
Prep/Total Time: 30 min.

   2 cups biscuit/baking mix
   2 tablespoons sugar
  1/4 cup cold butter, cubed
  2/3 cup 2% milk
  1/4 cup raspberry jam
GLAZE:
  1/2 cup confectioners' sugar
   2 teaspoons warm water
  1/4 teaspoon vanilla extract

1 In a large bowl, combine biscuit mix and sugar. Cut in butter until the mixture resembles coarse crumbs. Stir in milk just until moistened (batter will be thick).

2 Spoon about 1 tablespoon of batter into 12 paper-lined muffin cups. Top with 1 teaspoon jam. Spoon the remaining batter (about 1 tablespoon each) over jam.

3 Bake at 425° for 12-14 minutes or until a toothpick inserted near the center comes out clean. Cool in pans for 5 minutes.

4 Meanwhile, in a small bowl, combine glaze ingredients until smooth. Remove muffins to a wire rack. Drizzle glaze over warm muffins. Serve warm. **YIELD:** 1 dozen.

BACON QUICHE
Prep: 10 min. **Bake:** 30 min. + standing

Enjoy the traditional flavor of a bacon quiche without the effort by preparing this quick version. Using baking mix means there's no need to fuss over a pastry crust.

Helen Hoppes // Wabash, Indiana

   3 eggs
1-1/2 cups 2% milk
  1/4 cup butter, melted
  1/2 cup biscuit/baking mix
Dash pepper
   8 bacon strips, cooked and crumbled
  3/4 cup shredded cheddar cheese

1 In a blender, combine the eggs, milk and butter. Add biscuit mix and pepper; cover and process for 15 seconds. Pour into a greased 9-in. pie plate. Top with bacon and cheese.

2 Bake at 350° for 30-35 minutes or until a knife inserted near the center comes out clean. Let stand for 10 minutes before cutting. **YIELD:** 6-8 servings.

For a quick breakfast, I make the crowd-pleasing pancake while I fix supper the night before, then cut it into squares. The next morning, I top them with butter and syrup before placing them in the microwave. This innovative way to make pancakes takes most of the fuss out of making breakfast.

Norna Detig // Lindenwood, Illinois

BAKED BLUEBERRY PANCAKE

Prep: 20 min. **Bake:** 40 min. + cooling

> 2 cups pancake mix
> 1-1/2 cups fat-free milk
> 1 egg
> 1 tablespoon canola oil
> 1 teaspoon ground cinnamon
> 1 cup fresh *or* frozen blueberries
> Butter and maple syrup

1 In a large bowl, combine the pancake mix, milk, egg, oil and cinnamon just until blended (batter will be lumpy). Fold in blueberries.

2 Spread into a greased 15-in. x 10-in. x 1-in. baking pan. Bake at 400° for 10-12 minutes or until golden brown. Serve with butter and syrup. **YIELD:** 6 servings.

HOLIDAY BRUNCH CASSEROLE PICTURED ON RIGHT

Prep: 15 min. + chilling
Bake: 30 min. + standing

If you'll be having overnight company during the holidays, you may want to consider this hearty casserole. Guests will be impressed with its bountiful filling and scrumptious flavor.

Nelda Cronbaugh // Belle Plaine, Iowa

> 4 cups frozen shredded hash brown potatoes
> 1 pound bulk pork sausage, cooked and drained
> 1/2 pound bacon strips, cooked and crumbled
> 1 medium green pepper, chopped
> 2 cups (8 ounces) shredded cheddar cheese, *divided*
> 1 green onion, chopped
> 1 cup reduced-fat biscuit/baking mix
> 1/2 teaspoon salt
> 4 eggs
> 3 cups 2% milk

1 In a large bowl, combine the hash browns, sausage, bacon, green pepper, 1 cup cheese and onion. Transfer to a greased 13-in. x 9-in. baking dish.

2 In another bowl, whisk the biscuit mix, salt, eggs and milk; pour over the top. Sprinkle with remaining cheese. Cover and refrigerate overnight.

3 Remove from the refrigerator 30 minutes before baking. Bake, uncovered, at 375° for 30-35 minutes or a knife inserted near the center comes out clean. Let stand for 10 minutes before cutting. **YIELD:** 12 servings.

This healthful recipe makes a lovely brunch bake or main dish for lunch. The cheese mix will convince anyone to eat their spinach. Plus it adds extra protein.

Betty B. Claycomb //
Alverton, Pennsylvania

BAKED SPINACH SUPREME

Prep: 20 min. **Bake:** 40 min. + cooling

      1 cup reduced-fat biscuit/baking mix
      2 egg whites
      1 egg
   1/4 cup fat-free milk
   1/4 cup finely chopped onion
FILLING:
      1 package (10 ounces) frozen chopped spinach,
          thawed and squeezed dry
1-1/2 cups fat-free cottage cheese
   3/4 cup shredded Monterey Jack cheese
   1/2 cup grated Parmesan cheese
      2 egg whites
      1 egg
      1 teaspoon dried minced onion

1 In a small bowl, combine the biscuit mix, egg whites, egg, milk and onion. Spread into a greased 11-in. x 7-in. baking dish.

2 In another bowl, combine the filling ingredients. Gently spoon over biscuit mixture.

3 Bake, uncovered, at 350° for 28-32 minutes or until golden brown and a knife inserted near the center comes out clean. **YIELD:** 6 servings.

MAPLE-BACON OVEN PANCAKE

Prep/Total Time: 25 min.

For years, my mother has served this tasty baked pancake as a main dish for dinner. But it's so quick and easy I like to make it for breakfast, too. Leftovers taste just as good the next morning warmed up in the microwave.

Kari Caven // Post Falls, Idaho

1-1/2 cups biscuit/baking mix
      1 tablespoon sugar
   3/4 cup 2% milk
      2 eggs
   1/4 cup maple syrup
1-1/2 cups (6 ounces) shredded cheddar
          cheese, *divided*
   1/2 pound sliced bacon, cooked and crumbled
Additional syrup, optional

1 In a large bowl, combine biscuit mix and sugar. In a small bowl, combine the milk, eggs, syrup and 1/2 cup cheese. Stir into dry ingredients just until moistened. Pour into a greased 13-in. x 9-in. baking dish.

2 Bake, uncovered, at 425° for 10-15 minutes or until a toothpick inserted near the center comes out clean. Sprinkle with bacon and remaining cheese. Bake 3-5 minutes longer or until cheese is melted. Serve with syrup if desired. **YIELD:** 12 servings.

PULL-APART BACON BREAD

Prep: 20 min. + rising **Bake:** 20 min.

I stumbled across the recipe for this savory breakfast bread while looking for something different to take to a brunch. Boy, am I glad I did! Everyone asked for the recipe and could not believe it only called for five ingredients. It's the perfect item to bake for a casual get-together.

Traci Collins // Cheyenne, Wyoming

- 12 bacon strips, diced
- 1 loaf (1 pound) frozen bread dough, thawed
- 2 tablespoons olive oil, *divided*
- 1 cup (4 ounces) shredded part-skim mozzarella cheese
- 1 envelope (1 ounce) ranch salad dressing mix

1 In a large skillet, cook bacon over medium heat for 5 minutes or until partially cooked; drain on paper towels. Roll out dough to 1/2-in. thickness; brush with 1 tablespoon of oil. Cut into 1-in. pieces; place in a large bowl. Add the bacon, cheese, dressing mix and remaining oil; toss to coat.

2 Arrange pieces in a 9-in. x 5-in. oval on a greased baking sheet, layering as needed. Cover and let rise in a warm place for 30 minutes or until doubled.

3 Bake at 350° for 15 minutes. Cover with foil; bake 5-10 minutes longer or until golden brown. **YIELD:** 1 loaf.

RHUBARB BERRY COFFEE CAKE

Prep: 20 min. **Bake:** 40 min.

I rely on a cake mix to stir up this moist streusel-topped treat that pairs tart rhubarb with sweet strawberries. I prefer it without the frosting so that it doesn't get too sweet.

Jackie Heyer // Cushing, Iowa

- 1 package (18-1/4 ounces) yellow cake mix, *divided*
- 2/3 cup packed brown sugar
- 2 tablespoons butter
- 3/4 cup chopped walnuts
- 1 cup (8 ounces) sour cream
- 2 eggs
- 1-1/2 cups finely chopped fresh *or* frozen rhubarb
- 1-1/2 cups sliced fresh strawberries
- 1/2 cup cream cheese frosting, optional

1 In a large bowl, combine 2/3 cup cake mix and sugar; cut in butter until crumbly. Add walnuts; set aside.

2 In another bowl, combine the sour cream, eggs and remaining cake mix; beat on low speed for 30 seconds. Beat on medium for 2 minutes. Fold in rhubarb and strawberries. Spread into a greased 13-in. x 9-in. baking dish. Sprinkle with reserved crumb mixture.

3 Bake at 350° for 40-50 minutes or until a toothpick inserted near the center comes out clean. Cool on a wire rack.

4 Place frosting in a microwave-safe bowl and heat for 15 seconds if desired. Drizzle over cake. **YIELD:** 12-15 servings.

EDITOR'S NOTE: If using frozen rhubarb, measure rhubarb while still frozen, then thaw completely. Drain in a colander, but do not press liquid out.

Salads & Side Dishes

BALSAMIC VEGETABLE SALAD, PG. 46

VEGGIE NOODLE SIDE DISH

Prep/Total Time: 20 min.

I love to cook with fresh vegetables, especially when they're from my garden. Pair this colorful side dish with grilled chicken for a meal.

Wendy Myers // Thompson Falls, Montana

- 1 small sweet red pepper, julienned
- 3/4 cup cut fresh green beans
- 3/4 cup thinly sliced fresh carrots
- 1/4 cup chopped red onion
- 1 tablespoon canola oil
- 1 package (3 ounces) ramen noodles
- 1 yellow summer squash, sliced
- 1 medium zucchini, sliced
- 1/4 cup chicken broth
- 1 tablespoon soy sauce
- 1 teaspoon fajita seasoning mix

1 In a large skillet or wok, stir-fry the pepper, green beans, carrots and onion in oil for 4 minutes. Meanwhile, cook noodles according to package directions (discard seasoning packet or save for another use).

2 Add the remaining ingredients to the vegetable mixture; cook and stir until vegetables are crisp-tender. Drain noodles; add to vegetables and stir until blended. **YIELD:** 4 servings.

I like to take advantage of gelatin mixes and pie fillings to make colorful salads that can be prepared the day before. These fruity squares are great for everyday suppers yet special enough for company.

Chris Rentmeister // Ripon, Wisconsin

CHERRY GELATIN SQUARES

Prep: 15 min. + chilling

    2 packages (3 ounces *each*) cherry gelatin
1-1/2 cups boiling water
    1 can (21 ounces) cherry pie filling
1-1/4 cups lemon-lime soda, chilled
Whipped topping, optional

1 In a large bowl, dissolve gelatin in water. Stir in the cherry pie filling and mix well. Slowly stir in soda (mixture will foam).

2 Pour into an 8-in. square dish. Cover and refrigerate until firm. Cut into squares. Garnish with whipped topping if desired. **YIELD:** 9 servings.

VEGETABLE WILD RICE

Prep: 20 min. **Cook:** 30 min.

A packaged rice mix gives a jump start to this simple side dish that's easy on the budget. A bright blend of veggies adds appealing color.

Helen Jacobs // Canton, Michigan

    1 package (6 ounces) long grain and wild rice mix
    2 medium carrots, cut into 1/4-inch slices
    1 cup diced yellow summer squash
2/3 cup chopped sweet red pepper
2/3 cup chopped green pepper
1/4 cup chopped onion
    2 tablespoons canola oil

1 In a large saucepan, place rice mix, contents of seasoning packet and water as directed on package. Bring to a boil. Add carrots. Reduce heat; cover and simmer for 30 minutes or until rice is tender and water is absorbed.

2 Meanwhile, in a skillet, saute squash, peppers and onion in oil until crisp-tender. Stir into rice mixture. **YIELD:** 6 servings.

SUMMER SQUASH

Summer squash have edible thin skins and soft seeds. Zucchini, pattypan and crookneck are the most common varieties. Choose firm summer squash with brightly colored skin that's free from spots and bruises. Generally, the smaller the squash, the more tender it will be.
—Taste of Home Test Kitchen

STUFFING BASKETS

Prep: 10 min. **Bake:** 30 min.

  1 medium green pepper, chopped
1/4 cup butter, cubed
  1 jar (4-1/2 ounces) sliced mushrooms
  1 package (6 ounces) instant stuffing mix
1/2 cup chopped pecans

1 In a large saucepan, saute green pepper in butter until crisp-tender. Drain mushrooms, reserving liquid; set mushrooms aside. Add water to liquid to measure 1-2/3 cups. Add to green pepper. Bring to a boil; stir in the stuffing mix. Remove from heat.

2 Cover; let mixture stand for about 5 minutes. Add mushrooms and pecans; fluff with a fork. Spoon into paper-lined muffin cups; pack lightly. Bake at 350° for 30-35 minutes. **YIELD:** 1 dozen.

PIZZA POTATOES

Prep: 15 min. **Bake:** 55 min.

For a savory side dish that's sure to appeal to kids, try this twist on traditional pizza.
Kathy White // Chicopee, Massachusetts

  1 package (4.9 ounces) scalloped potatoes
  1 can (14-1/2 ounces) Italian stewed tomatoes
1-1/2 cups water
1/4 teaspoon dried oregano
  1 package (3-1/2 ounces) sliced pepperoni
  1 cup (4 ounces) shredded mozzarella cheese

1 Combine the potatoes and contents of sauce mix in a greased 1-1/2-qt. baking dish. In a large saucepan, bring the tomatoes, water and oregano to a boil. Pour over potatoes. Top with pepperoni.

2 Bake, uncovered, at 375° for 50-60 minutes or until the potatoes are tender. Sprinkle with cheese. Bake 5-10 minutes longer or until cheese is melted. **YIELD:** 4 servings.

CHERRY BAKED BEANS

Prep: 20 min. **Bake:** 40 min.

Here's a perfect dish to bring to a family reunion or any get-together. You won't ever have to worry about bringing leftovers home...because there won't be any!

Margaret Smith // Superior, Wisconsin

- 1 pound lean ground beef (90% lean)
- 2 cans (15 ounces *each*) pork and beans
- 2 cups frozen pitted tart cherries, thawed
- 1 can (16 ounces) kidney beans, rinsed and drained
- 1 cup ketchup
- 1/2 cup water
- 1 envelope onion soup mix
- 2 tablespoons prepared mustard
- 2 teaspoons cider vinegar

1 In a large skillet, cook beef over medium heat until no longer pink; drain. In a large bowl, combine the remaining ingredients; stir in beef.

2 Transfer to an ungreased 2-1/2 qt. baking dish. Bake, uncovered, at 400° for 40-45 minutes or until heated through, stirring occasionally. **YIELD:** 12 servings.

I developed this recipe when my kids were toddlers. The veggies and rice were small enough for them to pick up with their fingers.
Coleen Martin // Brookfield, Wisconsin

VEGETABLE RICE MEDLEY
Prep/Total Time: 20 min.

> 1 cup uncooked long grain rice
> 2-1/4 cups water
> 2 to 3 tablespoons onion *or* vegetable soup mix
> 1/4 teaspoon salt
> 2 cups frozen corn, peas *or* mixed vegetables

1 In a large saucepan, combine the rice, water, soup mix and salt; bring to a boil. Add the vegetables; return to a boil. Reduce heat; cover and simmer for 15 minutes. Cook until rice and vegetables are tender. **YIELD:** 4-6 servings.

LEFTOVER VEGETABLE SOUP

There are just the two of us, so we sometimes end up with leftover vegetables after meals. I put them in a heavy-duty resealable plastic bag or freezer container and store in the freezer. When I have 3 to 4 cups, I make vegetable soup.
—Caroline W., Thermopolis, Wyoming

JAZZY GELATIN   PICTURED ON RIGHT

Prep: 10 min. + chilling

This colorful gelatin is garnished with a chorus of fresh grapes. Loaded with mandarin oranges and crushed pineapple, it's so refreshing that guests won't be able to refrain from seconds.
Taste of Home Test Kitchen

> 1 package (6 ounces) orange gelatin
> 2 cups boiling water
> 1 cup ice cubes
> 1 can (15 ounces) mandarin oranges, drained
> 1 can (8 ounces) unsweetened crushed pineapple, undrained

> 1 can (6 ounces) frozen orange juice concentrate, thawed
> Green grapes and fresh mint, optional

1 In a large bowl, dissolve gelatin in boiling water. Add ice cubes, oranges, pineapple and orange juice concentrate. Pour into a 6-cup ring mold coated with cooking spray. Refrigerate overnight or until firm.

2 Just before serving, unmold onto a serving plate. Fill center with grapes and garnish with mint if desired. **YIELD:** 12 servings.

ZUCCHINI PANCAKES

Prep/Total Time: 30 min.

In place of potato pancakes, try this no-fuss zucchini version. Not only are they tasty, the flecks of green make them look pretty, too.

Teressa Eastman // El Dorado, Kansas

- 1/3 cup biscuit/baking mix
- 1/4 cup grated Parmesan cheese
- 1/8 teaspoon pepper
- 2 eggs, lightly beaten
- 2 cups shredded zucchini
- 2 tablespoons butter

1 In a large bowl, combine the biscuit mix, cheese, pepper and eggs just until blended. Add the zucchini and mix well.

2 In a large skillet, melt butter. Drop batter by about 1/3 cupfuls into skillet; press lightly to flatten. Fry until golden brown, about 3 minutes on each side. **YIELD:** 5 pancakes.

This colorful and fruity gelatin ring gets extra flavor from an ambrosia-like mixture in the center. I've been bringing it to potlucks, buffets and showers for more than 20 years.

Janice Steinmetz //
Somers, Connecticut

FRUIT-FILLED RASPBERRY RING

Prep: 10 min. + chilling

    2 packages (6 ounces *each*) raspberry gelatin
    4 cups boiling water
    1 quart raspberry sherbet
    1 can (14 ounces) pineapple tidbits, drained
    1 can (11 ounces) mandarin oranges, drained
    1 cup flaked coconut
    1 cup miniature marshmallows
    1 cup (8 ounces) sour cream

1 In a large bowl, dissolve gelatin in boiling water. Stir in sherbet until melted. Pour into an 8-cup ring mold coated with cooking spray. Chill overnight or until firm.

2 In another large bowl, combine the pineapple, oranges, coconut, marshmallows and sour cream. Cover and chill. To serve, unmold gelatin onto a serving plate. Spoon fruit mixture into center of ring. **YIELD:** 12-16 servings.

VEGETABLE RICE SALAD

Prep: 5 min. + chilling

I always receive lots of compliments when I bring this salad to parties and get-togethers. The recipe combines leftover rice and crisp vegetables in a cool, creamy ranch-flavored dressing.

Cathy Sestak // Freeburg, Missouri

1-1/2 cups cooked rice
    1 cup broccoli florets
    1 cup cauliflowerets
    3 green onions, thinly sliced
  1/2 cup mayonnaise
    2 tablespoons ranch salad dressing mix
    2 tablespoons 2% milk
    1 tablespoon vinegar
    2 teaspoons sugar

1 In a large bowl, combine the rice, broccoli, cauliflower and onions. In a small bowl, combine the remaining ingredients. Stir in rice mixture. Cover and refrigerate for 1 hour or until serving. **YIELD:** 6 servings.

RICE RESCUE

Brown rice has a nut-like flavor and chewy texture. When you substitute cooked brown rice in recipes that use cooked white rice, keep in mind these simple steps: Use a heavy pan with a tight-fitting lid and plenty of room above the rice for steam. Once all the ingredients are combined and brought to a boil, cover and reduce the heat to a low simmer for 35-45 minutes.
—Taste of Home Test Kitchen

Ranch salad dressing mix flavors these tasty veggies in a flash. By using packages of baby carrots, you can forget any time-consuming peeling or slicing.

Marion Reed // Omak, Washington

GLAZED CARROTS
Prep/Total Time: 25 min.

- 2 **pounds fresh baby carrots**
- 1/2 **cup butter, cubed**
- 1/2 **cup packed brown sugar**
- 2 **envelopes ranch salad dressing mix**

1 Place carrots in a saucepan; add 1 in. of water. Bring to a boil. Reduce heat. Cover; cook for 8-10 minutes or until crisp-tender. Drain and set aside.

2 In the same pan, combine the butter, brown sugar and salad dressing mix until blended. Add carrots. Cook and stir over medium heat for 5 minutes or until glazed. **YIELD:** 10-12 servings.

BALSAMIC VEGETABLE SALAD
Prep/Total Time: 10 min.

Looking for a refreshing and colorful salad? Look no further. This concoction has a tang from balsamic vinegar and couldn't be easier to prepare.

Emily Paluszak // Spartanburg, South Carolina

- 3 **large tomatoes, cut into wedges**
- 3 **medium cucumbers, peeled, halved and sliced**
- 1/2 **cup olive oil**
- 1/4 **cup balsamic vinegar**
- 3 **tablespoons water**
- 1 **envelope Italian salad dressing mix**

1 In a salad bowl, combine tomatoes and cucumbers. In a small bowl, whisk the oil, vinegar, water and dressing mix. Pour over vegetables and toss to coat. **YIELD:** 6 servings.

BALSAMIC VINEGAR

Balsamic vinegar is made from sweet white grapes and aged in wooden barrels for at least 10 years (that explains the hefty price!). You can substitute cider vinegar or a mild red wine vinegar. White wine vinegar is much stronger and sharper and should be used sparingly if it's your only substitute. —Taste of Home Test Kitchen

VEGGIE RICE BOWL

Prep/Total Time: 20 min.

This yummy recipe makes a lot, so it's great for a gathering. Packed with vegetables and two kinds of rice, it's a quick and easy dish.

Sherry Hulsman // Elkton, Florida

- 1 package (6.2 ounces) fast-cooking long grain and wild rice mix
- 2 cups uncooked instant rice
- 1/2 cup chopped green onions
- 1/2 cup chopped celery
- 1/2 cup chopped fresh mushrooms
- 1/2 cup chopped carrot
- 3 tablespoons butter
- 1 cup frozen peas

1 Prepare rice mix and instant rice separately according to package directions. Meanwhile, in a large skillet, saute the onions, celery, mushrooms and carrot in butter for 4-6 minutes or until tender.

2 Stir in peas and prepared rice; cook for 2-4 minutes or until heated through. **YIELD:** 12 servings.

PREPARING MUSHROOMS

Gently remove dirt by rubbing with a mushroom brush or wipe mushrooms with a damp paper towel. Or quickly rinse under cold water, drain and pat dry with paper towels. Do not peel mushrooms. Trim stems. —Taste of Home Test Kitchen

SLOW COOKER MASHED POTATOES

Prep: 5 min. **Cook:** 2 hours

Sour cream and cream cheese add richness to these smooth, make-ahead potatoes. They're wonderful when time is tight because they don't require any last-minute mashing.

Trudy Vincent // Valles Mines, Missouri

- 1 package (3 ounces) cream cheese, softened
- 1/2 cup sour cream
- 1/4 cup butter, softened
- 1 envelope ranch salad dressing mix
- 1 teaspoon dried parsley flakes
- 6 cups warm mashed potatoes (without added milk and butter)

1 In a large bowl, combine the cream cheese, sour cream, butter, salad dressing mix and parsley; stir in potatoes. Transfer to a 3-qt. slow cooker. Cover and cook on low for 2-3 hours. **YIELD:** 8-10 servings.

HOLIDAY BUFFETS

We feed a lot of people at Thanksgiving and Christmas dinner, so my sisters and I always set up a big buffet on the kitchen counter. We put each side dish in a slow cooker (mashed potatoes, scalloped corn, squash, gravy and so forth) to keep everything warm. Guests bring the breads, rolls, salads and pies. —Marla C., Smyrna, New York

A friend shared this recipe with me years ago. My family enjoys it with meat dishes as a substitute for potatoes. It's great to take to a potluck, but be prepared to also pass along the recipe!

Melba Cleveland //
Groveland, California

MUSHROOM BARLEY CASSEROLE

Prep: 10 min. **Bake:** 1-1/4 hours

1 cup medium pearl barley
1 small onion, chopped
1/4 cup butter
1-1/2 cups sliced fresh mushrooms
1 cup slivered almonds, toasted
1 envelope onion soup mix
2 tablespoons minced fresh parsley
or 2 teaspoons dried parsley flakes
3 to 3-1/2 cups chicken broth

1 In a small skillet, saute barley and onion in butter for 5 minutes or until onion is tender. Transfer to an ungreased 2-qt. baking dish. Stir in the mushrooms, almonds, soup mix and parsley. Add 3 cups broth.

2 Bake, uncovered, at 350° for 1-1/4 hours or until barley is tender, adding more broth if needed. **YIELD:** 8-10 servings.

COTTAGE CHEESE FLUFF

Prep/Total Time: 5 min.

Canned fruit and packaged gelatin are the convenient keys to this dish that's not your ordinary salad. You can vary the flavor of gelatin or the type of fruits to suit your family's tastes.

Annette Self // Junction City, Ohio

1 cup (8 ounces) 4% cottage cheese
1 package (3 ounces) gelatin flavor of your choice
1 can (11 ounces) mandarin oranges, drained
1 cup unsweetened crushed pineapple, drained
1/2 cup chopped pecans, optional
1 carton (8 ounces) frozen whipped topping, thawed

1 In a large bowl, combine cottage cheese and gelatin powder. Stir in the oranges, pineapple and pecans if desired. Just before serving, fold in the whipped topping. **YIELD:** 8 servings.

Whenever I take this time-saving side-dish casserole to a potluck, I seldom bring any home, and folks often ask for the recipe. If I have fresh dill, I'll substitute a couple tablespoons for the dill weed.

Esther Kilborn // Bridgton, Maine

DILLY ZUCCHINI CASSEROLE

Prep: 15 min. **Bake:** 25 min.

      1 cup biscuit/baking mix
  1/2 cup grated Parmesan cheese
      1 tablespoon dill weed
      1 teaspoon salt
  1/8 teaspoon pepper
      4 eggs, lightly beaten
  1/2 cup canola oil
      3 cups chopped zucchini
      1 large onion, chopped

1 In a large bowl, combine the biscuit mix, Parmesan cheese, dill, salt and pepper. Add eggs and oil. Stir in zucchini and onion until blended. Pour into a greased 1-1/2-qt. baking dish.

2 Bake, uncovered, at 375° for 25-30 minutes or until golden brown. **YIELD:** 5 servings.

HASH BROWN BAKE

Prep: 20 min. **Bake:** 45 min.

My family has no idea they're eating a low-fat recipe with this hearty side dish. It's creamy, cheesy and simply delicious!

Darla Kahler // Bison, South Dakota

1-1/4 cups fat-free milk
      3 ounces reduced-fat cream cheese
      1 envelope ranch salad dressing mix
      6 cups frozen shredded hash brown
         potatoes, thawed
  1/2 cup shredded reduced-fat cheddar cheese
      1 bacon strip, cooked and crumbled

1 In a blender, combine the milk, cream cheese and salad dressing mix. Cover and process until smooth. Place potatoes in an 8-in. square baking dish coated with cooking spray; top with milk mixture. Cover and bake at 350° for 35 minutes.

2 Sprinkle with cheddar cheese and bacon. Bake, uncovered, 8-10 minutes longer or until cheese is melted and potatoes are tender. **YIELD:** 6 servings.

HUSH PUPPY MIX

Prep: 15 min. **Cook:** 20 min.

I add garlic powder and red pepper flakes to the cornmeal that creates these golden hush puppies. You'll win rave reviews for the crunchy crust and spicy flavor.

Edna Bullett // Wilburton, Oklahoma

4-1/3 cups cornmeal
  3/4 cup all-purpose flour
6-1/2 teaspoons baking powder
    2 tablespoons sugar
    2 tablespoons garlic powder
    1 tablespoon pepper
    1 tablespoon salt
  1/2 teaspoon crushed red pepper flakes

ADDITIONAL INGREDIENTS:
    1 can (8-1/4 ounces) cream-style corn
  1/2 cup chopped onion
    1 egg
Oil for deep-fat frying

1 In a large bowl, combine the first eight ingredients. Store the mix in an airtight container in a cool dry place for up to 6 months. **YIELD:** 3 batches (4-1/2 cups total).

2 **TO PREPARE HUSH PUPPIES:** In a large bowl, combine 1-1/2 cups mix, corn, onion and egg; stir just until moistened. In an electric skillet or deep-fat fryer, heat 1-1/2 in. of oil to 375°. Drop batter by teaspoonfuls into oil; fry until golden brown. Drain on paper towels. Serve warm. **YIELD:** about 4 dozen per batch.

This crunchy cabbage salad comes together so quickly we often have it for spur-of-the-moment picnics or whenever unexpected guests stop by. Sliced almonds lend a fabulous nutty flavor.

Julie Vavroch // Montezuma, Iowa

CRUNCHY COLESLAW
Prep/Total Time: 10 min.

    1/3 cup canola oil
      1 package (3 ounces) beef ramen noodles
    1/2 teaspoon garlic salt
      1 package (16 ounces) shredded coleslaw mix
      1 package (5 ounces) sliced almonds

1 In a small saucepan, heat oil. Stir in contents of noodle seasoning packet and garlic salt; cook for 3-4 minutes or until blended.

2 Meanwhile, crush the noodles and place in a large salad bowl. Add coleslaw mix and almonds. Drizzle with oil mixture; toss to coat. Serve immediately. **YIELD:** 6-8 servings.

CANOLA VS. VEGETABLE OIL

When a recipe calls for vegetable oil, canola oil can be substituted in equal amounts. There should be no difference in the final product.
—*Taste of Home Test Kitchen*

OUT TO SEA PASTA SHELL SALAD   PICTURED ON RIGHT

Prep/Total Time: 20 min.

Here's a healthier version of a popular boxed salad mix you can buy at the store. We absolutely love it! You can also add a little cooked chicken breast to make it heartier.

Ann Timmerman // Northfield, Minnesota

      3 cups uncooked medium pasta shells
    2/3 cup shredded carrots
    2/3 cup frozen peas, thawed
      4 turkey bacon strips, diced and cooked
      4 ounces reduced-fat cream cheese
    1/2 cup reduced-fat sour cream
    3/4 cup fat-free milk
      1 envelope ranch salad dressing mix

1 Cook shells according to package directions. Meanwhile, in a large bowl, combine the carrots, peas and bacon. In a small bowl, beat cream cheese and sour cream. Add milk and dressing mix; beat until combined.

2 Drain pasta and rinse in cold water; add to vegetable mixture. Add dressing mixture; toss to coat. Chill until serving. **YIELD:** 8 servings.

HERBED TOSSED SALAD

Prep/Total Time: 15 min.

Basil from my herb garden boosts the fresh flavor of this speedy dressing when drizzled over colorful salad fixings.

Deb Morrison // Skiatook, Oklahoma

- 8 cups torn lettuce
- 1 cup coarsely chopped fresh cilantro
- 1 cup sliced fresh mushrooms
- 2 medium tomatoes, chopped
- 1 medium carrot, shredded
- 2 radishes, sliced
- 1 envelope Italian salad dressing mix
- 1 tablespoon minced fresh basil *or* 1 teaspoon dried basil
- 1 garlic clove, minced

1 In a large bowl, toss the lettuce, cilantro, mushrooms, tomatoes, carrot and radishes. Prepare salad dressing according to package directions; add basil and garlic. Pour over salad and toss to coat. **YIELD:** 6-8 servings.

STORING LETTUCE

Iceberg lettuce should be washed before storing. First, remove the core by grasping the head in your hand and hitting the core area against the counter-top; lift out the core. Rinse the head under running water and drain core side down in a colander. Dry thoroughly with paper towels or in a salad spinner. Wrap lettuce in dry paper towels and place in a resealable plastic bag, removing as much air as possible. Store in the refrigerator.
—Taste of Home Test Kitchen

My husband's grandmother receives the credit for this zippy dish. Corn bread stuffing mix and a can of green chilies give fast flavor to sliced summer squash.

Tatra Kay Cottingham //
Munday, Texas

SQUASH STUFFING CASSEROLE

Prep: 20 min. **Bake:** 25 min.

  3/4 cup water
  1/4 teaspoon salt
    6 cups sliced yellow summer squash
      (1/4 inch thick)
    1 small onion, halved and sliced
    1 can (10-3/4 ounces) condensed cream
      of mushroom soup, undiluted
    1 cup (8 ounces) sour cream
    1 package (6 ounces) corn bread stuffing mix
    1 can (4 ounces) chopped green chilies
Salt and pepper to taste
    1 cup (4 ounces) shredded cheddar cheese

1 In a large saucepan, bring water and salt to a boil. Add squash and onion. Reduce heat; cover and cook until squash is crisp-tender, about 6 minutes. Drain well; set aside.

2 In a large bowl, combine the soup, sour cream, stuffing and the contents of seasoning packet, chilies, salt and pepper. Fold in squash mixture.

3 Pour into a greased shallow 2-qt. baking dish. Sprinkle with cheese. Bake, uncovered, at 350° for 25-30 minutes or until heated through. **YIELD:** 8-10 servings.

CORN BREAD PUDDING

Prep: 5 min. **Bake:** 40 min.

This comforting side dish pairs perfectly with shrimp and other seafood. I adapted the dish from my mom's recipe. It never fails to please.

Bob Gebhardt // Wausau, Wisconsin

    2 eggs
    1 cup (8 ounces) sour cream
    1 can (15-1/4 ounces) whole kernel corn, drained
    1 can (14-3/4 ounces) cream-style corn
  1/2 cup butter, melted
    1 package (8-1/2 ounces) corn bread/muffin mix
  1/4 teaspoon paprika

1 In a large bowl, combine the first five ingredients. Stir in corn bread mix just until blended. Pour into a greased 3-qt. baking dish. Sprinkle with paprika.

2 Bake, uncovered, at 350° for 40-45 minutes or until a knife inserted near the center. Serve warm. **YIELD:** 12 servings.

A friend fixed this for a company outing years ago, and it has since become my favorite picnic salad. Jars of marinated mushrooms and artichoke hearts, along with fresh vegetables, turn prepared rice mix into something special.

Suzanne Strocsher //
Bothell, Washington

SPECIAL WILD RICE SALAD
Prep: 15 min. + chilling **Cook:** 25 min.

2 packages (6 ounces *each*) long grain and wild rice mix
2 to 3 ripe avocados, peeled and chopped
1 jar (8 ounces) marinated whole mushrooms, undrained
1 jar (6-1/2 ounces) marinated artichoke hearts, undrained
1 to 2 medium tomatoes, diced
2 celery ribs, chopped
2 to 3 green onions, chopped
1/2 cup Italian salad dressing

1 Prepare rice according to package directions. Cool; place in a large bowl. Add remaining ingredients and toss to coat. Cover and refrigerate overnight. **YIELD:** 10-12 servings.

CREAMY ITALIAN NOODLES
Prep/Total Time: 25 min.

These no-fail noodles are a flavorful accompaniment to most any meat. Rich and creamy, they're special enough for company, too.
Linda Hendrix // Moundville, Missouri

1 package (8 ounces) wide egg noodles
1/4 cup butter, melted
1/2 cup heavy whipping cream, half-and-half cream *or* evaporated milk
1/4 cup grated Parmesan cheese
2-1/4 teaspoons Italian salad dressing mix

1 Cook noodles according to package directions; drain and place in a bowl. Drizzle with butter. Add the remaining ingredients; toss to coat. Serve immediately. **YIELD:** 4-6 servings.

HALF & HALF SUBSTITUTE

For dishes that are cooked or baked, you may substitute 4-1/2 teaspoons melted butter plus enough whole milk to equal 1 cup. One cup of evaporated milk may also be substituted for each cup of half-and-half cream.
—*Taste of Home Test Kitchen*

COLORFUL VEGETABLE BAKE

Prep: 10 min. **Bake:** 55 min. + standing

My sister gave me the recipe for this side dish years ago, and it's become a favorite in our household. Chock-full of colorful veggies, it's delicious and feeds a crowd.

Betty Brown // Buckley, Washington

- 3 cups frozen cut green beans, thawed and drained
- 2 medium green peppers, chopped
- 6 plum tomatoes, chopped and seeded
- 2 to 3 cups (8 to 12 ounces) shredded cheddar cheese
- 3 cups chopped zucchini
- 1 cup biscuit/baking mix
- 1/2 teaspoon salt
- 1/2 teaspoon cayenne pepper
- 6 eggs, lightly beaten
- 1 cup 2% milk

1 Place beans and peppers in a greased 13-in. x 9-in. baking dish. Layer with tomatoes, cheese and zucchini. In a large bowl, combine the biscuit mix, salt, cayenne, eggs and milk just until moistened. Pour over the vegetables.

2 Bake, uncovered, at 350° for 55-60 minutes or until puffed and a knife inserted near the center comes out clean. Let stand for 10 minutes before serving. **YIELD:** 12 servings.

CRISPY CAJUN POTATO WEDGES

Prep: 15 min. **Bake:** 45 min.

A sprinkle of Cajun seasoning lends spunk to these hearty, cornflake-coated wedges.

LaDonna Reed // Ponca City, Oklahoma

      1/4 cup 2% milk
      1/4 cup mayonnaise
    4-1/2 teaspoons ranch salad dressing mix
      3/4 teaspoon Cajun seasoning, *divided*
      3/4 cup crushed cornflakes
        2 medium russet potatoes

1 In a shallow bowl, combine the milk, mayonnaise, dressing mix and 1/2 teaspoon Cajun seasoning. In another shallow bowl, combine cornflakes and remaining Cajun seasoning.

2 Cut each potato into eight wedges; dip wedges in mayonnaise mixture, then coat with crumbs.

3 Arrange in a single layer in a 15-in. x 10-in. x 1-in. baking pan coated with cooking spray. Bake at 375° for 45-50 minutes or until tender and lightly browned, turning once. **YIELD:** 2 servings.

Main Dishes

PLANTATION HAM PIE, PG. 61

ITALIAN BEEF SANDWICHES

Prep: 15 min. **Cook:** 7 hours

Before leaving for work, I often put these ingredients in the slow cooker. Supper is ready when I get home. This recipe is also good to take to a get-together.

Carol Allen // McLeansboro, Illinois

- 1 boneless beef chuck roast (3 to 4 pounds)
- 3 tablespoons dried basil
- 3 tablespoons dried oregano
- 1 cup water
- 1 envelope onion soup mix
- 10 to 12 Italian rolls *or* sandwich buns

1 Cut the roast in half; place in a 5-qt. slow cooker. Combine the basil, oregano and water; pour over roast. Sprinkle with soup mix.

2 Cover and cook on low for 8-10 hours or until meat is tender. Remove meat; shred with two forks and keep warm. Strain broth and skim fat. Serve meat on rolls; use broth for dipping if desired. **YIELD:** 10-12 servings.

Everyone who tries these potatoes likes them. They're almost a meal by themselves, but I usually serve them with breadsticks, a green salad and dessert.

Kaleta Shepperson // Ozona, Texas

IDAHO TACOS

Prep/Total Time: 20 min.

    1 pound ground beef
    1 envelope taco seasoning
    4 hot baked potatoes
    1/2 cup shredded cheddar cheese
    1 cup chopped green onions
Salsa, optional

1 In a large skillet, cook beef over medium heat until no longer pink; drain. Add taco seasoning; prepare according to package directions.

2 With a sharp knife, cut an X in the top of each potato; fluff pulp with a fork. Top with taco meat, cheese and onions. Serve with salsa if desired. **YIELD:** 4 servings.

PLANTATION HAM PIE

Prep: 20 min. **Bake:** 20 min.

Pretty parsley pinwheels top this hearty casserole filled with a saucy mixture of broccoli, ham and onion. It also can be made with asparagus instead of broccoli.

Sharon White // Morden, Manitoba

    4 cups cubed fully cooked ham (2 pounds)
    1 medium onion, chopped
    2 tablespoons butter
    2 cans (10-3/4 ounces *each*) condensed cream
      of chicken soup, undiluted
    1 cup 2% milk
    2 cups fresh *or* frozen broccoli florets
    2 cups biscuit/baking mix
    1/2 cup water
    1/2 cup minced fresh parsley

1 In a skillet, saute ham and onion in butter until onion is tender. Combine soup and milk; stir into ham mixture. Add broccoli; heat through. Pour into an ungreased shallow 2-1/2-qt. baking dish.

2 Combine biscuit mix and water until a soft dough forms. On a lightly floured surface, knead dough 10 times. Roll out into a 12-in. square; sprinkle with parsley.

3 Roll up jelly-roll style. Cut into 12 pieces; place over the ham mixture. Bake, uncovered, at 425° for 20-25 minutes or until biscuits are golden and ham mixture is bubbly. **YIELD:** 6 servings.

If you're a fan of the classic tuna melt, you won't want to pass up this innovative twist. A cool slice of avocado is a delicious addition.
Taste of Home Test Kitchen

TUNA MELT ON CORN BREAD
Prep/Total Time: 30 min.

- 1 package (8-1/2 ounces) corn bread/muffin mix
- 2 cans (6 ounces *each*) light water-packed tuna, drained and flaked
- 1/3 cup mayonnaise
- 1/3 cup chopped celery
- 2 tablespoons finely chopped onion
- 1 hard-cooked egg, chopped
- 1 teaspoon dill weed
- 1/4 teaspoon salt
- 1/8 teaspoon pepper
- 6 slices cheddar cheese
- 1 medium tomato, sliced
- 1 medium ripe avocado, peeled and sliced

1 Prepare and bake corn bread according to package directions, using a greased 8-in. square baking pan. Cool on a wire rack.

2 In a small bowl, combine the tuna, mayonnaise, celery, onion, egg, dill, salt and pepper. Cut corn bread into six pieces; place on an ungreased baking sheet. Top each with 1/4 cup tuna mixture and a slice of cheese.

3 Broil 4-6 in. from the heat for 2-3 minutes or until cheese is melted. Top with tomato and avocado. **YIELD:** 6 servings.

BEEFY RICE DINNER
Prep/Total Time: 30 min.

To turn a boxed rice mix into a meal, I add ground beef, celery and green pepper. It's quick to fix and makes a flavorful, filling main dish.
Mildred Sherrer // Fort Worth, Texas

- 1 package (6.8 ounces) beef-flavored rice mix
- 1/2 pound lean ground beef (90% lean)
- 1/3 cup chopped celery
- 1/3 cup chopped green pepper
- 1/8 to 1/4 teaspoon salt
- 1/8 teaspoon pepper
- 1/3 cup shredded cheddar cheese

1 Prepared rice according to package directions. Meanwhile, in a large skillet, cook the beef, celery and green pepper until the meat is browned and vegetables are tender; drain. Add the rice, salt and pepper.

2 Transfer to a greased 2-qt. baking dish. Sprinkle with cheese. Bake, uncovered, at 350° for 10-15 minutes or until heated through and cheese is melted. **YIELD:** 4-6 servings.

CHICKEN MARSALA WITH PASTA

Prep/Total Time: 30 min.

My family always looks forward to this chicken. It's elegant enough for company, but quick and easy enough for a weeknight.

Trisha Kruse // Eagle, Idaho

    2 cups sliced fresh mushrooms
  1/4 cup butter, *divided*
    2 teaspoons minced garlic
2-1/4 cups hot water
  1/4 cup marsala wine *or* chicken broth
    1 envelope (4.3 ounces) fettuccini and
      chicken-flavored sauce mix
    4 boneless skinless chicken breast halves
      (4 ounces *each*)
  1/4 cup all-purpose flour
  1/4 teaspoon salt
  1/4 teaspoon pepper
    1 tablespoon canola oil
    2 tablespoons sour cream

1 In a large saucepan, saute mushrooms in 2 tablespoons butter for 4-5 minutes or until tender. Add garlic; cook 1 minute longer. Add water and wine. Bring to a boil; stir in pasta mix. Reduce heat; simmer, uncovered, for 10 minutes or until the pasta is tender.

2 Meanwhile, flatten chicken to 1/2-in. thickness. In a large resealable plastic bag, combine the flour, salt and pepper. Add chicken, a few pieces at a time, and shake to coat.

3 In a large skillet, cook chicken in oil and remaining butter over medium heat for 4-5 minutes on each side or until no longer pink. Remove pasta mixture from the heat. Stir in sour cream. Serve with chicken. **YIELD:** 4 servings.

CREOLE SHRIMP & RICE

Prep: 25 min. **Cook:** 20 min.

1 celery rib, chopped
1 small onion, chopped
1 small green pepper, chopped
1 tablespoon canola oil
1 can (14-1/2 ounces) diced tomatoes, undrained
2 tablespoons savory herb with garlic soup mix
1 garlic clove, minced
1 teaspoon Worcestershire sauce
1 bay leaf
1/8 teaspoon cayenne pepper
1 pound cooked medium shrimp, peeled and deveined
2 cups hot cooked rice

1 In a large skillet, saute the celery, onion and green pepper in oil until tender. Add the tomatoes, soup mix, garlic, Worcestershire sauce, bay leaf and cayenne. Bring to a boil. Reduce heat; cover and simmer for 15 minutes.

2 Add shrimp; heat through. Discard bay leaf. Serve with rice. **YIELD:** 4 servings.

MEATBALLS WITH PEPPER SAUCE   PICTURED ON RIGHT

Prep: 25 min. **Bake:** 1-1/4 hours

I've found these colorful meatballs keep well in a slow cooker for a no-fuss meal. We enjoy them served over pasta or rice.

Julie Neal // Green Bay, Wisconsin

1 cup evaporated milk
1 tablespoon Worcestershire sauce
1 envelope onion soup mix
2 pounds ground beef
SAUCE:
1/2 pound sliced fresh mushrooms
1-1/2 cups ketchup
3/4 cup packed brown sugar
3/4 cup water
1/2 cup chopped green pepper
1/2 cup chopped sweet red pepper
2 tablespoons chopped onion
1 tablespoon Worcestershire sauce

1 In a large bowl, combine the milk, Worcestershire sauce and soup mix. Crumble beef over mixture and mix well. Shape into 1-in. balls.

2 Place meatballs on a rack in a shallow baking pan. Broil 4-6 in. from the heat for 5-8 minutes or until browned. In a Dutch oven, combine sauce ingredients. Bring to a boil. Reduce heat; add meatballs. Simmer, uncovered, for 1 hour or until the meat is no longer pink. **YIELD:** 60 meatballs.

CITRUS FISH TACOS

Prep: 15 min. + chilling **Bake:** 15 min.

Fish tacos bring a deliciously different twist to the Southwest stand-by. I combine halibut or cod with a fruity salsa and a zesty seasoning.

Maria Baldwin // Mesa, Arizona

1-1/2 cups finely chopped fresh pineapple
1 can (11 ounces) mandarin oranges, drained and cut in half
1 envelope reduced-sodium taco seasoning, *divided*
3 tablespoons thawed orange juice concentrate, *divided*
3 tablespoons lime juice, *divided*
1 jalapeno pepper, seeded and finely chopped
1-1/2 pounds halibut *or* cod, cut into 3/4-inch cubes
8 corn tortillas (6 inches), warmed
3 cups shredded lettuce

1 In a large bowl, combine the pineapple, oranges, 1 tablespoon taco seasoning, 1 tablespoon orange juice concentrate, 1 tablespoon lime juice and jalapeno pepper. Cover and refrigerate.

2 Place fish in an ungreased shallow 2-qt. baking dish. In a small bowl, combine the remaining orange juice concentrate, lime juice and taco seasoning. Pour over fish; toss gently to coat. Cover and bake at 375° for 12-16 minutes or until fish flakes easily with a fork.

3 Place a spoonful of the fish mixture down the center of each tortilla. Top with lettuce and pineapple salsa: roll up. **YIELD:** 4 servings.

EDITOR'S NOTE: Wear disposable gloves when cutting hot peppers; the oils can burn skin. Avoid touching your face.

This satisfying stew is a breeze to fix because it uses leftover roast beef and refrigerated biscuits.
Patti Keith // Ebensburg, Pennsylvania

BEEF VEGGIE CASSEROLE
Prep/Total Time: 25 min.

    1 envelope mushroom gravy mix
3/4 cup water
    2 cups cubed cooked beef
    2 cups frozen mixed vegetables
    2 medium potatoes, peeled, cubed and cooked
    1 tube (12 ounces) refrigerated buttermilk
       biscuits, separated into 10 biscuits

1 In a large saucepan, combine gravy mix and water until smooth. Bring to a boil; cook and stir for 1 minute or until thickened. Stir in the beef, vegetables and potatoes; heat through.

2 Transfer to a greased 8-in. square baking dish. Top with biscuits. Bake, uncovered, at 400° for 12-16 minutes or until bubbly and biscuits are golden brown. **YIELD:** 5 servings.

HERBED PORK AND POTATOES
Prep/Total Time: 30 min.

With pork, stuffing and vegetables, this combination is a hearty meal in one. Plus, red tomatoes and green parsley give great color.
Evelyn Harzbecker // Charlestown, Massachusetts

1/2 cup butter, *divided*
    3 cups cubed red potatoes (1-inch pieces)
    1 pound boneless pork loin, cut into 1-inch cubes
1/2 teaspoon dried rosemary, crushed
1/2 teaspoon rubbed sage
1/2 teaspoon salt
1/2 teaspoon pepper
    1 garlic clove, minced
    2 cups crushed herb-seasoned stuffing
    1 cup sliced celery
    1 cup chopped onion
1/2 cup apple juice
    3 medium tomatoes, chopped
1/4 cup minced fresh parsley

1 In a large skillet, melt 1/4 cup butter. Add potatoes; cook over medium heat, stirring occasionally, until lightly browned. Add the pork, rosemary, sage, salt and pepper. Cook and stir until pork is browned, about 12 minutes. Add garlic; cook 1 minute longer. Stir in the stuffing, celery, onion, apple juice and remaining butter.

2 Cover and cook for 7 minutes or until heated through. Stir in tomatoes and parsley. Remove from the heat; cover and let stand for 2 minutes. **YIELD:** 4 servings.

I'm always trying new recipes on my family. This easy, quick and delicious one is a keeper and a nice change from pork roast or pork chops.

Carol Heim // Nokesville, Virginia

HONEY PORK AND PEPPERS

Prep: 25 min. **Cook:** 40 min.

1-1/2 pounds boneless pork, cut into 1-inch cubes
   2 tablespoons canola oil
   1 envelope (.87 ounce) brown gravy mix
   1 cup water
1/4 cup honey
   3 tablespoons soy sauce
   2 tablespoons red wine vinegar
1/2 teaspoon ground ginger
1/8 teaspoon garlic powder
   1 medium onion, cut into wedges
   1 medium sweet red pepper, cut into 1-inch pieces
   1 medium green pepper, cut into 1-inch pieces
Hot cooked rice

1 In a large skillet over medium heat, cook pork in oil until browned, about 15 minutes. In a small bowl, combine gravy mix, water, honey, soy sauce, vinegar, ginger and garlic powder; add to pork.

2 Cover; simmer for 20 minutes, stirring occasionally. Add onion and peppers; cook 5-10 minutes longer. Serve with rice. **YIELD:** 4-6 servings.

ROAST BEEF WITH GRAVY

Prep: 5 min. **Cook:** 6 hours

Start this simple roast in the morning and you'll have savory slices of meat and gravy ready at suppertime. The tender beef is loaded with homemade taste and leaves plenty for main dishes later in the week.

Tracy Ashbeck // Wisconsin Rapids, Wisconsin

   1 beef sirloin tip roast (4 pounds)
1/2 cup all-purpose flour, *divided*
   1 envelope onion soup mix
   1 envelope brown gravy mix
   2 cups cold water
Hot mashed potatoes

1 Cut roast in half; rub with 1/4 cup flour. Place in 5-qt. slow cooker. In a small bowl, combine soup and gravy mixes with remaining flour; stir in water until blended. Pour over roast.

2 Cover and cook on low for 6-8 hours or until meat is tender. Slice roast; serve with mashed potatoes and gravy. **YIELD:** 16 servings.

SAVORY ONION CHICKEN

Prep/Total Time: 30 min.

Dinner doesn't get any easier than this tasty chicken entree. Buy chicken that's already cut up to save even more time.

Julia Anderson // Ringgold, Georgia

- 1/4 **cup all-purpose flour,** *divided*
- 1 **broiler/fryer chicken (3 to 4 pounds), skin removed and cut up**
- 2 **tablespoons olive oil**
- 1 **envelope onion soup mix**
- 1 **bottle (12 ounces) beer** *or* **nonalcoholic beer**

1 Place 2 tablespoons flour in a large resealable plastic bag. Add chicken, a few pieces at a time, and shake to coat. In a large skillet, brown chicken in oil on all sides. Remove and keep warm.

2 Add soup mix and remaining flour, stirring to loosen browned bits from pan. Gradually whisk in beer. Bring to a boil; cook and stir for 2 minutes or until thickened.

3 Return chicken to the pan. Bring to a boil. Reduce heat; cover and simmer for 12-15 minutes or until chicken juices run clear. **YIELD:** 6 servings.

BAVARIAN SAUSAGE SUPPER

Prep/Total Time: 20 min.

My mom, who's a great cook, shared the recipe for this easy skillet meal. Spicy kielbasa makes a flavored noodle and sauce mix truly delicious.

Pat Frankovich // North Olmsted, Ohio

2 cups coleslaw mix
1 cup thinly sliced carrots
2 tablespoons butter
2-1/4 cups water
3/4 pound smoked kielbasa *or* Polish sausage, sliced into 1/4-inch pieces
1 package (4.9 ounces) quick-cooking noodles and sour cream and chive sauce mix
1/2 teaspoon caraway seeds, optional

1 In a large skillet, saute coleslaw mix and carrots in butter until crisp-tender. Add water; bring to a boil. Stir in remaining ingredients. Return to a boil. Reduce heat; cover and cook, for 8 minutes or until noodles are tender, stirring occasionally. **YIELD:** 5 servings.

The first time I tasted this creamy casserole at a friend's get-together, I noted how much everyone loved it. All of the party guests went for seconds...and thirds.
Todd Richards // West Allis, Wisconsin

CHICKEN ARTICHOKE BAKE

Prep: 15 min. **Bake:** 55 min.

- 2 cans (10-3/4 ounces *each*) condensed cream of celery soup, undiluted
- 1 cup mayonnaise
- 3 cups cubed cooked chicken
- 1 can (14 ounces) water-packed artichoke hearts, rinsed, drained and chopped
- 1 can (8 ounces) sliced water chestnuts, drained
- 1 package (6 ounces) long grain and wild rice mix
- 1 cup sliced fresh mushrooms
- 1 medium onion, finely chopped
- 1 jar (2 ounces) diced pimientos, drained
- 1/4 teaspoon pepper
- 1 cup seasoned stuffing cubes

1 In a large bowl, combine soup and mayonnaise. Stir in the chicken, artichokes, water chestnuts, rice mix with contents of seasoning packet, mushrooms, onion, pimientos and pepper.

2 Spoon into a greased 2-1/2-qt. baking dish. Sprinkle with stuffing cubes. Bake, uncovered, at 350° for 55-65 minutes or until edges are bubbly and rice is tender. **YIELD:** 6 servings.

PORK AND CABBAGE DINNER

Prep: 15 min. **Cook:** 4 hours

I put on this pork roast in the morning to avoid that evening dinner rush so common on busy weeknights. All I do is fix a side of family-favorite potatoes and we can sit down to a satisfying supper.
Trina Hinkel // Minneapolis, Minnesota

- 1 pound carrots
- 1-1/2 cups water
- 1 envelope onion soup mix
- 2 garlic cloves, minced
- 1/2 teaspoon celery seed
- 1 boneless pork shoulder butt roast (4 to 6 pounds)
- 1/2 teaspoon salt
- 1/4 teaspoon pepper
- 1-1/2 pounds, cabbage, cut into 2-inch pieces

1 Cut carrots in half lengthwise and then into 2-in. pieces. Place in a 5-qt. slow cooker. Add the water, soup mix, garlic and celery seed. Cut roast in half; place over carrot mixture. Sprinkle with salt and pepper. Cover and cook on high for 2 hours.

2 Reduce heat to low; cook for 4 hours. Add cabbage; cook 2 hours longer or until the meat and cabbage are tender.

3 Remove the meat and vegetables to a serving plate; keep warm. If desired, thicken pan drippings for gravy and serve with the roast. **YIELD:** 8-10 servings.

Slow cook your way to a tasty, crowd-pleasing entree! Ground beef is transformed into a classic sandwich filling with just a few pantry staples.

**Joeanne Steras //
Garrett, Pennsylvania**

SLOW COOKER SLOPPY JOES
Prep: 15 min. **Cook:** 4 hours

2 pounds ground beef
1 cup chopped green pepper
2/3 cup chopped onion
2 cups ketchup
2 envelopes sloppy joe mix
2 tablespoons brown sugar
1 teaspoon prepared mustard
12 hamburger buns, split

1 In a large skillet, cook the beef, pepper and onion over medium heat until meat is no longer pink; drain. Stir in the ketchup, sloppy joe mix, brown sugar and mustard.

2 Transfer to a 3-qt. slow cooker. Cover and cook on low for 4-5 hours or until flavors are blended. Spoon 1/2 cup onto each bun. **YIELD:** 12 servings.

LAMB RATATOUILLE
Prep: 30 min. **Cook:** 20 min.

This quick-and-easy recipe is a great way to use up leftover lamb.

Maxine Cenker // Weirton, West Virginia

1 package (6.8 ounces) beef-flavored rice and vermicelli mix
2 tablespoons butter
2-1/2 cups water
3 medium tomatoes, peeled, seeded and chopped
1 medium zucchini, sliced
1-1/2 cups sliced fresh mushrooms
1 small onion, chopped
6 green onions, sliced
3 garlic cloves, minced
2 tablespoons olive oil
1 pound cooked lamb *or* beef, cut into thin strips

1 Set rice seasoning packet aside. In a large skillet, saute the rice mix in butter until browned. Stir in water and contents of seasoning packet; bring to a boil. Reduce heat. Cover; simmer for 15 minutes.

2 Meanwhile, in another skillet, saute vegetables in oil until crisp-tender. Add lamb and vegetables to the rice. Cover and simmer for 5-10 minutes or until the meat is no longer pink and rice is tender. **YIELD:** 6 servings.

TUNA MAC AND CHEESE BAKE

Prep: 15 min. **Bake:** 30 min.

Tuna lovers will gobble up this easy and fast casserole. Chances are, you've already got the ingredients in your pantry.

Bonnie Hord // Lee's Summit, Missouri

- 1 package (7-1/4 ounces) macaroni and cheese dinner mix
- 1 can (12 ounces) light water-packed tuna, drained and flaked
- 1 can (10-3/4 ounces) condensed cream of mushroom soup, undiluted
- 1-1/3 cups 2% milk
- 2 packages (9 ounces *each*) frozen peas and pearl onions
- 1 can (4 ounces) mushroom stems and pieces, drained
- 1 can (2.8 ounces) French-fried onions, *divided*

1 Prepare the macaroni and cheese according to package directions. Stir in the tuna, soup, milk, peas, mushrooms and half of the fried onions.

2 Place in a greased 11-in. x 7-in. baking dish. Bake, uncovered, at 325° for 25 minutes. Sprinkle with remaining fried onions; bake 5 minutes longer or until heated through. **YIELD:** 8 servings.

An onion soup and sour cream mixture really adds zip to this beautiful baked fish. Your family will never guess how quick and easy it comes together.

Beverly Krueger // Yamhill, Oregon

BUSY-DAY BAKED FISH

Prep/Total Time: 30 min.

    1 cup (8 ounces) sour cream
    2 tablespoons onion soup mix
1-1/2 cups seasoned bread crumbs
2-1/2 pounds fish fillets
    1/4 cup butter, melted
    1/3 cup shredded Parmesan cheese

1 In a shallow bowl, combine sour cream and soup mix. Place bread crumbs in another shallow bowl. Cut fish into serving-size pieces; coat with sour cream mixture, then roll in crumbs.

2 Place in two greased 13-in. x 9-in. baking dishes. Drizzle with butter. Bake, uncovered, at 425° for 12 minutes. Sprinkle with cheese; bake 2-6 minutes longer or until fish flakes easily with a fork. **YIELD:** 6-8 servings.

AU GRATIN TACO BAKE PICTURED ON RIGHT

Prep: 15 min. Bake: 70 min.

This hearty hot dish relies on a package of au gratin potatoes for simple preparation. Chock-full of tender beef, potatoes, corn, tomatoes and cheese, the southwestern supper is sure to be a hit in your home.

Linda Muir // Big Lake, Minnesota

    1 pound ground beef
    1 package (4.9 ounces) au gratin potatoes
    1 can (15-1/4 ounces) whole kernel
       corn, undrained
    1 can (14-1/2 ounces) no-salt-added stewed
       tomatoes, undrained
3/4 cup 2% milk
1/2 cup water
    2 tablespoons taco seasoning
    1 cup (4 ounces) shredded cheddar cheese

1 In a large skillet, cook the beef over medium heat until no longer pink; drain. Stir in the potatoes and contents of sauce mix, corn, tomatoes, milk, water and taco seasoning. Transfer to a greased 2-qt. baking dish.

2 Cover and bake at 350° for 65-70 minutes or until potatoes are tender. Sprinkle with cheese. Bake, uncovered, 5 minutes longer or until the cheese is melted. **YIELD:** 4-6 servings.

CONVECTION OVENS

Convection ovens have a fan that continuously circulates hot air around the food. Foods cook up to 25% faster. In general, to adapt a recipe for a convection oven, heat the oven 25° lower than the recipe suggests and expect foods to cook in about 25% less time. —Taste of Home Test Kitchen

TACO-FILLED PASTA SHELLS

Prep: 20 min. + chilling **Bake:** 45 min.

I've been stuffing pasta shells with different fillings for years, but my family enjoys this version with taco-seasoned meat the most.

Marge Hodel // Roanoke, Illinois

- 2 pounds ground beef
- 2 envelopes taco seasoning
- 1 package (8 ounces) cream cheese, cubed
- 24 uncooked jumbo pasta shells
- 1/4 cup butter, melted

ADDITIONAL INGREDIENTS
(for each casserole):
- 1 cup salsa
- 1 cup taco sauce
- 1 cup (4 ounces) shredded cheddar cheese
- 1 cup (4 ounces) shredded Monterey Jack cheese
- 1-1/2 cups crushed tortilla chips
- 1 cup (8 ounces) sour cream
- 3 green onions, chopped

1 In a Dutch oven, cook beef over medium heat until no longer pink; drain. Add taco seasoning; prepare according to package directions. Add cream cheese; cook and stir for 5-10 minutes or until melted. Transfer to a bowl; chill for 1 hour.

2 Cook pasta according to package directions; drain. Gently toss with butter. Fill each shell with about 3 tablespoons of meat mixture. Place 12 shells in a freezer container. Cover and freeze for up to 3 months.

3 To prepare remaining shells, spoon salsa into a greased 9-in. square baking dish. Top with stuffed shells and taco sauce. Cover and bake at 350° for 30 minutes. Uncover; sprinkle with cheeses and chips. Bake 15 minutes longer or until heated through. Serve with sour cream and onions.

4 **TO USE FROZEN SHELLS:** Thaw in the refrigerator for 24 hours (shells will be partially frozen). Spoon salsa into a greased 9-in. square baking dish; top with shells and taco sauce. Cover and bake at 350° for 40 minutes. Uncover and continue as above. **YIELD:** 2 casseroles (6 servings each).

Leftover chicken, ham and a wild rice mix make this comforting dish quick to assemble. If you have extra turkey, you can use it instead of the chicken.

Lovetta Breshears // Nixa, Missouri

CHICKEN HAM CASSEROLE

Prep: 15 min. **Bake:** 25 min.

- 1 package (6 ounces) long grain and wild rice mix
- 2 cups cubed cooked chicken
- 1 cup cubed fully cooked ham
- 1 can (10-3/4 ounces) condensed cream of chicken soup, undiluted
- 1 can (12 ounces) evaporated milk
- 1 cup (4 ounces) shredded Colby cheese
- 1/8 teaspoon pepper
- 1/4 cup grated Parmesan cheese

1 Cook the rice mix according to package directions. Transfer to a greased 2-qt. baking dish. Top with chicken and ham.

2 In a large bowl, combine the soup, milk, Colby cheese and pepper; pour over chicken mixture. Sprinkle with Parmesan cheese.

3 Bake, uncovered, at 350° for 25-30 minutes or until bubbly. **YIELD:** 6 servings.

PIGGIES IN BLANKIES

Prep/Total Time: 30 min.

Pigs-in-a-blanket is a super simple supper standby for many families. In this version, sauerkraut adds a tangy touch.

Iola Egle // Bella Vista, Arkansas

- 2 cups biscuit/baking mix
- 1/2 cup water
- 1 can (14 ounces) sauerkraut, rinsed and drained, *divided*
- 1 pound hot dogs

1 In a large bowl, combine biscuit mix and water until a soft dough forms. Turn onto a floured surface; knead 5-10 times. Roll dough into a 13-in. circle; cut into 10 wedges.

2 Place 1 tablespoon sauerkraut on each wedge. Place a hot dog at the wide end; roll up each wedge tightly. Place on an ungreased baking sheet.

3 Bake at 450° for 12-15 minutes or until golden brown. Heat remaining sauerkraut; serve with the hot dogs. **YIELD:** 10 servings.

I've been part of the food services staff at a local university for a long time. One summer we created this flavorful sandwich. Thousands of students have enjoyed it since then.

Jane Hollar // Vilas, North Carolina

CHEESY CHICKEN SUBS
Prep/Total Time: 25 min.

12 ounces boneless skinless chicken breasts, cut into strips
1 envelope Parmesan Italian *or* Caesar salad dressing mix
1 cup sliced fresh mushrooms
1/2 cup sliced red onion
1/4 cup olive oil

4 submarine buns, split and toasted
4 slices Swiss cheese

1 Place chicken in a large bowl; sprinkle with salad dressing mix. In a large skillet, saute mushrooms and onion in oil for 3 minutes. Add chicken; saute for 6 minutes or until chicken is no longer pink.

2 Spoon mixture onto roll bottoms; top with cheese. Broil 4 in. from the heat for 4 minutes or until cheese is melted. Replace tops. **YIELD:** 4 servings.

PORK CHOPS WITH APPLES AND STUFFING PICTURED ON RIGHT

Prep: 15 min. Bake: 45 min.

The heartwarming taste of cinnamon and apples is the perfect accompaniment to these tender pork chops. Because it calls for only four ingredients, it's a main course I can serve with little preparation.

Joan Hamilton // Worcester, Massachusetts

6 boneless pork loin chops (1-inch thick and 4 ounces *each*)
1 tablespoon canola oil
1 package (6 ounces) crushed stuffing mix
1 can (21 ounces) apple pie filling with cinnamon

1 In a large skillet, brown pork chops in oil over medium-high heat. Meanwhile, prepare stuffing according to package directions. Spread pie filling into a greased 13-in. x 9-in. baking dish. Place the pork chops on top; spoon stuffing over chops.

2 Cover and bake at 350° for 35 minutes. Uncover; bake 10 minutes longer or until a meat thermometer reads 160°. **YIELD:** 6 servings.

TACO CASSEROLE

Prep: 20 min. **Bake:** 20 min.

When you're bored with traditional tacos, give this filling main dish a try. It puts the same Southwestern taste into a comforting casserole.

Bonnie King // Lansing, Michigan

2-1/2 pounds ground beef
   2 packages taco seasoning
2/3 cup water
   1 can (16 ounces) kidney beans, rinsed
     and drained
   1 cup (4 ounces) shredded Monterey Jack
     or pepper Jack cheese
   2 eggs, lightly beaten
   1 cup 2% milk
1-1/2 cups biscuit/baking mix
   1 cup (8 ounces) sour cream

   1 cup (4 ounces) shredded cheddar cheese
   2 cups shredded lettuce
   1 medium tomato, diced
   1 can (2-1/4 ounces) sliced ripe olives, drained

1 In a large skillet, cook beef over medium heat until meat is no longer pink; drain. Stir in taco seasoning and water. Bring to a boil. Reduce heat and simmer for 5 minutes. Stir in beans.

2 Spoon meat mixture into a greased 8-in. square baking dish. Sprinkle with Monterey Jack cheese. In a large bowl, combine the eggs, milk and biscuit mix until moistened. Pour over cheese.

3 Bake, uncovered, at 400° for 20-25 minutes or until lightly browned and a knife inserted near the center comes out clean. Spread with sour cream. Top with cheddar, lettuce, tomato and olives.
YIELD: 6-8 servings.

I have been making this recipe for years, changing it here and there until this delicious version is now what I serve. It's a favorite of company and family alike.

Sharon Belmont // Lincoln, Nebraska

PORK BURRITOS
Prep: 20 min. **Cook:** 8 hours

1 boneless pork sirloin roast (3 pounds)
1/4 cup reduced-sodium chicken broth
1 envelope reduced-sodium taco seasoning
1 tablespoon dried parsley flakes
2 garlic cloves, minced
1/2 teaspoon pepper
1/4 teaspoon salt
1 can (16 ounces) refried beans
1 can (4 ounces) chopped green chilies
14 flour tortillas (8 inches), warmed
Optional toppings: shredded lettuce, chopped
    tomatoes, chopped green pepper, guacamole,
    reduced-fat sour cream and shredded reduced-
    fat cheddar cheese

1 Cut roast in half; place in a 4- or 5-qt. slow cooker. In a small bowl, combine the broth, taco seasoning, parsley, garlic, pepper and salt. Pour over roast. Cover and cook on low for 8-10 hours or until meat is very tender.

2 Remove pork from the slow cooker; cool slightly. Shred with two forks; set aside. Skim fat from the liquid; stir in beans and chilies. Return pork to the slow cooker; heat through.

3 Spoon 1/2 cup pork mixture down the center of each tortilla; add toppings of your choice. Carefully fold sides and ends over filling; roll up. **YIELD:** 14 servings.

SALMON MACARONI BAKE
Prep: 20 min. **Bake:** 30 min.

A neighbor brought us this creamy casserole the night after our newborn daughter came home from the hospital.

Carrie Mitchell // Raleigh, North Carolina

1 package (14 ounces) deluxe macaroni and
    cheese dinner mix
1 can (10-3/4 ounces) condensed cream of
    mushroom soup, undiluted
1/2 cup 2% milk
1 pouch (6 ounces) boneless skinless pink salmon

1 tablespoon grated onion *or* 1/2 teaspoon
    onion powder
1/2 cup shredded cheddar cheese
1/2 cup dry bread crumbs
2 tablespoons butter, cubed

1 Prepare macaroni and cheese according to package directions. Stir in the soup, milk, salmon, onion and cheddar cheese.

2 Transfer to a greased 1-1/2-qt. baking dish. Sprinkle with bread crumbs; dot with butter. Bake, uncovered, at 375° for 30 minutes or until heated through. **YIELD:** 4 servings.

Not even finicky eaters can resist the veggies in this main dish when they're seasoned with soup mix. I sometimes replace the ham with cooked kielbasa or smoked sausage.

Melody Williamson //
Blaine, Washington

GARLIC POTATOES AND HAM
Prep: 10 min. **Cook:** 35 min.

- 8 small red potatoes, cut into wedges
- 1 tablespoon canola oil
- 1 package (16 ounces) frozen broccoli cuts, partially thawed
- 1 cup cubed fully cooked ham
- 1 envelope herb with garlic soup mix

1 In a large skillet, cook potatoes in oil over medium-high heat for 10 minutes or until lightly browned. Stir in the broccoli, ham and dry soup mix. Reduce heat; cover and cook for 25 minutes or until potatoes are tender. **YIELD:** 4 servings.

CAVATINI PASTA   PICTURED ON RIGHT

Prep: 30 min. + simmering **Bake:** 35 min.

This recipe has been in my family as long as I can remember, and it is still a favorite. I love to make it when we have company since it's always a hit.
Russ Palmer // Saranac, Michigan

- 2 pounds ground beef
- 2 medium onions, chopped
- 1 medium green pepper, chopped
- 6 garlic cloves, minced
- 4 cups water
- 1 can (12 ounces) tomato paste
- 1 can (4 ounces) mushroom stems and pieces, drained
- 1 package (3-1/2 ounces) sliced pepperoni
- 2 envelopes spaghetti sauce mix
- 1 teaspoon Italian seasoning
PASTA:
- 8 cups water
- 1 cup *each* uncooked elbow macaroni, bow tie pasta and medium pasta shells
- 2 cups (8 ounces) shredded part-skim mozzarella cheese

1 In a Dutch oven, cook the beef, onions and pepper over medium heat until meat is no longer pink; drain. Add garlic; cook 1 minute longer. Stir in the water, tomato paste, mushrooms, pepperoni, sauce mix and Italian seasoning. Bring to a boil. Reduce heat; simmer, uncovered, for 1 hour.

2 Meanwhile, for pasta, bring water to a boil in a large saucepan. Add macaroni and pastas. Return to a boil, stirring occasionally. Cook, uncovered, for 10-12 minutes or until tender; drain. Stir into tomato sauce. Transfer to a greased 13-in. x 9-in. baking dish (dish will be full).

3 Bake at 350° for 30 minutes. Sprinkle with cheese. Bake 5-10 minutes longer or until cheese is melted. **YIELD:** 14 servings.

This is one of my gang's favorite sandwiches. The zesty salad dressing makes it tastier than just plain mayonnaise. This is also good using canned chicken for the tuna, or using French dressing for the ranch dressing.

Heidi Wilcox // Lapeer, Michigan

OPEN-FACED TUNA BURGERS
Prep/Total Time: 15 min.

   3 slices bread, crusts removed, cubed
1/2 cup evaporated milk
4-1/2 teaspoons ranch salad dressing mix
   2 cans (6 ounces *each*) tuna, drained and flaked
   1 jar (2 ounces) chopped pimientos, drained
   4 hamburger buns, split and toasted

1 In a large bowl, soak bread cubes in evaporated milk; let stand for 5 minutes. Stir in the salad dressing mix, tuna and pimientos. Spoon about 1/4 cup onto each bun half.

2 Place on a baking sheet. Broil 5-6 in. from the heat for 4 minutes or until golden brown. **YIELD:** 4 servings.

ITALIAN CHICKEN AND RICE
Prep: 10 min. Bake: 25 min.

I combined the best of three different recipes to come up with this tender and tasty dish. It's become my family's favorite way to eat chicken.

Cathee Bethel // Lebanon, Oregon

2/3 cup biscuit/baking mix
1/3 cup grated Parmesan cheese
   2 teaspoons Italian seasoning
   1 teaspoon paprika
   1 can (5 ounces) evaporated milk, *divided*
   6 boneless skinless chicken breast halves
   2 cups boiling water
   2 cups uncooked instant rice
   1 teaspoon salt, optional
   2 tablespoons butter, melted

1 In a shallow bowl, combine the first four ingredients. Place 1/3 cup milk in another bowl. Dip chicken in milk, then coat with the cheese mixture.

2 In a greased 13-in. x 9-in. baking dish, combine the water, rice, salt if desired and remaining milk. Top with chicken. Drizzle with butter.

3 Bake, uncovered, at 425° for 25-30 minutes or until the rice is tender and a meat thermometer reads 170°. **YIELD:** 6 servings.

ITALIAN SEASONING

Italian seasoning can be found in the spice aisle of most grocery stores. A basic blend might contain marjoram, thyme, rosemary, savory, sage, oregano and basil. —Taste of Home Test Kitchen

SPANISH SAUSAGE SUPPER

Prep/Total Time: 25 min.

A pastor's wife shared her recipe for this colorful all in one skillet meal that she frequently brings to church dinners. Hearty chunks of smoked sausage and canned tomatoes with chilies add just the right amount of zip.

Gene Pitts // Wilsonville, Alabama

1/2 cup chopped green pepper
1/3 cup chopped celery
1/4 cup chopped onion
  1 tablespoon canola oil

1 pound fully cooked smoked sausage, sliced
2 cups water
1 can (10 ounces) diced tomatoes and green chilies, undrained
1 package (6.0 ounces) Spanish rice and pasta mix
1/4 cup sliced pimiento-stuffed olives
1/8 teaspoon pepper

1 In a large skillet, saute the green pepper, celery and onion in oil until tender. Stir in the remaining ingredients. Cover and simmer for 15-20 minutes or until rice is tender and liquid is absorbed, stirring occasionally. **YIELD:** 4 servings.

SOUTHWEST TORTILLA-TURKEY SKILLET

Prep/Total Time: 25 min.

I wanted to cut back on red meat, but my husband thinks ground turkey can be dry. I think the taco seasoning and jalapeno juice in this recipe give the turkey added flavor and moistness—and he agrees.

Lindsay Ludden // Omaha, Nebraska

1/2 **pound ground turkey**
3/4 **cup black beans, rinsed and drained**
1/2 **cup water**
1/3 **cup sliced ripe olives**
  2 **tablespoons reduced-sodium taco seasoning**
  1 **tablespoon juice from pickled jalapeno slices**
  1 **flour tortillas (10 inches), cut into 1-inch pieces**
1/2 **cup shredded reduced-fat Mexican cheese blend**
  2 **tablespoons pickled jalapeno slices**
  2 **tablespoons reduced-fat sour cream**

1 In a large skillet, cook turkey over medium heat until no longer pink; drain. Stir in the beans, water, olives, taco seasoning and juice from jalapenos. Bring to a boil. Reduce heat; simmer, uncovered, for 6-7 minutes or until thickened.

2 Stir in tortilla. Sprinkle with cheese and jalapeno. Remove from the heat and cover for 1-2 minutes or until cheese is melted. Serve with sour cream. **YIELD:** 2 servings.

Taco seasoning mix adds fast flavor to this speedy skillet dish. Because it comes together quickly, I fix it frequently.
Leota Shaffer // Sterling, Virginia

FIESTA FRY PAN DINNER
Prep/Total Time: 30 min.

  1 pound ground turkey *or* beef
1/2 cup chopped onion
  1 envelope taco seasoning
1-1/2 cups water
1-1/2 cups sliced zucchini
  1 can (14-1/2 ounces) stewed tomatoes, undrained
  1 cup frozen corn
1-1/2 cups uncooked instant rice
  1 cup (4 ounces) shredded cheddar cheese

1 In a skillet, cook turkey and onion until meat is no longer pink; drain if necessary. Stir in the taco seasoning, water, zucchini, tomatoes and corn; bring to a boil. Add rice. Reduce heat; cover and simmer for 5 minutes or until rice is tender and liquid is absorbed. Sprinkle with cheese; cover and let stand until the cheese is melted. **YIELD:** 6 servings.

CHICKEN STEW OVER BISCUITS
Prep: 5 min. **Cook:** 8 hours

A pleasant sauce coats this chicken and veggie dinner that's slow-cooked to tender perfection, then served over biscuits. My family can't get enough of it.
Kathy Garrett // Browns Mills, New Jersey

  2 envelopes chicken gravy mix
  2 cups water
3/4 cup white wine
  1 tablespoon minced fresh parsley
  1 to 2 teaspoons chicken bouillon granules
  1 teaspoon minced garlic
1/2 teaspoon pepper
  5 medium carrots, cut into 1-inch chunks
  1 large onion, cut into eight wedges
  1 broiler/fryer chicken (3 to 4 pounds), cut up, skin removed
  3 tablespoons all-purpose flour
1/3 cup cold water
  1 tube (7-1/2 ounces) refrigerated buttermilk biscuits

1 In a 5-qt. slow cooker, combine the gravy mix, water, wine, parsley, bouillon, garlic and pepper until blended. Add the carrots, onion and chicken. Cover and cook on low for 6-8 hours.

2 In a small bowl, combine flour and cold water until smooth; gradually stir into slow cooker. Cover and cook on high for 1 hour or until thickened.

3 Meanwhile, bake biscuits according to package directions. Place the biscuits in soup bowls; top with stew. **YIELD:** 5 servings.

My sister gave me this recipe a while ago. The filling one-dish meal has a fun popover crust—and the pizza flavor makes it a hit with all ages.

**Linda Wilkens //
Maple Grove, Minnesota**

PUFFED PIZZA CASSEROLE
Prep: 25 min. **Bake:** 20 min.

  1/3 pound lean ground beef (90% lean)
  1/4 cup chopped onion
  1/2 cup tomato sauce
    3 tablespoons water
    3 teaspoons spaghetti sauce mix
  1/3 cup all-purpose flour
  1/3 cup 2% milk
    2 tablespoons beaten egg
    1 teaspoon canola oil
  1/2 cup shredded part-skim mozzarella cheese
    2 tablespoons grated Parmesan cheese

1 In a large skillet, cook beef and onion over medium heat until meat is no longer pink; drain. Add the tomato sauce, water and spaghetti sauce mix. Bring to a boil. Reduce heat; simmer, uncovered, for 5 minutes. Meanwhile, place flour in a small bowl. Combine the milk, egg and oil; whisk into flour just until blended.

2 Pour meat mixture into a 3-cup baking dish coated with cooking spray. Sprinkle with mozzarella cheese. Pour flour mixture over top. Sprinkle with Parmesan cheese.

3 Bake, uncovered, at 400° for 20-25 minutes or until golden brown and center is set. **YIELD:** 2 servings.

CRUMB-COATED COD
Prep/Total Time: 30 min.

Fish fillets get fast flavor from Italian salad dressing mix and a breading made with seasoned stuffing mix. I serve this baked fish with a tossed salad or relishes.

Julia Bruce // Tuscola, Illinois

  2 tablespoons canola oil
  2 tablespoons water
  1 envelope Italian salad dressing mix
  2 cups crushed stuffing mix
  4 cod fillets (about 6 ounces *each*)

1 In a shallow bowl, combine the oil, water and salad dressing mix. Place the stuffing mix in another bowl. Dip fillets in salad dressing mixture, then in stuffing.

2 Place on a greased baking sheet. Bake at 425° for 15-20 minutes or until fish flakes easily with a fork. **YIELD:** 4 servings.

PINEAPPLE CHICKEN FAJITAS

Prep: 25 min. **Cook:** 15 min.

Honey and pineapple add a sweet twist to these fajitas that my family frequently requests. I like to serve them with coleslaw and baked or fried potatoes.

Raymonde Bourgeois // Swastika, Ontario

- 2 pounds boneless skinless chicken breasts, cut into strips
- 1 tablespoon olive oil
- 1 *each* medium green, sweet red and yellow pepper, julienned
- 1 medium onion, cut into thin wedges
- 2 tablespoons fajita seasoning mix
- 1/4 cup water
- 2 tablespoons honey
- 1 tablespoon dried parsley flakes
- 1 teaspoon garlic powder
- 1/2 teaspoon salt
- 1/2 cup unsweetened pineapple chunks, drained
- 8 flour tortillas (10 inches), warmed

1 In a large nonstick skillet, cook chicken in oil for 4-5 minutes. Add peppers and onion; cook and stir 4-5 minutes longer.

2 In a small bowl, combine seasoning mix and water; stir in the honey, parsley, garlic powder and salt. Stir into skillet. Add pineapple. Cook and stir for 1-2 minutes or until chicken is no longer pink and vegetables are tender.

3 Place chicken mixture on one side of each tortilla; fold tortillas over filling. **YIELD:** 8 fajitas.

I made some changes to the original recipe by adding extra tomatoes, more color, celery for crunch, relish for a hint of sweetness and ham to make it more filling.

Karen Ballance // Wolf Lake, Illinois

HAM MACARONI SALAD

Prep: 15 min. + chilling

- 1 package (7-1/2 ounces) macaroni and cheese
- 1/2 cup mayonnaise
- 2 tablespoon Dijon mustard
- 3 medium tomatoes, seeded and chopped
- 1 medium cucumber, peeled and chopped
- 1 cup diced fully cooked ham
- 4 hard-cooked eggs, chopped
- 1/2 cup chopped celery
- 1/4 cup sweet pickle relish
- 2 tablespoons chopped onion
- 1/2 teaspoon salt
- 1/8 teaspoon pepper

1 Prepare macaroni and cheese according to package directions; cool for 20 minutes. Stir in mayonnaise and mustard. Fold in the remaining ingredients. Refrigerate for 2 hours or until chilled. **YIELD:** 8 servings.

WILD RICE MUSHROOM CHICKEN PICTURED ON RIGHT

Prep: 15 min. **Cook:** 30 min. + freezing

I use a wild rice mix to put a tasty spin on a traditional chicken and rice bake. It's simple and delicious with leftover chicken or turkey.

Jacqueline Graves // Lawrenceville, Georgia

- 2 packages (6 ounces *each*) long grain and wild rice mix
- 8 bone-in chicken breast halves (8 ounces *each*)
- 5 tablespoons butter, *divided*
- 1 large sweet red pepper, chopped
- 2 jars (4-1/2 ounces *each*) sliced mushrooms, drained

1 Prepare rice according to package directions. Meanwhile, in a large skillet, cook chicken in 3 tablespoons butter for 10 minutes on each side or until browned and a meat thermometer reads 170°. Remove chicken and keep warm.

2 Add remaining butter to pan drippings; saute red pepper until tender. Stir in mushrooms; heat through. Add to rice. Serve four chicken breasts with half of the rice mixture.

3 Place remaining chicken in a greased 11-in. x 7-in. baking dish; top with remaining rice mixture. Cool. Cover and freeze for up to 3 months.

4 **TO USE FROZEN CASSEROLE:** Thaw in the refrigerator. Cover; bake at 350° for 35-40 minutes. **YIELD:** 2 casseroles (4 servings each).

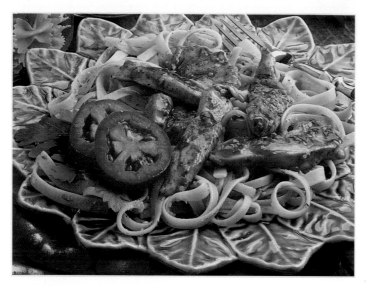

Savory seasonings add zip to these moist chicken strips tossed with pasta. It goes well with steamed broccoli and glazed carrots to make a quick and colorful meal.

Kathy Kirkland //
Denham Springs, Louisiana

HERBED CHICKEN FETTUCCINE

Prep: 25 min. **Cook:** 15 min.

- 1 to 2 teaspoons salt-free seasoning blend
- 1 teaspoon poultry seasoning
- 1 pound boneless skinless chicken breast, cut into 1-inch strips
- 2 tablespoons olive oil
- 4 tablespoons butter, *divided*
- 2/3 cup water
- 2 tablespoons teriyaki sauce
- 2 tablespoons onion soup mix
- 1 envelope savory herb and garlic soup mix, *divided*
- 8 ounces uncooked fettuccine *or* pasta of your choice
- 2 tablespoons grated Parmesan cheese
- 1 tablespoon Worcestershire sauce

1 Combine seasoning blend and poultry seasoning; sprinkle over chicken. In a large skillet, saute chicken in oil and 2 tablespoons butter for about 5 minutes or until chicken is no longer pink. Add the water, teriyaki sauce, onion soup mix and 2 tablespoons herb and garlic soup mix. Bring to a boil. Reduce the heat; cover and simmer for 15 minutes.

2 Meanwhile, cook fettuccine according to package directions. Drain; add to chicken mixture. Stir in the cheese, Worcestershire sauce, remaining butter, and remaining herb and garlic soup mix; toss to coat. **YIELD:** 4 servings.

PANTRY SKILLET

Prep/Total Time: 30 min.

I came up with this all-in-one dish by using whatever ingredients I had on hand one day.

Susie Smith // Sauk Village, Illinois

- 1 pound ground beef
- 1 can (10-3/4 ounces) condensed tomato soup, undiluted
- 1-1/2 cups water
- 1 envelope onion mushroom soup mix
- 1/2 pound fresh mushrooms, sliced
- 1-1/2 cups frozen cut green beans
- 3 medium carrots, grated
- 1 cup cooked rice
- 2 slices process American cheese, cut into strips

1 In a large skillet over medium heat, cook beef until no longer pink; drain. Stir in the soup, water and soup mix. Stir in the mushrooms, beans, carrots and rice. Bring to a boil. Reduce heat; cover and simmer for 5-7 minutes or until beans are tender. Top with cheese; cover and let stand until cheese is melted. **YIELD:** 6 servings.

LEMON GARLIC SHRIMP

Prep: 15 min. + marinating **Cook:** 30 min.

*This was the meal I cooked for my husband on
our first date. To this day, he still remembers that
night whenever I cook it for him.*

Kristine DeGaetano // Brick, New Jersey

- 1 small onion, chopped
- 2 garlic cloves, minced
- 3 tablespoons canola oil
- 2 tablespoons lemon juice
- 4 teaspoons reduced-sodium soy sauce
- 1 teaspoon ground ginger
- 3/4 pound uncooked large shrimp, peeled and deveined
- 1 package (6 ounces) long grain and wild rice mix

1 In a large bowl, combine the first six ingredients. Pour 1/2 cup marinade into a large resealable plastic bag; add shrimp. Seal bag and turn to coat; refrigerate for 2-3 hours, turning occasionally. Cover and refrigerate remaining marinade.

2 Cook rice according to package directions. Cover and refrigerate 1 cup cooked rice for another use. Drain and discard marinade from shrimp.

3 In a large skillet, saute shrimp in reserved marinade for 3-4 minutes or until shrimp turn pink. Serve shrimp with remaining rice. **YIELD:** 2 servings.

LASAGNA IN A BUN

Prep: 25 min. **Bake:** 20 min.

This mouthwatering recipe is always a hit because it's a little like traditional lasagna and a little like a sandwich. What could be better than that combination?

Margaret Peterson // Forest City, Iowa

- 3/4 **pound ground beef**
- 1 **can (14-1/2 ounces) diced tomatoes, drained**
- 2 **tablespoons onion soup mix**
- 1/4 **teaspoon dried basil**
- 1/4 **teaspoon dried oregano**
- 8 **hoagie buns**
- 3/4 **cup 4% cottage cheese**
- 1 **egg, lightly beaten**
- 1 **cup (4 ounces) shredded part-skim mozzarella cheese,** *divided*

1 In a large skillet, cook beef over medium heat until no longer pink; drain. Stir in the tomatoes, soup mix, basil and oregano. Cook, uncovered, for 5 minutes or until heated through.

2 Cut a thin slice off the top of each bun. Carefully hollow out bun bottoms, leaving a 1/4-in. shell (discard removed bread or save for another use).

3 In a small bowl, combine the cottage cheese, egg and 1/4 cup mozzarella cheese; spoon into buns. Top with meat mixture; sprinkle with remaining mozzarella cheese. Replace bun tops.

4 Wrap each sandwich in heavy-duty foil; place on a baking sheet. Bake at 400° for 20-25 minutes or until heated through. **YIELD:** 8 servings.

Taco seasoning adds zip to this hearty main dish. It's easy to top with instant mashed potatoes, which I stir up while browning the beef.

Mary Malchow // Neenah, Wisconsin

SPICY SHEPHERD'S PIE

Prep/Total Time: 30 min.

1 package (6.6 ounces) instant mashed potatoes
1 pound ground beef
1 medium onion, chopped
1 can (14-1/2 ounces) diced tomatoes, undrained
1 can (11 ounces) Mexicorn, drained
1 can (2-1/4 ounces) sliced ripe olives, drained
1 envelope taco seasoning
1-1/2 teaspoons chili powder
1/2 teaspoon salt
1/8 teaspoon garlic powder
1 cup (4 ounces) shredded cheddar cheese, *divided*

1 Prepare mashed potatoes according to package directions. Meanwhile, in a large skillet, cook beef and onion over medium heat until meat is no longer pink; drain. Add the tomatoes, corn, olives, taco seasoning, chili powder, salt and garlic powder. Bring to a boil; cook and stir for 1-2 minutes.

2 Transfer to a greased 2-1/2-qt. baking dish. Top with 3/4 cup cheese. Spread mashed potatoes over the top; sprinkle with remaining cheese. Bake, uncovered, at 350° for 12-15 minutes or until cheese is melted. **YIELD:** 4-6 servings.

CHICKEN AND RICE

Prep: 15 min. **Bake:** 50 min.

Crunched for time? Consider this fast-to-fix chicken and rice bake. After popping it in the oven, you can toss together a salad and have dinner on the table in no time.

Doris Barb // El Dorado, Kansas

6 boneless skinless chicken breast halves
1-1/2 cups uncooked instant rice
1/2 cup boiling water
1 can (10-3/4 ounces) condensed cream of chicken soup, undiluted
1 can (10-3/4 ounces) condensed cream of celery soup, undiluted
2 tablespoons onion soup mix
1 package (10 ounces) frozen peas, thawed
1/2 cup minced fresh parsley

1 Place chicken in a greased 13-in. x 9-in. baking dish. In a small bowl, combine rice and water. In a large bowl, combine the soups, soup mix and peas; stir into rice mixture. Spread over chicken.

2 Cover and bake at 350° for 40 minutes. Uncover; sprinkle with parsley. Bake about 10-15 minutes longer or until a meat thermometer reads 170°. **YIELD:** 6 servings.

I created this recipe one Sunday afternoon to use up ingredients I had on hand. My husband and a guest loved the tasty combination of salmon, vegetables and noodles.

Jenny Kimberlin //
Overland Park, Kansas

SALMON PASTA PRIMAVERA

Prep/Total Time: 30 min.

8 ounces uncooked fettuccine, broken in half
1-1/2 cups fresh *or* frozen broccoli florets
1/4 cup chopped red onion
2 tablespoons chopped green pepper
4 tablespoons butter, *divided*
2 garlic cloves, minced
1 envelope Alfredo sauce mix
1/2 cup evaporated milk
1/2 cup water
Salt and pepper to taste

1 cup cubed cooked salmon
Crumbled cooked bacon, optional

1 Cook fettuccine according to package directions. Meanwhile, in a large skillet, saute the broccoli, onion and green pepper in 2 tablespoons butter until vegetables are tender. Add garlic; cook 1 minute longer.

2 In a large saucepan, combine the sauce mix, milk, water, salt, pepper and remaining butter. Cook over medium heat until thickened. Add the salmon and heat through. Drain pasta; add to vegetable mixture. Top with sauce and gently toss to coat. Sprinkle with bacon if desired. **YIELD:** 4 servings.

TACO NOODLE DINNER

Prep: 15 min. Cook: 35 min.

Taco seasoning provides the family-pleasing Tex-Mex flavor in this skillet supper. The topping of sour cream and fresh parsley is the perfect finishing touch.

Marcy Cella // L'Anse, Michigan

1 pound ground beef
1/4 cup chopped onion
3/4 cup water
1 envelope taco seasoning
1/2 teaspoon salt
1 can (4 ounces) mushroom stems and
    pieces, drained

3 cups uncooked fine egg noodles
2-1/2 to 3 cups tomato juice
1 cup (8 ounces) sour cream
1 tablespoon minced fresh parsley

1 In a skillet, cook the beef and onion over medium heat until meat is no longer pink; drain. Stir in the water, taco seasoning and salt. Reduce heat; simmer for 2-3 minutes. Add mushrooms. Sprinkle noodles over the top. Pour tomato juice over the noodles and stir gently. Cover and simmer for 20-25 minutes or until noodles are tender.

2 Remove from the heat. Combine sour cream and parsley; spread over the top. Cover and let stand for 5 minutes. **YIELD:** 6 servings.

PEPPER BEEF GOULASH

Prep: 10 min. **Cook:** 4 hours

I only need a couple of common ingredients to turn beef stew meat into a hearty entree. No one will ever guess the secret behind this great goulash.

Peggy Key // Grant, Alabama

1/2 cup water
1 can (6 ounces) tomato paste
2 tablespoons cider vinegar
1 envelope sloppy joe seasoning

2 to 2-1/4 pounds beef stew meat
  (3/4-inch cubes)
1 celery rib, cut into 1/2-inch slices
1 medium green pepper, cut
  into 1/2-inch chunks
Hot cooked rice or noodles

1 In a 3-qt. slow cooker, combine the water, tomato paste, vinegar and sloppy joe seasoning. Stir in the beef, celery and green pepper.

2 Cover and cook on high for 4-5 hours. Serve with rice. **YIELD:** 4-5 servings.

ITALIAN ORANGE ROUGHY

Prep: 5 min. + marinating **Cook:** 5 min.

My family really enjoys this moist and tender fish swimming in a flavorful sauce. It's easy to marinate first, and then cook quickly in the microwave.

Alice Mashek // Schaumburg, Illinois

- 1 pound orange roughy fillets
- 1/2 cup tomato juice
- 2 tablespoons white vinegar
- 1 envelope Italian salad dressing mix
- 1/4 cup chopped green onions
- 1/4 cup chopped green pepper

1 Place fish fillets in a shallow 2-qt. microwave-safe dish, positioning the thickest portion of fish toward the outside edges. In a small bowl, combine the tomato juice, vinegar and salad dressing mix; pour over fish. Cover and refrigerate for 30 minutes.

2 Sprinkle with onions and green pepper. Cover and microwave on high for 2 minutes. Turn fillets over; cook 1-3 minutes longer or until fish flakes easily with a fork. Let stand, covered, for 2 minutes.
YIELD: 4 servings.

EDITOR'S NOTE: This recipe was tested in a 1,100-watt microwave.

I sometimes treat my friends at work to these peppy pitas at lunchtime. I prepare everything in advance, so the spicy sandwiches can just be zapped in the microwave.

Helen Overman // Pottsborgo, Texas

TEX-MEX PITAS

Prep: 40 min. **Bake:** 10 min.

    2 pounds ground beef
    1 envelope taco seasoning
 1/3 cup water
    1 can (16 ounces) refried beans
    1 can (10 ounces) diced tomatoes and green
      chilies, undrained
Pinch ground cumin
    7 pita breads (6 inches), halved
    3 cups (12 ounces) shredded cheddar cheese
Sliced jalapenos

1 In a large skillet, cook beef over medium heat until no longer pink; drain. Stir in the taco seasoning, water, beans, tomatoes and cumin. Simmer, uncovered, for 20 minutes, stirring occasionally.

2 Spoon about 1/3 cup into each pita half; top with about 2 tablespoons cheese and a few jalapeno slices. Place in an ungreased 13-in. x 9-in. baking pan.

3 Bake at 350° for 10 minutes or until cheese is melted. **YIELD:** 7 servings.

EDITOR'S NOTE: Wear disposable gloves when cutting hot peppers; the oils can burn skin. Avoid touching your face.

TURKEY STUFFING ROLL-UPS

Prep: 15 min. **Bake:** 25 min.

When I worked at a local deli, a customer gave me this family-pleasing recipe. After a busy day, I tried it with boxed stuffing mix in place of homemade dressing. It's wonderful with salad and green beans.

Darlene Ward // Hot Springs, Arkansas

    1 package (6 ounces) stuffing mix
    1 can (10-3/4 ounces) condensed cream of
      chicken soup, undiluted
 3/4 cup 2% milk
    1 pound sliced deli smoked turkey
    1 can (2.8 ounces) french-fried onions, crushed

1 Prepare the stuffing mix according to package directions. Meanwhile, in a small bowl, combine soup and milk; set aside. Spoon about 1/4 cup stuffing onto each turkey slice.

2 Roll up and place in a greased 13-in. x 9-in. baking dish. Pour soup mixture over roll-ups. Bake, uncovered, at 350° for 20 minutes. Sprinkle with onions. Bake 5 minutes longer or until heated through. **YIELD:** 6 servings.

Biscuit mix really speeds up the preparation of this can't-miss casserole. You just pour the batter over the beef mixture and pop the dish into the oven.

Taste of Home Test Kitchen

MEAT BUN BAKE

Prep: 20 min. **Bake:** 20 min.

1-1/2 pounds ground beef
   2 cups chopped cabbage
  1/4 cup chopped onion
  1/2 teaspoon salt
  1/4 teaspoon pepper
  1/2 to 1 cup shredded cheddar cheese
1-1/2 cups biscuit/baking mix
   1 cup 2% milk
   2 eggs

1 In a large skillet, cook beef over medium heat until no longer pink; drain. Add the cabbage, onion, salt and pepper; cook over medium heat for 15 minutes or until the cabbage and onion are tender. Stir in cheese.

2 Spoon into a greased 13-in. x 9-in. baking dish. In a large bowl, blend the biscuit mix, milk and eggs. Pour over beef mixture. Bake, uncovered, at 400° for 20-25 minutes or until golden brown. **YIELD:** 6 servings.

HERBED CHICKEN WITH WILD RICE PICTURED ON RIGHT

Prep: 20 min. **Cook:** 4 hours

My family is always very busy, so it's nice to come home to a meal that's already prepared and ready to eat.

Becky Gifford // Conway, Arkansas

   1 package (6 ounces) long grain and wild rice mix
   6 boneless skinless chicken breast halves (5 ounces *each*)
   1 tablespoon canola oil
   1 teaspoon butter
  1/2 pound sliced fresh mushrooms
   1 can (10-3/4 ounces) condensed cream of chicken soup, undiluted

   1 cup water
   3 bacon strips, cooked and crumbled
   1 teaspoon dried parsley flakes
  1/2 teaspoon dried thyme
  1/4 teaspoon dried tarragon

1 Place rice in a 5-qt. slow cooker; set aside seasoning packet. In a large skillet, brown chicken in oil and butter. Add to slow cooker. In the same skillet, saute mushrooms until tender; place over chicken.

2 In a small bowl, combine the soup, water, bacon, herbs and contents of seasoning packet. Pour over top. Cover and cook on low for 4-5 hours or until meat is tender. **YIELD:** 6 servings.

HOT HOAGIES

Prep/Total Time: 15 min.

I use my family's favorite combination of meats and cheeses in these broiled sandwiches, and then serve them with chips and pickles. They're a hit every time.

Paula Hadley // Somerville, Louisiana

3/4 cup butter, softened
1 envelope Italian salad dressing mix
6 hoagie buns, split
12 to 16 ounces sliced luncheon meat (salami, ham and/*or* turkey)
12 thin slices cheese (Swiss, cheddar and/*or* brick)

1 In a small bowl, combine butter and salad dressing mix; spread 1 tablespoonful inside each bun. On bottom of each bun, layer one slice of meat, two slices of cheese and another slice of meat; replace tops. Spread 1 tablespoon butter mixture over top of each bun.

2 Place on a baking sheet. Broil 6 in. from the heat for 2-3 minutes or until tops are lightly browned. **YIELD:** 6 servings.

I don't have a lot of time to cook, so I came up with this tasty way to beef up a box of macaroni and cheese. The hearty mixture gets extra flavor from corn, ripe olives and zippy salsa.

Charlotte Kremer // Pahrump, Nevada

MEATY MAC 'N' CHEESE

Prep/Total Time: 20 min.

    1 package (7-1/4 ounces) macaroni and cheese
    1 pound ground beef
1/4 cup chopped onion
1-1/2 cups salsa
  1/2 cup fresh *or* frozen corn
    1 can (2-1/4 ounces) sliced ripe olives, drained
    3 tablespoons diced pimientos
Shredded cheddar cheese
Chopped tomato

1 Set aside cheese sauce mix from macaroni and cheese; cook macaroni according to package directions.

2 Meanwhile, in a large saucepan, cook beef and onion over medium heat until meat is no longer pink; drain. Add the salsa, corn, olives and pimientos; cook until heated through.

3 Drain macaroni; add to beef mixture with contents of cheese sauce mix. Cook and stir until blended and heated through. Sprinkle with cheese and tomato. **YIELD:** 4-6 servings.

CREAMED HAM ON CORN BREAD

Prep/Total Time: 30 min.

To make a satisfying and economical supper, I top pieces of corn bread with a cheesy sauce chock-full of ham. This is one meal my family asks for over and over again.

Denise Hershman // Cromwell, Indiana

    1 package (8-1/2 ounces) corn bread/muffin mix
    1 egg
1/3 cup 2% milk
CREAMED HAM:
    2 tablespoons butter
    2 tablespoons all-purpose flour

  1/2 teaspoon ground mustard
  1/4 teaspoon salt
1-1/2 cups 2% milk
  3/4 cup shredded cheddar cheese
1-1/2 cups cubed fully cooked ham

1 In a large bowl, combine the corn bread mix, egg and milk until blended. Spread into a greased 8-in. square baking pan. Bake at 400° for 18-20 minutes.

2 Meanwhile, in a large saucepan, melt butter; stir in the flour, mustard and salt until smooth. Add milk. Bring to a boil; cook and stir for 2 minutes or until thickened. Stir in cheese until melted. Add ham and heat through. Cut corn bread into squares; top with creamed ham. **YIELD:** 6 servings.

Packed with meat, cheese and olives, these roll-ups are always a hit at parties. Experiment with different lunch meat and salad dressing flavors.

Linda Searl // Pampa, Texas

CLUB ROLL-UPS
Prep/Total Time: 25 min.

- 1 package (3 ounces) cream cheese, softened
- 1/2 cup ranch salad dressing
- 2 tablespoons ranch salad dressing mix
- 8 bacon strips, cooked and crumbled
- 1/2 cup finely chopped onion
- 1 can (2-1/4 ounces) sliced ripe olives, drained
- 1 jar (2 ounces) diced pimientos, drained
- 1/4 cup diced canned jalapeno peppers
- 8 flour tortillas (10 inches), room temperature
- 8 thin slices deli ham
- 8 thin slices deli turkey
- 8 thin slices deli roast beef
- 2 cups (8 ounces) shredded cheddar cheese

1 In a small bowl, beat the cream cheese, ranch dressing and dressing mix until well blended. In another bowl, combine the bacon, onion, olives, pimientos and jalapenos.

2 Spread cream cheese mixture over tortillas; layer with ham, turkey and roast beef. Sprinkle with bacon mixture and cheddar cheese; roll up. **YIELD:** 8 servings.

ARTICHOKE TUNA TOSS
Prep/Total Time: 30 min.

I do volunteer work one evening a week and leave a meal behind for my family. On one occasion, I left this made-in-minutes medley. When I came home, my husband said it was the best pasta dish I'd ever fixed!

Emily Perez // Alexandra, Virginia

- 3-1/2 cups water
- 1/4 cup butter, cubed
- 2 packages (4.6 ounces *each*) garlic and olive oil vermicelli mix
- 1 can (14 ounces) water-packed artichoke hearts, rinsed, drained and quartered
- 2 cans (6 ounces *each*) light water-packed tuna
- 1 package (10 ounces) frozen peas
- 1 tablespoon olive oil
- 1 tablespoon red wine vinegar
- 4 to 6 garlic cloves, minced

1 In a saucepan, bring water and butter to a boil. Stir in the vermicelli with contents of seasoning packets, artichokes, tuna, peas, oil, vinegar and garlic.

2 Return to a boil; cook, uncovered, for 8-10 minutes or until vermicelli is tender. Let stand for 5 minutes. **YIELD:** 6 servings.

HOME-STYLE STEW

Prep: 20 min. **Cook:** 6 hours

My husband and I both work full time, so quick meals are important. Because this stew always tastes great, it's a regular menu item for us.

Marie Shanks // Terre Haute, Indiana

- 2 **packages (16 ounces** *each*) **frozen vegetables for stew**
- 1-1/2 **pounds beef stew meat, cut into 1-inch cubes**
- 1 **can (10-3/4 ounces) condensed cream of mushroom soup, undiluted**
- 1 **can (10-3/4 ounces) condensed tomato soup, undiluted**
- 1 **envelope reduced-sodium onion soup mix**

1 Place vegetables in a 5-qt. slow cooker. In a large nonstick skillet coated with cooking spray, brown beef on all sides.

2 Transfer to slow cooker. Combine the remaining ingredients; pour over top.

3 Cover and cook on low for 6-8 hours or until beef is tender. **YIELD:** 5 servings.

I couldn't wait to try out our microwave after we first purchased the appliance. And this was the first recipe I tried. Guess what? My husband still thinks it is a great dinner!

Donna Garvin // Glens Falls, New York

PORK CHOPS WITH APPLE DRESSING

Prep/Total Time: 25 min.

1-1/2 cups crushed seasoned stuffing
  1 medium tart apple, peeled and chopped
  3 tablespoons butter, melted
  2 tablespoons chopped onion
  1 tablespoon sugar
1/4 teaspoon rubbed sage
1/4 teaspoon salt
1/4 cup raisins
  4 boneless pork loin chops (1/2 inch thick and 6 ounces *each*)
  1 envelope pork gravy mix

1 In a small bowl, combine the first eight ingredients. Place in a greased 11-in. x 7-in. microwave-safe dish. Top with pork chops. Cover and microwave on high for 8-12 minutes or until a meat thermometer reads 160°. Prepare the gravy mix according to package directions. Serve with pork chops. **YIELD:** 4 servings.

EDITOR'S NOTE: This recipe was tested in a 1,100-watt microwave.

TACO PIZZA   PICTURED ON RIGHT

Prep: 30 min. Bake: 10 min.

Convenient prebaked crust makes this tasty taco pizza as easy as can be. I keep the ingredients on hand so that we can whip up this filling meal anytime.

Mary Cass // Baltimore, Maryland

  1 pound ground beef
  1 envelope taco seasoning
  1 cup water
  2 prebaked 12-inch pizza crusts
  1 can (16 ounces) refried beans
3/4 cup salsa
  2 cups coarsely crushed tortilla chips
  2 cups (8 ounces) shredded cheddar cheese
  2 medium tomatoes, chopped, optional
  1 cup shredded lettuce, optional

1 In a large saucepan, cook beef over medium heat until no longer pink; drain. Stir in taco seasoning and water. Bring to a boil; reduce heat. Simmer, uncovered, for 10 minutes; set aside.

2 Place crusts on ungreased pizza pans or baking sheets. Combine beans and salsa; spread over crusts. Top with beef mixture, chips and cheese.

3 Bake at 350° for 13-16 minutes or until cheese is melted. Sprinkle with tomatoes and lettuce if desired. **YIELD:** 2 pizzas (6-8 servings each).

HONEY MUSTARD CHICKEN

Prep: 15 min. **Bake:** 45 min.

Moist and flavorful, this chicken is a real treat. With just 15 minutes of prep time, you'll be out of the kitchen quick!

Richard Gallop // Pueblo, Colorado

- 1/2 cup honey
- 1/4 cup prepared mustard
- 1 envelope ranch salad dressing mix
- 1 tablespoon dried parsley flakes
- 1-1/2 teaspoons Italian seasoning
- 1/2 teaspoon dried basil
- 1/2 teaspoon chili powder
- 1/4 teaspoon garlic powder
- 1/4 teaspoon pepper
- 6 chicken drumsticks
- 6 bone-in chicken thighs

1 For sauce, in a small bowl, combine the first nine ingredients. Set aside 1/2 cup for serving. Place chicken in a greased 15-in. x 10-in. x 1-in. baking pan; brush with remaining sauce.

2 Bake, uncovered, at 350° for 45-50 minutes or until a meat thermometer reads 180° and chicken juices run clear, basting occasionally with pan juices. Warm reserved sauce; serve with chicken. **YIELD:** 6 servings.

By using frozen vegetables and a package of au gratin potatoes, I can get this satisfying stovetop supper on the table in no time. It's an excellent way of getting kids to eat their vegetables.

Penny Greene // Lancaster, Ohio

AU GRATIN SAUSAGE SKILLET

Prep: 15 min. **Cook:** 30 min.

> 1 pound smoked kielbasa *or* Polish sausage, halved and sliced 1/2 inch thick
> 2 tablespoons canola oil
> 1 package (4.9 ounces) au gratin potatoes
> 2-1/2 cups water
> 1 package (8 ounces) frozen California-blend vegetables
> 1 to 2 cups (4 to 8 ounces) shredded cheddar cheese

1 In a large skillet, cook sausage in oil until lightly browned; drain. Add potatoes with contents of sauce mix and water. Cover and cook over medium heat for 18-20 minutes or until the potatoes are almost tender, stirring occasionally.

2 Add vegetables; cover and cook for 8-10 minutes or until potatoes and vegetables are tender. Sprinkle with cheese. Remove from the heat; cover and let stand for 2 minutes or until the cheese is melted. **YIELD:** 4 servings.

BEEFY HASH BROWN BAKE

Prep: 15 min. **Bake:** 25 min.

A topping of french-fried onions provides a little crunch to this meaty main dish. Since this casserole is practically a meal in itself, I simply accompany it with a fruit salad and dessert.

Rochelle Boucher // Brooklyn, Wisconsin

> 4 cups frozen shredded hash brown potatoes
> 3 tablespoons canola oil
> 1/8 teaspoon pepper
> 1 pound ground beef
> 1 cup water
> 1 envelope brown gravy mix
> 1/2 teaspoon garlic salt
> 2 cups frozen mixed vegetables
> 1 can (2.8 ounces) french-fried onions, *divided*

> 1 cup (4 ounces) shredded cheddar cheese, *divided*

1 In a large bowl, combine the potatoes, oil and pepper. Press into a greased 8-in. square baking dish. Bake, uncovered, at 350° for 15-20 minutes or until potatoes are thawed and set.

2 Meanwhile, in a large saucepan over medium heat, cook beef until no longer pink; drain. Stir in water, gravy mix and garlic salt. Bring to a boil; cook and stir for 2 minutes. Add vegetables; cook and stir for 5 minutes. Stir in half of the onions and cheese.

3 Pour over potatoes. Bake for 5-10 minutes. Sprinkle with remaining onions and cheese; bake 5 minutes longer or until cheese is melted. **YIELD:** 4 servings.

A *packaged pesto mix tastefully replaces traditional tomato sauce in this tempting pizza. Served alongside a simple, tossed green salad, this is one of my husband's favorite meals.*

Juanita Fleck // Bullhead City, Arizona

CHICKEN-PESTO PAN PIZZA

Prep/Total Time: 30 min.

   1 tube (13.8 ounces) refrigerated pizza crust
1/2 cup water
   3 tablespoons olive oil
   1 envelope pesto sauce mix
   1 package (10 ounces) frozen chopped spinach,
      thawed and squeezed dry
1/2 cup ricotta cheese
1/4 cup chopped onion
   2 cups shredded cooked chicken
   1 jar (4-1/2 ounces) sliced mushrooms, drained
   4 plum tomatoes, sliced
   1 cup (4 ounces) shredded Swiss cheese
1/4 cup grated Romano cheese

1 Unroll pizza crust into an ungreased 15-in. x 10-in. x 1-in. baking pan; flatten dough and build up edges slightly. Prick dough several times with a fork. Bake at 425° for 7 minutes or until lightly browned.

2 Meanwhile, combine the water, oil and pesto sauce mix in a saucepan. Cook until heated through (do not boil). Add the spinach, ricotta and onion.

3 Spread over crust. Top with chicken, mushrooms, tomatoes and Swiss and Romano cheeses. Bake at 425° for 7 minutes or until crust is golden and cheese is melted. **YIELD:** 8 servings.

TURKEY BURGER PIE

Prep/Total Time: 30 min.

This recipe requires just six ingredients and bakes in less that half an hour, so I can have this hearty dinner on the table in a jiffy.

Danielle Monai // Brooklyn Heights, Ohio

   1 pound lean ground turkey
   1 cup chopped onion
   1 cup shredded reduced-fat cheddar cheese
1/2 cup egg substitute
   1 cup fat-free milk
1/2 cup reduced-fat biscuit/baking mix

1 In a large skillet over medium heat, cook turkey and onion until meat is no longer pink; drain. Transfer to a 9-in. pie plate coated with cooking spray. Sprinkle with cheese.

2 In a small bowl, combine the egg substitute, milk and baking mix. Pour over cheese. Bake at 400° for 20-25 minutes or until golden brown and a knife inserted near the center comes out clean. **YIELD:** 6 servings.

HEARTY BEEF AND NOODLES

Prep: 10 min. **Cook:** 25 min.

This is a longtime family favorite, and my kids always asked to bring home friends on nights we served it. Plus, it's hefty man food at its easy best!

Sylvia Streu // Norman, Oklahoma

1-1/2 pounds beef top sirloin steak,
    cut into 1/2-inch strips
   2 teaspoons olive oil
 1/2 cup chopped onion
1-1/2 teaspoons minced garlic
   1 can (10-3/4 ounces) condensed cream
    of mushroom soup, undiluted
   1 cup water
   1 cup half-and-half cream
 1/3 cup brewed coffee
   2 envelopes brown gravy mix
   5 cups uncooked egg noodles
   1 cup (8 ounces) sour cream
 1/2 teaspoon paprika
 1/4 teaspoon pepper

1 In a large skillet, brown beef in oil on all sides; remove and keep warm. In the same skillet, saute onion until tender. Add garlic; cook 1 minute longer. Return beef to the pan; stir in the soup, water, cream, coffee and gravy mix. Bring to a boil. Reduce heat; cover and simmer for 20-25 minutes or until meat is tender, stirring occasionally.

2 Meanwhile, cook noodles according to package directions. Add the sour cream, paprika and pepper to skillet; heat through. Drain noodles. Serve with beef. **YIELD:** 6 servings.

This cheesy chicken casserole gets its vibrant color from frozen vegetables and its unique flavor from crumbled bacon. The biscuit-topped dish is a regular at our dinner table.

Debbie Vannette // Zeeland, Michigan

CHICKEN 'N' BISCUITS

Prep: 15 min. **Bake:** 40 min.

  1 package (16 ounces) frozen mixed vegetables
2-1/2 cups cubed cooked chicken
  1 can (10-3/4 ounces) condensed cream of chicken soup, undiluted
  3/4 cup 2% milk
1-1/2 cups (6 ounces) shredded cheddar cheese, *divided*
  8 bacon strips, cooked and crumbled, optional

BISCUITS:

1-1/2 cups biscuit/baking mix
  2/3 cup 2% milk
  1 can (2.8 ounces) french-fried onions

1 In a large bowl, combine the vegetables, chicken, soup, milk, 1 cup cheese and bacon if desired. Pour into an ungreased 13-in. x 9-in. baking dish. Cover and bake at 400° for 15 minutes.

2 Meanwhile, in another bowl, combine biscuit mix and milk. Drop batter by tablespoonfuls onto chicken mixture.

3 Bake, uncovered, for 20-22 minutes or until biscuits are golden brown. Top with onions and remaining cheese. Bake 3-4 minutes longer or until the cheese is melted. **YIELD:** 6 servings.

STEAK BURRITOS   PICTURED ON RIGHT

Prep: 15 min. **Cook:** 8 hours

Slowly simmered all day, the beef is tender and a snap to shred. Just fill flour tortillas and add toppings for a tasty, time-easing meal.

Valerie Jones // Portland, Maine

  2 beef flank steaks (about 1 pound *each*)
  2 envelopes taco seasoning
  1 medium onion, chopped
  1 can (4 ounces) chopped green chilies
  1 tablespoon white vinegar
 10 flour tortillas (8 inches), warmed
1-1/2 cups (6 ounces) shredded Monterey Jack cheese
1-1/2 cups chopped seeded plum tomatoes
  3/4 cup sour cream

1 Cut steaks in half; rub with taco seasoning. Place in a 3-qt. slow cooker coated with cooking spray. Top with onion, chilies and vinegar. Cover and cook on low for 8-9 hours or until meat is tender.

2 Remove steaks and cool slightly; shred meat with two forks. Return to slow cooker; heat through.

3 Spoon about 1/2 cup meat mixture down the center of each tortilla. Top with cheese, tomato and sour cream. Fold ends and sides over filling. **YIELD:** 10 servings.

CORN DOG CASSEROLE

Prep: 25 min. **Bake:** 30 min.

Reminiscent of traditional corn dogs, this fun main dish really hits the spot. It tastes especially good right from the oven.

Marcy Suzanne Olipane // Belleville, Illinois

- 2 cups thinly sliced celery
- 2 tablespoons butter
- 1-1/2 cups sliced green onions
- 1-1/2 pounds hot dogs
- 2 eggs
- 1-1/2 cups 2% milk
- 2 teaspoons rubbed sage
- 1/4 teaspoon pepper
- 2 packages (8-1/2 ounces *each*) corn bread/muffin mix
- 2 cups (8 ounces) shredded sharp cheddar cheese, *divided*

1 In a skillet, saute celery in butter for 5 minutes. Add onions; saute for 5 minutes longer or until vegetables are tender. Place in a bowl; set aside.

2 Cut hot dogs lengthwise into quarters, then cut into thirds. In the same skillet, saute hot dogs for 5 minutes or until lightly browned; add to vegetables. Set aside 1 cup.

3 In a large bowl, whisk the eggs, milk, sage and pepper. Add the remaining hot dog mixture. Stir in corn bread mixes. Add 1-1/2 cups of cheese. Spread into a shallow 3-qt. baking dish. Top with reserved hot dog mixture and remaining cheese.

4 Bake, uncovered, at 400° for 30 minutes or until golden brown. **YIELD:** 12 servings.

I created this main-dish salad to satisfy our family's love of shrimp. It has lots of contrasting textures, including firm taco-seasoned shrimp, crispy tortilla strips and hearty black beans.

Ellen Morrell // Hazleton, Pennsylvania

SHRIMP TACO SALAD
Prep/Total Time: 30 min.

- 1 pound uncooked large shrimp, peeled and deveined
- 1 envelope taco seasoning, *divided*
- 1/2 cup plus 3 tablespoons olive oil, *divided*
- 1 small onion, finely chopped
- 3 tablespoons cider vinegar
- 2 tablespoons diced green *or* sweet red pepepr
- 6 garlic cloves, minced
- 1/2 teaspoon ground coriander
- 1/4 teaspoon sugar
- 3 corn tortillas (6 inches), cut into 1/4-inch strips
- 1 package (8 ounces) ready-to-serve salad greens
- 1 medium tomato, chopped
- 1 can (8 ounces) black beans, rinsed and drained
- 2 cups (8 ounces) finely shredded Colby-Monterey Jack cheese

1 Remove shrimp tails if desired. Place shrimp in a large bowl; sprinkle with half of the taco seasoning. Set aside. In a small bowl, whisk 1/2 cup oil, onion, vinegar, green pepper, garlic, coriander and sugar; set aside.

2 In a large skillet, stir-fry tortilla strips in remaining oil; drain on paper towels. Sprinkle with remaining taco seasoning. In the same skillet, saute shrimp for 8-10 minutes or until shrimp turn pink.

3 In a large bowl, combine the greens, tomato, beans, shrimp and tortilla strips. Just before serving, whisk dressing and pour over salad; sprinkle with cheese and toss to coat. **YIELD:** 6-8 servings.

OREGANO CHICKEN
Prep: 10 min. **Bake:** 1 hour

Salad dressing mix and a generous sprinkling of oregano add the rich herb flavor to this tender baked chicken. It's tasty over rice or noodles.

Nancy Moore // Candler, North Carolina

- 1/4 cup butter, melted
- 1 envelope Italian salad dressing mix
- 2 tablespoons lemon juice
- 1 broiler/fryer chicken (3-1/2 to 4 pounds), cut up
- 1 to 2 tablespoons dried oregano

1 In a small bowl, combine the butter, salad dressing mix and lemon juice. Place chicken in an ungreased 13-in. x 9-in. baking dish. Spoon butter mixture over chicken.

2 Cover and bake at 350° for 45 minutes. Uncover. Baste with pan drippings; sprinkle with oregano. Bake 15-20 minutes longer or until chicken juices run clear. **YIELD:** 6 servings.

As a teenager, I created this layered casserole one day when my mom asked me what I wanted for supper. Using packaged potatoes speeds up the preparation.

Nicole Rute // Fall River, Wisconsin

CHEESY POTATO BEEF BAKE

Prep: 10 min. **Bake:** 35 min. + standing

- 1 pound ground beef
- 2 cans (4 ounces *each*) mushroom stems and pieces, drained, optional
- 2 packages (5-1/4 ounces *each*) au gratin potatoes
- 4 cups boiling water
- 1-1/3 cups 2% milk
- 2 teaspoons butter
- 1 teaspoon salt
- 1/2 teaspoon seasoned salt
- 1/2 teaspoon pepper
- 1 cup (4 ounces) shredded cheddar cheese

1 In a large skillet over medium heat, cook beef until no longer pink; drain. Place in a greased 13-in. x 9-in. baking pan. Top with mushrooms.

2 In a small bowl, combine the potatoes and contents of sauce mix packets, water, milk, butter, salt, seasoned salt and pepper. Pour over beef and mushrooms. Cover and bake at 400° for 30 minutes or until heated through.

3 Sprinkle with cheese. Bake, uncovered, for 5 minutes longer or until cheese is melted. Let stand 10 minutes before serving. **YIELD:** 8 servings.

CHICKEN FRIED RICE

Prep/Total Time: 30 min.

I make the most of leftover cooked chicken and a can of crunchy water chestnuts by adding them to a fried rice mix. We love this speedy skillet supper!

Kathy Hoyt // Maplecrest, New York

- 1 package (6.2 ounces) fried rice mix
- 2 cups cubed cooked chicken
- 1-1/2 cups cooked broccoli florets
- 1 can (8 ounces) sliced water chestnuts, drained
- 1 cup (4 ounces) shredded mozzarella cheese

1 Cook rice according to package directions. Stir in the chicken, broccoli and water chestnuts; heat through. Sprinkle with cheese. **YIELD:** 4 servings.

SAUSAGE NOODLE SUPPER

Prep/Total Time: 25 min.

I can't recall how I came up with this main dish, but it's a staple in my house. With packaged coleslaw mix and noodles in a flavorful sauce, it's always on the table in less than 30 minutes.

Mary Jo Miller // Mansfield, Ohio

- 1 cup thinly sliced fresh carrots
- 3 tablespoons butter
- 1/2 pound smoked sausage, thinly sliced
- 3/4 cup green thinly sliced onions
- 4 cups coleslaw mix
- 2-1/4 cups water
- 1 package (4.9 ounces) quick-cooking noodles and sour cream and chive sauce mix

1 In a skillet, cook carrots in butter for 2 minutes. Add sausage and onions; cook for 2 minutes. Stir in coleslaw mix; cook 1-2 minutes longer. Add water; bring to a boil.

2 Stir in noodles and sauce mix. Return to a boil; cook and stir for 7-9 minutes or until noodles are tender, stirring occasionally. Let stand for 2-3 minutes before serving. **YIELD**: 3-4 servings.

TACO MEAT LOAF

Prep: 10 min. **Bake:** 1 hour

Even your kids will enjoy this tasty meat loaf. I like to serve it with shredded cheese, salsa and sour cream.

Cathy Streeter // De Kalb Junction, New York

- 1 cup crushed saltines (about 30 crackers)
- 1 envelope taco seasoning
- 1/2 cup ketchup
- 1 can (4 ounces) mushroom stems and pieces, drained
- 1 can (2-1/4 ounces) sliced ripe olives, drained
- 1 small onion, chopped
- 2 eggs, lightly beaten
- 2 tablespoons Worcestershire sauce
- 2 pounds lean ground beef (90% lean)

Salsa, sour cream, shredded cheddar cheese and additional olives, optional

1 In a large bowl, combine the first eight ingredients. Crumble beef over mixture and mix well. Press into a greased 9-in. x 5-in. loaf pan.

2 Bake, uncovered, at 350° for 1-1/2 hours or until no pink remains and a meat thermometer reads 160°. Serve with salsa, sour cream, cheese and olives if desired. **YIELD:** 8 servings.

This fast dinner for two is one of my favorites. It's a simple way to dress up a boxed pasta mix. While it's cooking, I toast some garlic bread and warm up some green beans.

Cindy Preston // Benkelman, Nebraska

SHRIMP AND HAM ALFREDO
Prep/Total Time: 20 min.

- 1 package (4.7 ounces) fettuccine noodles and Alfredo sauce mix
- 10 frozen peeled cooked medium shrimp, thawed
- 1/2 cup cubed fully cooked ham (1/2-inch pieces)
- 1/4 teaspoon garlic powder
- Dash cayenne pepper
- 1 green onion, chopped

1 In a large saucepan, prepare noodles and sauce mix according to package directions. Stir in the shrimp, ham, garlic powder and cayenne; heat through. Sprinkle with onion. **YIELD:** 2 servings.

SPICY JAMBALAYA
Prep/Total Time: 30 min.

My family says I use just the right amount of seasonings to spice up this memorable main dish. It's loaded with zesty sausage, tender chicken and tasty shrimp, too.

Amy Chop // Oak Grove, Louisiana

- 1 package (4.4 ounces) chicken-flavored rice and sauce mix
- 1/2 pound boneless skinless chicken breasts, cubed
- 1/4 pound bulk Italian sausage
- 2 tablespoons butter
- 2 garlic cloves, minced
- 1 medium green pepper, chopped
- 1 celery rib, thinly sliced
- 1 small onion, chopped
- 1 medium tomato, chopped
- 1/2 to 1 teaspoon ground cumin
- 1/2 teaspoon dried oregano
- 1/2 teaspoon salt
- 1/2 teaspoon pepper
- 1/8 teaspoon hot pepper sauce
- 1/4 pound uncooked medium shrimp, peeled, deveined and chopped

1 Prepare rice mix according to package directions. Meanwhile, in a large skillet, cook chicken and sausage in butter for 5 minutes. Add garlic; cook 1 minute longer. Add the green pepper, celery and onion; cook and stir until meat is no longer pink and vegetables are tender.

2 Stir in tomato and seasonings; heat through. Add the shrimp; cook an stir for 3-4 minutes or until shrimp turn pink. Serve with the prepared rice. **YIELD:** 4 servings.

This deliciously moist chicken is a longtime favorite with family and friends. It's so easy, comforting and rich. A friend shared the recipe years ago, and I adapted it by adding a few new ingredients. I like to serve it over mashed potatoes or rice.

Darolyn Jones // Fishers, Indiana

CHICKEN WITH MUSHROOM GRAVY

Prep: 10 min. **Cook:** 4-1/4 hours

4 boneless skinless chicken breast halves
1 can (12 ounces) mushroom gravy
1 cup 2% milk
1 can (8 ounces) mushroom stems and pieces, drained
1 can (4 ounces) chopped green chilies
1 envelope Italian salad dressing mix
1 package (8 ounces) cream cheese, cubed

1 In a 3-qt. slow cooker, combine chicken, gravy, milk, mushrooms, chilies and dressing mix. Cover; cook on low 4-5 hours or until chicken is tender.

2 Stir in cream cheese; cover and cook 15 minutes longer or until cheese is melted. **YIELD:** 4 servings.

CORN BREAD SLOPPY JOES PICTURED ON RIGHT

Prep/Total Time: 30 min.

Purchase ready-to-eat corn bread from the bakery section in your local grocery store for this easy recipe. It's a tasty take on sloppy joes.

Taste of Home Test Kitchen

1 package (8-1/2 ounces) corn bread/muffin mix
1 egg
1/3 cup 2% milk
2 pounds ground beef
1/2 cup chopped onion
1 jar (24 ounces) meatless spaghetti sauce
1 cup frozen corn
1 can (4 ounces) chopped green chilies, drained
2 envelopes sloppy joe mix
1 cup (4 ounces) shredded cheddar cheese

1 Prepare and bake corn bread according to package directions, using the egg and milk. Meanwhile, in a large skillet, cook beef and onion over medium heat until meat is no longer pink; drain. Stir in the spaghetti sauce, corn, chilies and sloppy joe mix. Bring to a boil. Reduce heat; simmer, uncovered, for 10 minutes.

2 Sprinkle with cheese; cover and cook for 1 minute or until cheese is melted. Cut corn bread into six pieces; cut each piece in half. Top with sloppy joe mixture. **YIELD:** 6 servings.

TACO MAC

Prep/Total Time: 30 min.

Pork sausage, taco seasoning and taco sauce add plenty of zip to easy macaroni and cheese. This zesty dish is just as yummy the next day.

JoLynn Fribley // Nokomis, Illinois

- 1 package (24 ounces) shells and cheese dinner mix
- 1/2 pound bulk pork sausage, cooked and drained
- 1/3 cup taco sauce
- 1 tablespoon taco seasoning
- 4 cups shredded lettuce
- 2 medium tomatoes, chopped
- 1 cup (4 ounces) shredded cheddar cheese, optional

1 Prepare shells and cheese mix according to package directions. Stir in the sausage, taco sauce and seasoning. Garnish with lettuce, tomatoes and cheddar cheese if desired. **YIELD:** 6 servings.

Soups

HEARTY TACO CHILI, PG. 125

CHEESY WILD RICE

Prep/Total Time: 30 min.

We often eat no-fuss soups when there's not a lot of time to cook. I replaced the wild rice requested in the original recipe with a boxed rice mix.

Lisa Hofer // Hitchcock, South Dakota

- 1 package (6.2 ounces) fast-cooking long grain and wild rice mix
- 4 cups 2% milk
- 1 can (10-3/4 ounces) condensed cream of potato soup, undiluted
- 8 ounces process cheese (Velveeta), cubed
- 1/2 pound sliced bacon, cooked and crumbled

1 In a large saucepan, prepare rice according to package directions. Stir in the milk, soup and cheese. Cook and stir until cheese is melted. Garnish with bacon. **YIELD:** 8 servings.

Because this quick-to-fix soup starts with a box of au gratin potatoes, you don't have to spend time peeling and slicing them. A co-worker shared the recipe with me. My husband requests it often.

Sherry Dickerson //
Sebastopol, Mississippi

NACHO POTATO SOUP

Prep/Total Time: 25 min.

 1 package (5-1/4 ounces) au gratin potatoes
 1 can (11 ounces) whole kernel corn, drained
 1 can (10 ounces) diced tomatoes and green chilies, undrained
 2 cups water
 2 cups 2% milk
 2 cups cubed process American cheese (Velveeta)

Dash hot pepper sauce, optional
Minced fresh parsley, optional

1 In a 3-qt. saucepan, combine the contents of potato package, corn, tomatoes and water. Bring to a boil. Reduce heat; cover and simmer for 15-18 minutes or until potatoes are tender. Add the milk, cheese and hot pepper sauce if desired; cook and stir until the cheese is melted. Garnish with parsley if desired. **YIELD:** 6-8 servings (2 quarts).

HEARTY TACO CHILI

Prep: 30 min. **Cook:** 6 hours

Ranch dressing mix and taco seasoning give this Southwestern-style chili extraordinary taste. Double the recipe because folks will come back for seconds...and thirds!

Julie Neuhalfen // Glenwood, Iowa

 2 pounds ground beef
 1 can (16 ounces) kidney beans, rinsed and drained
 1 can (15 ounces) pinto beans, rinsed and drained
 1 can (15 ounces) black beans, rinsed and drained
 1 can (14 ounces) hominy, rinsed and drained
 1 can (10 ounces) diced tomatoes and green chilies, undrained
 1 can (8 ounces) tomato sauce
 1 small onion, chopped
 1 envelope ranch salad dressing mix
 1 envelope taco seasoning
 1/2 teaspoon pepper
 2 cans (14-1/2 ounces *each*) diced tomatoes, undrained
 1 can (4 ounces) chopped green chilies
Corn chips, sour cream and shredded cheddar cheese, optional

1 In a large skillet, cook beef over medium heat until no longer pink; drain. Transfer to a 5-qt. slow cooker. Add the beans, hominy, tomatoes, tomato sauce, onion, salad dressing mix, taco seasoning and pepper.

2 In a blender, combine diced tomatoes and green chilies; cover and process until smooth. Add to the slow cooker. Cover and cook on low for 6-8 hours.

3 Serve with corn chips, sour cream and cheese if desired. **YIELD:** 11 servings (2-3/4 quarts).

CHICKEN WILD RICE SOUP

Prep: 30 min. **Cook:** 15 min.

    1 package (6 ounces) long grain and wild
      rice mix
1/2 pound boneless skinless chicken breasts, cubed
1/2 pound sliced fresh mushrooms
1-1/4 cups chopped onions
    1 tablespoon canola oil
    2 garlic cloves, minced
    2 cans (14-1/2 ounces *each*) chicken broth
1/2 teaspoon dried tarragon
1/4 teaspoon dried thyme
1/8 teaspoon pepper
    2 tablespoons cornstarch

    1 can (12 ounces) evaporated milk
    6 tablespoons sliced green onions

1 Prepare rice mix according to package directions, omitting butter. Meanwhile, in a large saucepan, saute the chicken, mushrooms and onions in oil until chicken is no longer pink and vegetables are tender. Add garlic; cook 1 minute longer.

2 Add the prepared rice, broth, tarragon, thyme and pepper; bring to a boil. Combine cornstarch and evaporated milk until smooth; stir into rice mixture. Return to a boil; cook for 1-2 minutes or until slightly thickened. Garnish with green onions. **YIELD:** 10 servings (2-1/2 quarts).

BEEFY TOMATO SOUP

Prep/Total Time: 30 min.

Who says soup has to simmer for hours in order to be satisfying? This hearty dish, featuring ground beef and macaroni, takes just 30 minutes from start to finish.
Patricia Staudt // Marble Rock, Iowa

    1 pound lean ground beef (90% lean)
    4 cups reduced-sodium tomato juice

    3 cups water
3/4 cup uncooked elbow macaroni
    1 envelope onion soup mix
1/4 teaspoon chili powder

1 In a large saucepan, cook beef over medium heat until no longer pink; drain. Add the remaining ingredients. Bring to a boil. Reduce heat; simmer, uncovered, for 15-20 minutes or until macaroni is tender. **YIELD:** 8 servings.

TEX-MEX CHILI

Prep: 20 min. **Cook:** 6 hours

*Hearty and spicy, this is a man's chili for sure!
The slow-cooker preparation is a real plus for
cooks on the go.*

Eric Hayes // Antioch, California

- 3 **pounds beef stew meat**
- 1 **tablespoon canola oil**
- 3 **garlic cloves, minced**
- 3 **cans (16 ounces *each*) kidney beans, rinsed
  and drained**
- 3 **cans (15 ounces *each*) tomato sauce**
- 1 **can (14-1/2 ounces) diced tomatoes, undrained**
- 1 **cup water**
- 1 **can (6 ounces) tomato paste**
- 3/4 **cup salsa verde**
- 1 **envelope chili seasoning**
- 2 **teaspoons dried minced onion**
- 1 **teaspoon chili powder**
- 1/2 **teaspoon crushed red pepper flakes**
- 1/2 **teaspoon ground cumin**
- 1/2 **teaspoon cayenne pepper**

Shredded cheddar cheese and minced fresh cilantro

1 In a large skillet, brown beef in oil in batches. Add
garlic to the pan; cook and stir for 1 minute longer.
Transfer to a 6-qt. slow cooker.

2 Stir in the remaining ingredients. Cover and cook
on low for 6-8 hours or until meat is tender.
Garnish each serving with cheese and cilantro.
YIELD: 12 servings (1-1/3 cups each).

This meaty meal-in-one is very versatile. Sometimes I make it without beans and serve it on hot dogs or over rice as a main dish.

Christine Panzarella //
Buena Park, California

HEARTWARMING CHILI

Prep/Total Time: 30 min.

- 1 pound ground beef
- 1 pound ground pork
- 1 medium onion, chopped
- 1/2 cup chopped green pepper
- 1-1/2 to 2 cups water
- 1 can (15 ounces) tomato sauce
- 1 can (15 ounces) pinto beans, rinsed and drained
- 1 can (14-1/2 ounces) diced tomatoes, undrained
- 1 envelope chili seasoning
- 1/4 teaspoon garlic salt
- Shredded cheddar cheese, sour cream, chopped green onions *and/or* hot pepper slices, optional

1 In a large saucepan, cook the beef, pork, onion and green pepper over medium heat until meat is no longer pink and vegetables are tender; drain.

2 Add water, tomato sauce, beans, tomatoes, chili seasoning and garlic salt. Bring to a boil. Reduce heat; simmer, uncovered, until heated through. Serve with cheese, sour cream, green onions and/ or hot peppers if desired. **YIELD:** 8-10 servings.

ZIPPY SPANISH RICE SOUP PICTURED ON RIGHT

Prep: 25 min. **Cook:** 4 hours

I created this recipe by accident after ruining a dinner of Spanish rice. I tried to salvage the dish by adding more water, cilantro and green chilies. Surprisingly, it was a hit with the whole family!

Marilyn Schetz // Cuyahoga Falls, Ohio

- 1 pound lean ground beef (90% lean)
- 1 medium onion, chopped
- 3 cups water
- 1 jar (16 ounces) salsa
- 1 can (14-1/2 ounces) diced tomatoes, undrained
- 1 jar (7 ounces) roasted sweet red peppers, drained and chopped
- 1 can (4 ounces) chopped green chilies
- 1 envelope taco seasoning
- 1 tablespoon dried cilantro flakes
- 1/2 cup uncooked converted rice

1 In a large skillet, cook beef and onion over medium heat until meat is no longer pink; drain.

2 Transfer beef and onion to a 4- or 5-qt. slow cooker. Add water, salsa, tomatoes, red peppers, chilies, taco seasoning and cilantro. Stir in rice. Cover and cook on low for 4-5 hours or until the rice is tender. **YIELD:** 8 servings (about 2 quarts).

DUMPLING VEGETABLE SOUP

Prep: 15 min. **Cook:** 1 hour

Fabulous rice dumplings give a homemade touch to this speedy soup that takes advantage of canned goods, frozen vegetables and dry soup mix. My mom found this to be a quick, nourishing all-in-one-pot meal...and so do I.

Peggy Linton // Cobourg, Ontario

1/2 pound ground beef
  4 cups water
  1 can (28 ounces) diced tomatoes, undrained
  1 package (10 ounces) frozen mixed vegetables
  1 envelope onion soup mix
1/2 teaspoon dried oregano
1/4 teaspoon pepper
RICE DUMPLINGS:
1-1/4 cups all-purpose flour
  1 teaspoon baking powder
1/2 teaspoon salt
  1 tablespoon shortening
1/3 cup cooked rice, room temperature
  1 tablespoon minced fresh parsley
  1 egg, lightly beaten
1/2 cup milk

1 In a Dutch oven, cook beef over medium heat until no longer pink; drain. Add the water, tomatoes, vegetables, soup mix, oregano and pepper; bring to a boil. Reduce heat; cover and simmer for 30-40 minutes or until the vegetables are tender.

2 For dumplings, combine the flour, baking powder and salt in a bowl. Cut in shortening until the mixture resembles coarse crumbs. Add rice and parsley; toss. In a small bowl, combine egg and milk. Stir into rice mixture just until moistened.

3 Drop by teaspoonfuls onto simmering soup. Cover and simmer for 15 minutes or until a toothpick inserted in a dumpling comes out clean (do not lift the cover while simmering). **YIELD:** 6-8 servings (2 quarts).

My daughter turns to a boxed rice mix to get a head start on this rich and colorful soup. She likes to serve it to friends after football games in autumn, but it's a favorite with our family anytime of year.

Janet Sawyer // Dysart, Iowa

BROCCOLI WILD RICE SOUP
Prep/Total Time: 30 min.

- 1 package (6 ounces) chicken and wild rice mix
- 5 cups water
- 3 cups frozen chopped broccoli, thawed
- 1 medium carrot, shredded
- 2 teaspoons dried minced onion
- 1 can (10-3/4 ounces) condensed cream of chicken soup, undiluted
- 1 package (8 ounces) cream cheese, cubed
- 1/4 cup slivered almonds, optional

1 In a large saucepan, combine the rice, contents of seasoning packet and water; bring to a boil. Reduce heat; cover and simmer for 10 minutes, stirring once. Stir in the broccoli, carrot and onion. Cover and simmer for 5 minutes. Stir in soup and cream cheese. Cook and stir until cheese is melted. Stir in almonds if desired. **YIELD**: 8 servings (about 2 quarts).

CHICKEN AND DUMPLING SOUP
Prep/Total Time: 10 min.

Our five kids are grown and live away from the farm, but I still frequently serve this soup for Sunday dinner.

Joey Ann Mostowy // Bruin, Pennsylvania

- 6 pieces bone-in chicken
- 1-1/2 quarts water
- 2 celery ribs, cut into chunks
- 1 medium onion, cut into chunks
- 1/2 cup diced green pepper
- 1 garlic clove, minced
- 1 tablespoon minced fresh dill
- 1 teaspoon salt
- 1/2 teaspoon pepper
- 1 can (10-3/4 ounces) condensed cream of potato soup, undiluted
- 1 can (10-3/4 ounces) condensed cream of chicken soup, undiluted
- 1 package (10 ounces) frozen mixed vegetables, thawed
- 1 tube (7-1/2 ounces) refrigerated buttermilk biscuits

1 In a soup kettle or Dutch oven, combine first nine ingredients; bring to a boil. Reduce heat; cover and simmer for 50-60 minutes or until chicken is tender. Remove chicken; allow to cool. Debone and cut into chunks; set aside. Strain broth and set aside.

2 In a large saucepan, combine soups. Gradually add broth, stirring constantly. Add mixed vegetables and chicken; cook over medium heat for 20-30 minutes or until vegetables are tender.

3 On a floured surface, pat the biscuits to 1/4-in. thickness; cut into 1/4-in. strips. Bring soup to boil; drop in strips. Cover and cook for 15-18 minutes. **YIELD**: 8-10 servings (2-1/2 quarts).

Pork sausage, ground beef and plenty of beans make this chili a marvelous meal. I keep serving-size containers of it in my freezer at all times so I can quickly warm up bowls on busy days.

Margie Shaw // Greenbrier, Arkansas

SLOW-COOKED CHUNKY CHILI

Prep: 15 min. **Cook:** 4 hours

- 1 pound ground beef
- 1 pound bulk pork sausage
- 4 cans (16 ounces *each*) kidney beans, rinsed and drained
- 2 cans (14-1/2 ounces *each*) diced tomatoes, undrained
- 2 cans (10 ounces *each*) diced tomatoes and green chilies, undrained
- 1 large onion, chopped
- 1 medium green pepper, chopped
- 1 envelope taco seasoning
- 1/2 teaspoon salt
- 1/4 teaspoon pepper

1 In a large skillet, cook ground beef and sausage over medium heat until meat is no longer pink; drain. Transfer to a 5-qt. slow cooker. Stir in the remaining ingredients.

2 Cover and cook on high for 4-5 hours or until vegetables are tender. Serve desired amount. Cool the remaining chili; transfer to freezer bags or containers. Freeze for up to 3 months.

3 TO USE FROZEN CHILI: Thaw in the refrigerator; place in saucepan and heat through. Add water if desired. YIELD: 3 quarts.

CHICKEN DUMPLING SOUP

Prep/Total Time: 30 min.

This comforting soup with soft dumplings was one of Mom's mainstays.

Brenda Risser // Willard, Ohio

- 2 cans (10-3/4 ounces *each*) condensed cream of chicken soup, undiluted
- 3-1/3 cups 2% milk, *divided*
- 1-2/3 cups biscuit/baking mix

1 In a 3-qt. saucepan, combine cream of chicken soup and 2-2/3 cups of milk. Bring to a boil over medium heat; reduce heat.

2 Meanwhile, in a large bowl, combine biscuit mix with remaining milk just until blended. Drop by rounded tablespoons onto simmering soup. Cook, uncovered, for 10 minutes.

3 Cover; simmer for 10-12 minutes or until a toothpick inserted in a dumpling comes out clean (do not lift the cover while simmering). YIELD: 4 servings.

MACARONI VEGETABLE SOUP

Prep/Total Time: 25 min.

With just moments of prep time, this soup truly couldn't be easier to make. Simply open up the ingredients, pour 'em in and dinner is practically done!

Metzel Turley // South Charleston, West Virginia

1 package (1.4 ounces) vegetable soup mix
1 envelope (.6 ounce) cream of chicken soup mix
2 cans (5-1/2 ounces *each*) spicy tomato juice
4 cups water
2 cans (15 ounces *each*) mixed vegetables, drained
Dash crushed red pepper flakes
Dash dried minced garlic
1/2 cup uncooked elbow macaroni

1 In a Dutch oven, combine soup mixes and tomato juice. Stir in the water, mixed vegetables, pepper flakes and garlic; bring to a boil. Add macaroni. Reduce heat; cook, uncovered, for 10-15 minutes or until macaroni is tender, stirring occasionally. **YIELD:** 7 servings.

EASY VEGETABLE SOUP

Prep: 5 min. **Cook:** 30 min.

Canned tomatoes and beans and frozen veggies serve as the no-fuss base for this crowd-pleasing kettle creation. Set a bowl of tortilla chips next to the soup for a fun alternative to crackers.

Jan Sharp // Blue Springs, Missouri

- 1 **pound ground beef**
- 1 **medium onion, chopped**
- 1 **can (28 ounces) diced tomatoes, undrained**
- 1 **package (16 ounces) frozen vegetable blend of your choice**
- 1 **can (16 ounces) kidney beans, undrained**
- 1 **can (14-1/2 ounces) beef broth**
- 1 **envelope taco seasoning**
- 1 **garlic clove, minced**

Shredded cheddar cheese, optional

1 In a saucepan, cook beef and onion over medium heat until meat is no longer pink; drain. Add the tomatoes, vegetables, beans, broth, taco seasoning and garlic; bring to a boil.

2 Reduce heat; simmer, uncovered, for 10 minutes. Garnish with cheese if desired. **YIELD:** 10-12 servings (2-3/4 quarts).

We first sampled this chili-like soup at a church dinner. It's a warming dish on a cold day. And since it uses packaged seasonings and several cans of vegetables, it's a snap to prepare.

Glenda Taylor //
Sand Springs, Oklahoma

SIMPLE TACO SOUP
Prep/Total Time: 25 min.

2 pounds ground beef
1 envelope taco seasoning
1-1/2 cups water
1 can (16 ounces) mild chili beans, undrained
1 can (15-1/4 ounces) whole kernel corn, drained
1 can (15 ounces) pinto beans, rinsed and drained
1 can (14-1/2 ounces) stewed tomatoes
1 can (10 ounces) diced tomato with green chilies
1 can (4 ounces) chopped green chilies, optional
1 envelope ranch salad dressing mix

1 In a Dutch oven, cook beef over medium heat until no longer pink; drain. Add taco seasoning and mix well. Stir in the remaining ingredients. Bring to a boil.

2 Reduce heat; simmer, uncovered, for 15 minutes or until heated through, stirring occasionally. **YIELD**: 6-8 servings (about 2 quarts).

SMOKED SAUSAGE SOUP
Prep: 15 min. Cook: 25 min.

Whenever I serve this thick stew-like soup to new friends, they never fail to ask for the recipe.
Marge Wheeler // San Benito, Texas

4-1/2 cups water
1 can (28 ounces) diced tomatoes, undrained
1 envelope onion soup mix
1 package (9 ounces) frozen cut green beans
3 small carrots, halved and thinly sliced
2 celery ribs, thinly sliced
1 tablespoon sugar
1/2 teaspoon salt
1/2 teaspoon dried oregano
1/8 teaspoon hot pepper sauce
1 pound smoked sausage, halved and thinly sliced
2-1/2 cups frozen shredded hash brown potatoes

1 In a Dutch oven, combine the first 10 ingredients. bring to a boil. reduce heat; cover and simmer for 20-25 minutes or until the vegetables are tender.

2 Stir in sausage and hash browns. Bring to a boil. Reduce heat; cover and cook for 5 minutes or until heated through. **YIELD**: 12 servings.

Pasta and corn give this zesty chili-like soup some texture and heft. Try garnishing individual bowls with dollops of salsa con queso and sliced jalapenos.

Joan Hallford //
North Richland Hills, Texas

ZESTY MACARONI SOUP

Prep/Total Time: 30 min.

- 1 pound ground beef
- 1 medium onion, chopped
- 5 cups water
- 1 can (15 ounces) pinto beans, rinsed and drained
- 1 can (14-1/2 ounces) diced tomatoes, undrained
- 1 can (7 ounces) whole kernel corn, drained
- 1 can (4 ounces) chopped green chilies, optional
- 1/2 teaspoon ground mustard
- 1/2 teaspoon salt
- 1/8 teaspoon pepper
- 1 package (7-1/2 ounces) chili macaroni dinner mix
- Salsa con queso dip

1 In a large saucepan, cook beef and onion over medium heat until meat is no longer pink; drain. Stir in the water, beans, tomatoes, corn and chilies if desired. Stir in the mustard, salt, pepper and contents of macaroni sauce mix. Bring to a boil. Reduce heat; cover and simmer for 10 minutes.

2 Stir in the contents of macaroni packet. Cover; simmer 10-14 minutes longer or until the macaroni is tender, stirring occasionally. Serve soup with salsa con queso dip. **YIELD:** 8-10 servings (about 2-1/2 quarts).

TASTY TURKEY SOUP

Prep/Total Time: 10 min.

You'll love this quick-and-easy way to jazz up a can of soup. Enjoy the comforting results in a snap by using leftover turkey and convenient ramen noodles.

Laurie Todd // Columbus, Mississippi

- 2 tablespoons chopped celery
- 2 tablespoons chopped onion
- 1 tablespoon butter
- 1 package (3 ounces) chicken-flavored ramen noodles
- 1-1/2 cups water
- 1 can (10-3/4 ounces) condensed turkey noodle soup, undiluted
- 1 cup chicken broth
- 1 cup cubed cooked turkey
- Pepper to taste

1 In a large saucepan, saute celery and onion in butter until tender. Discard seasoning packet from ramen noodles or save for another use.

2 Stir the noodles, water, soup, broth, turkey and pepper into celery mixture. Cook for 3 minutes or until noodles are tender and heated through. **YIELD:** 4 servings.

GROUND BEEF NOODLE SOUP

Prep: 15 min. **Cook:** 20 min.

My savory specialty combines ground beef with onions, celery and carrots. Whip it up any day of the week for a satisfying quick meal.

Judy Brander // Two Harbors, Minnesota

1-1/2 pounds lean ground beef (90% lean)
  1/2 cup *each* chopped onion, celery and carrot
    7 cups water
    1 envelope au jus mix
    2 tablespoons beef bouillon granules
    2 bay leaves
  1/8 teaspoon pepper
1-1/2 cups uncooked egg noodles

1 In a large saucepan, cook the beef, onion, celery and carrot over medium heat until meat is no longer pink; drain.

2 Add the water, au jus mix, bouillon, bay leaves and pepper; bring to a boil. Stir in the noodles. Return to a boil. Cook, uncovered, for 15 minutes or until noodles are tender, stirring occasionally. Discard bay leaves. **YIELD:** 8 servings (2 quarts).

BEEF NOODLE SOUP

Prep/Total Time: 30 min.

I take advantage of convenience items to prepare this hearty soup in a hurry. Bowls of the chunky mixture are chock-full of ground beef, noodles and vegetables.

Arlene Lynn // Lincoln, Nebraska

1 pound ground beef
1 can (46 ounces) V8 juice
1 envelope onion soup mix

1 package (3 ounces) beef ramen noodles
1 package (16 ounces) frozen mixed vegetables

1 In a large saucepan, cook beef over medium heat until no longer pink; drain. Stir in the V8 juice, soup mix, contents of noodle seasoning packet and mixed vegetables.

2 Bring to a boil. Reduce heat; simmer, uncovered, for 6 minutes or until vegetables are tender. Return to a boil; stir in noodles. Cook for 3 minutes or until noodles are tender. **YIELD:** 8 servings.

Breads

ROUND CHEESE BREAD, PG. 147

GREEN CHILI CORN MUFFINS

Prep: 15 min. **Bake:** 20 min.

The addition of cake mix makes these corn muffins a little more moist than most. With zesty green chilies, they really round out a Mexican dinner.

Melissa Cook // Chico, California

- 1 package (8-1/2 ounces) corn bread/muffin mix
- 1 package (9 ounces) yellow cake mix
- 2 eggs
- 1/2 cup 2% milk
- 1/3 cup water
- 2 tablespoons canola oil
- 1 can (4 ounces) chopped green chilies, drained
- 1 cup (4 ounces) shredded cheddar cheese, *divided*

1 In a large bowl, combine corn bread and cake mixes. In another bowl, combine the eggs, milk, water and oil. Stir into the dry ingredients just until moistened. Add chilies and 3/4 cup cheese.

2 Fill greased or paper-lined muffin cups two-thirds full. Bake at 350° for 20-22 minutes or until a toothpick inserted near the center comes out clean. Immediately sprinkle with remaining cheese. Cool for 5 minutes before removing from pans to wire racks. Serve warm. **YIELD:** 16 servings.

My recipe for this flavorful round bread is so simple. All I have to do is stir together biscuit mix, zucchini, cheddar cheese and toasted almonds. The golden wedges look as appealing as they taste.

Vevie Clarke //
Camano Island, Washington

CHEDDAR ZUCCHINI WEDGES

Prep: 20 min. **Bake:** 25 min.

1 medium onion, chopped
1/4 cup butter, cubed
2-1/2 cups biscuit/baking mix
1 tablespoon minced fresh parsley
1/2 teaspoon dried basil
1/2 teaspoon dried thyme
3 eggs, lightly beaten
1/4 cup 2% milk
1-1/2 cups shredded zucchini
1 cup (4 ounces) shredded cheddar cheese
3/4 cup chopped almonds, toasted

1 In a large skillet, saute onion in butter until tender. In a large bowl, combine the biscuit mix, parsley, basil, thyme and onion mixture. Stir in eggs and milk just until combined. Fold in the zucchini, cheese and almonds.

2 Transfer to a greased 9-in. round baking pan. Bake at 400° for 25-30 minutes or until a toothpick inserted near the center comes out clean. Cool for about 1 minute before cutting into wedges. Remove to wire rack to cool. **YIELD:** 6-8 servings.

ITALIAN SEASONED BREAD

Prep: 10 min. **Bake:** 3 hours

When I didn't have the onion soup mix called for in the original recipe, I used Italian salad dressing mix instead. Now this mildly seasoned bread is my family's favorite.

Jill Dickinson // Aurora, Minnesota

1 cup plus 3 tablespoons water (70° to 80°)
4-1/2 teaspoons butter
1/2 teaspoon salt
1 envelope zesty Italian salad dressing mix
1 tablespoon sugar
3 cups bread flour
4-1/2 teaspoons nonfat dry milk powder
2-1/4 teaspoons active dry yeast

1 In bread machine pan, place all ingredients in the order suggested by the manufacturer. Select basic bread setting. Choose the crust color and loaf size if available.

2 Bake according to the bread machine directions (check the dough after 5 minutes of mixing; add about 1 to 2 tablespoons of water or flour if needed). **YIELD:** 1 loaf (1-1/2 pounds).

APPLESAUCE BREAD

I use unsweetened applesauce instead of butter in bread machine recipes. My bread comes out just the same as if I'd used butter.
—Ronda V., Columbus, Nebraska

POPPY SEED BISCUITS

Prep/Total Time: 25 min.

  1/4 **cup 2% milk**
   2 **tablespoons honey**
  1/2 **cup cream-style cottage cheese**
2-1/4 **cups biscuit/baking mix**
   1 **tablespoon poppy seeds**

1 In a blender, combine the milk, honey and cottage cheese. Cover and process until smooth. In a large bowl, combine biscuit mix and poppy seeds. Stir in cottage cheese mixture just until blended.

2 Turn dough onto a floured surface; pat to 1/2-in. thickness. Cut with a 2-1/2-in. biscuit cutter. Place on an ungreased baking sheet. Bake at 425° for 8-10 minutes or until golden brown. Cool for 1 minute before removing to wire rack. Serve warm. **YIELD:** about 1 dozen.

ITALIAN SAUSAGE BREAD

Prep: 25 min. + rising **Bake:** 25 min.

This Italian-style stuffed bread is packed with eggs, sausage, pepperoni and cheese. If pressed for time, prepare it ahead of time and reheat slices.

Debbie Connett // Painted Post, New York

   1 **package (16 ounces) hot roll mix**
   6 **eggs**
   1 **tablespoon butter**
   1 **pound bulk Italian sausage, cooked and drained**
   8 **ounces pepperoni, thinly sliced**
   2 **cups (8 ounces) shredded part-skim mozzarella cheese**
   2 **cups (8 ounces) shredded provolone cheese**
Garlic powder to taste
   1 **egg yolk**
   1 **tablespoon water**

1 Prepare roll mix and knead dough according to package directions. Cover and let rise for 30 minutes. Meanwhile, in a large bowl, whisk eggs. In a large skillet, heat butter until hot. Add eggs; cook and stir over medium heat until eggs are completely set. In a large bowl, combine the scrambled eggs, sausage, pepperoni and cheeses.

2 Punch dough down. Turn onto a floured surface; roll into a 14-in. x 12-in. rectangle. Sprinkle with garlic powder. Spread filling to within 1/2 in. of edges. Roll up, jelly-roll style, starting with a short side; pinch seams to seal. Place, seam side down, on a greased baking sheet.

3 Beat egg yolk and water; brush over bread. Bake at 350° for 25-30 minutes or until golden brown. Serve warm. Refrigerate leftovers. **YIELD:** 1 loaf (12 slices).

ONION SANDWICH ROLLS

Prep: 25 min. + rising **Bake:** 20 min.

These tempting rolls have a mild onion flavor from handy dry soup mix. They are great with Italian meals or as sandwich rolls or hamburger buns. Plus, they freeze well, so you can prepare them ahead and take them out when needed.

Josie-Lynn Belmont // Woodbine, Georgia

    1 envelope onion soup mix
  1/2 cup boiling water
    1 tablespoon butter
3-1/2 to 4 cups all-purpose flour, *divided*
    2 packages (1/4 ounce *each*) quick-rise yeast
    1 tablespoon sugar
    1 cup warm water (120° to 130°)

1 In a small bowl, combine soup mix, boiling water and butter; cool to 120°-130°. In a large bowl, combine 1 cup flour, yeast and sugar. Add warm water; beat until smooth. Stir in 1 cup flour. Beat in onion soup mixture and enough remaining flour to form a soft dough.

2 Turn onto a floured surface; knead until smooth and elastic, about 6 minutes. Cover and let stand for 10 minutes. Divide dough into 12 portions and shape each into a ball. Place on greased baking sheets; flatten slightly.

3 Place two large shallow pans on the work surface; fill half full with boiling water. Place baking pans with rolls over water-filled pans. Cover and let rise for 15 minutes.

4 Bake at 375° for 16-19 minutes or until rolls are golden brown. Remove from pans to a wire rack. **YIELD:** 1 dozen.

When my sister and I spent the night at our grandmother's house, we often requested these muffins for breakfast. Today, I bake them for my kids. The very aroma is a trip down memory lane.

Kris Michels // Walled Lake, Michigan

LEMON BLUEBERRY MUFFINS

Prep/Total Time: 30 min.

> 2 cups biscuit/baking mix
> 1/2 cup plus 2 tablespoons sugar, *divided*
> 1 egg
> 1 cup (8 ounces) sour cream
> 1 cup fresh *or* frozen blueberries
> 2 teaspoons grated lemon peel

1 In a large bowl, combine the biscuit/baking mix and 1/2 cup sugar. Whisk egg and sour cream; stir into dry ingredients just until moistened. Fold in the blueberries.

2 Fill greased or paper-lined muffin cups half full. Combine lemon peel and remaining sugar; sprinkle over batter.

3 Bake at 400° for 20-25 minutes or until a toothpick inserted near the center comes out clean. Cool for 5 minutes before removing from pan to a wire rack. Serve warm. **YIELD:** 1 dozen.

EDITOR'S NOTE: If using frozen blueberries, use without thawing to avoid discoloring the batter.

MEXICAN SUNSET BREAD   PICTURED ON RIGHT

Prep: 5 min. **Bake:** 3-4 hours

I serve this tasty taco-seasoned bread with chili or cream soups. With its slightly chewy crust and wonderful texture inside, you'll love it, too.

Bobbie Hruska // Montgomery, Minnesota

> 2/3 cup water (70° to 80°)
> 1/2 cup sour cream
> 3 tablespoons chunky salsa
> 2 tablespoons plus 1-1/2 teaspoons taco seasoning
> 4-1/2 teaspoons sugar
> 1-1/2 teaspoons dried parsley flakes
> 1 teaspoon salt
> 3-1/3 cups bread flour
> 1-1/2 teaspoons active dry yeast

1 In bread machine pan, place all the ingredients in order suggested by manufacturer. Select basic bread setting. Choose crust color and loaf size if available.

2 Bake according to bread machine directions (check dough after 5 minutes of mixing; add 1 to 2 tablespoons of water or flour if needed). **YIELD:** 1 loaf (about 2 pounds).

EDITOR'S NOTE: We recommend you do not use a bread machine's time-delay feature for this recipe.

BACON CHEDDAR MUFFINS

Prep: 15 min. **Bake:** 20 min. + cooling

Cheddar cheese and bacon add hearty breakfast flavor to these tasty muffins. With just six ingredients, they're quick to stir up and handy to eat on the run.

Suzanne McKinley // Lyons, Georgia

2 cups biscuit/baking mix
2/3 cup 2% milk
1/4 cup canola oil
1 egg

1 cup (4 ounces) finely shredded sharp cheddar cheese
8 bacon strips, cooked and crumbled

1 In a large bowl, combine the biscuit mix, milk, oil and egg just until moistened. Fold in cheese and bacon. Fill greased muffin cups three-fourths full.

2 Bake at 375° for 20 minutes or until a toothpick inserted near the center comes out clean. Cool for 10 minutes; remove from pan to a wire rack. Serve warm. Refrigerate leftovers. **YIELD:** about 1 dozen.

Biscuit mix hurries along these nutmeg-spiced buttons and bows. This recipe remains a Saturday morning favorite at our house. Serve the sugar-coated treats with hot coffee for dunking.

Marcie Holladay // Irving, Texas

BUTTONS AND BOWS

Prep: 20 min. **Bake:** 10 min.

    2 cups biscuit/baking mix
    2 tablespoons plus 1/4 cup sugar, *divided*
    1 teaspoon ground nutmeg
  1/8 teaspoon ground cinnamon
    1 egg
  1/3 cup 2% milk
  1/4 cup butter, melted

1 In a large bowl, thoroughly combine the biscuit mix, 2 tablespoons sugar, nutmeg and cinnamon. Combine egg and milk; stir into dry ingredients just until moistened.

2 Turn onto a heavily floured surface; knead 5-6 times. Roll out to 1/4-in. thickness. Cut with a floured 2-1/2-in. doughnut cutter; set centers aside for buttons.

3 For bows, twist each circle to form a figure eight; place on a greased baking sheet. Bake at 400° for 8-10 minutes or until golden brown.

4 Place buttons on another greased baking sheet. Bake for 6-7 minutes. Brush tops with butter; sprinkle with remaining sugar. Remove from pans to wire racks. Serve warm. **YIELD:** 1 dozen buttons and bows.

ROUND CHEESE BREAD

Prep: 10 min. **Bake:** 20 min. + cooling

This savory loaf has a touch of Italian flair. Warm buttery wedges are tasty with a pasta dinner or tossed salad.

Deborah Bitz // Medicine Hat, Alberta

1-1/2 cups biscuit/baking mix
    1 cup (4 ounces) shredded part-skim mozzarella cheese
  1/4 cup grated Parmesan cheese
  1/2 teaspoon dried oregano
  1/2 cup 2% milk
    1 egg, lightly beaten
    2 tablespoons butter, melted
Additional Parmesan cheese

1 In a large bowl, combine the biscuit mix, mozzarella cheese, Parmesan cheese, oregano, milk and egg (batter will be thick).

2 Spoon mixture into a greased 9-in. round baking pan. Drizzle with butter; sprinkle with additional Parmesan cheese.

3 Bake at 400° for 20-25 minutes or until a toothpick inserted near the center comes out clean. Cool for 10 minutes. Cut into wedges. Serve warm. **YIELD:** 6-8 servings.

My husband grows a big garden, and our squash crop always seems to multiply! We give squash to everyone but still have plenty left over for making jelly, relish, pickles, breads, cakes and brownies.

Jean Moore // Pliny, West Virginia

ZUCCHINI CHEDDAR BISCUITS

Prep/Total Time: 25 min.

- 1 large onion, chopped
- 1/4 cup butter, cubed
- 2-1/2 cups biscuit/baking mix
- 1 tablespoon minced fresh parsley
- 1/2 teaspoon dried basil
- 1/2 teaspoon dried thyme
- 3 eggs, lightly beaten
- 1/4 cup 2% milk
- 1-1/2 cups shredded zucchini
- 1 cup (4 ounces) shredded cheddar cheese

1 In a large skillet, saute onion in butter until tender. In a large bowl, combine the biscuit mix, parsley, basil, thyme and onion mixture. In another bowl, whisk eggs and milk. Stir into biscuit mixture just until combined. Fold in zucchini and cheese.

2 Drop by 1/4 cupfuls 2 in. apart onto greased baking sheets. Bake biscuits at 400° for 10-14 minutes or until golden brown. Serve warm. Refrigerate leftovers. **YIELD:** 16 biscuits.

PIMIENTO-STUFFED OLIVE BREAD

Prep: 10 min. **Bake:** 50 min. + cooling

Salty olives pair well with this bread's cream cheese and chives. Even folks who normally avoid olives can't resist slices of this colorful bread.

Val Wilson // Wabasha, Minnesota

- 3 cups biscuit/baking mix
- 2 tablespoons sugar
- 1 egg
- 1-1/2 cups buttermilk
- 1 cup (4 ounces) shredded Swiss cheese
- 1 cup pimiento-stuffed olives
- 3/4 cup chopped walnuts
- 1 package (8 ounces) cream cheese, softened
- 1 teaspoon minced chives

1 In a large bowl, combine biscuit mix and sugar. In another bowl, whisk egg and buttermilk. Stir into dry ingredients just until moistened. Fold in the Swiss cheese, olives and walnuts.

2 Transfer to a greased 9-in. x 5-in. loaf pan. Bake at 350° for 50-55 minutes or until a toothpick inserted near the center comes out clean. Cool for 10 minutes before removing from pan to a wire rack.

3 In a small bowl, combine cream cheese and chives. Serve cream cheese mixture with the bread. Refrigerate leftovers. **YIELD:** 1 loaf (16 slices).

SUNSHINE MUFFINS

Prep/Total Time: 30 min.

The base for these sweet corn bread muffins is a cake mix and corn bread mix combined. The cake mix is the secret to the smoother texture than traditional corn bread.

Linnea Rein // Topeka, Kansas

- 1 package (9 ounces) yellow cake mix
- 1 package (8-1/2 ounces) corn bread/muffin mix
- 2 eggs
- 1/2 cup water
- 1/3 cup 2% milk
- 2 tablespoons canola oil

1 In a large bowl, combine the mixes. In a small bowl, combine the eggs, water, milk and oil. Stir into dry ingredients just until moistened.

2 Fill greased and floured muffin cups half full. Bake at 350° for 18-22 minutes or until a toothpick inserted near the center comes out clean. Cool for 5 minutes; remove from pans to wire racks. Serve warm. **YIELD:** 14 muffins.

This corn bread is richer and sweeter than others I've tried, and especially luscious alongside ham and beans.

Karen Ann Bland // Gove, Kansas

COWBOY CORN BREAD
Prep/Total Time: 25 min.

- 2 cups biscuit/baking mix
- 1 cup yellow cornmeal
- 3/4 cup sugar
- 1/2 teaspoon baking soda
- 1/2 teaspoon salt
- 2 eggs
- 1 cup butter, melted
- 1 cup half-and-half cream

1 In a large bowl, combine the first five ingredients. In another bowl, combine the eggs, butter and cream; stir into the dry ingredients just until moistened. Spread into a greased 13-in. x 9-in. baking pan.

2 Bake at 350° for 25-30 minutes or until a toothpick inserted near the center comes out clean. Serve warm. **YIELD:** 12 servings.

SMOKY ONION BISCUIT SQUARES PICTURED ON RIGHT

Prep: 20 min. **Bake:** 20 min.

Whip up a batch of my savory, biscuit-like squares to complement dinner or whenever you need a yummy bit of comfort.

Donna Marie Ryan // Topsfield, Massachusetts

- 1 small onion, chopped
- 2 tablespoons butter
- 1/4 teaspoon sugar
- 1 garlic clove, minced
- 1-1/2 cups biscuit/baking mix
- 1/2 cup 2% milk
- 1 egg
- 1/4 pound smoked mozzarella cheese, shredded, *divided*
- 1 teaspoon salt-free Southwest chipotle seasoning blend

1 In a small skillet, cook onion in butter over medium heat until tender. Add sugar; cook 10-15 minutes longer or until golden brown. Add garlic; cook for 1 minute. Cool slightly.

2 In a small bowl, combine the biscuit mix, milk and egg. Fold in 1/2 cup cheese, seasoning blend and onion mixture. Transfer to an 8-in. square baking dish coated with cooking spray. Sprinkle with remaining cheese.

3 Bake at 400° for 18-22 minutes or until a toothpick inserted near the center comes out clean. Cut into squares; serve warm. **YIELD:** 16 servings.

TEX-MEX BISCUITS

Prep/Total Time: 20 min.

I love cooking with green chilies because they add so much flavor to ordinary dishes. Once while making a pot of chili, I had some green chilies left over and mixed them into my biscuit dough, creating this recipe. The fresh-from-the-oven treats are a wonderful accompaniment to chili.

Angie Trolz // Jackson, Michigan

   2 cups biscuit/baking mix
2/3 cup 2% milk
   1 cup (4 ounces) finely shredded cheddar cheese
   1 can (4 ounces) chopped green chilies, drained

1 In a large bowl, combine biscuit mix and milk until a soft dough forms. Stir in cheese and chilies. Turn onto a floured surface; knead 10 times. Roll out to 1/2-in. thickness; cut with a 2-1/2-in. biscuit cutter.

2 Place on an ungreased baking sheet. Bake at 450° for 8-10 minutes or until golden brown. Serve biscuits warm. **YIELD:** about 1 dozen.

Colorful gumdrops make these fun miniature loaves just perfect for holiday gift-giving. I usually bake this moist bread at Christmas, but I also get requests to bring it for Easter dinner.

Linda Samaan // Fort Wayne, Indiana

GUMDROP BREAD

Prep: 15 min. **Bake:** 35 min. + cooling

    3 cups biscuit/baking mix
  2/3 cup sugar
    1 egg
1-1/4 cups 2% milk
1-1/2 cups chopped nuts
    1 cup chopped gumdrops

1 In a large bowl, combine biscuit mix and sugar. In another bowl, beat egg and milk; add to dry ingredients and stir well. Add nuts and gumdrops; stir just until mixed. Pour into three greased 5-3/4-in. x 3-in. x 2-in. loaf pans.

2 Bake at 350° for 35 minutes or until a toothpick inserted near the center comes out clean. Cool for 10 minutes; remove from pans to wire racks to cool completely. **YIELD:** 3 mini loaves.

CHEDDAR SAUSAGE MUFFINS

Prep: 20 min. **Bake:** 20 min.

Handy biscuit mix and cheese soup hurry along these hearty muffins. The golden muffins are great at breakfast, brunch or a soup lunch.

Melissa Vannoy // Childress, Texas

    1 pound bulk pork sausage
    1 can (10-3/4 ounces) condensed cheddar
      cheese soup, undiluted
    1 cup (4 ounces) shredded cheddar cheese
  2/3 cup water
    3 cups biscuit/baking mix

1 In a large skillet over medium heat, cook sausage until no longer pink; drain. In a large bowl, combine the soup, cheese and water. Stir in biscuit mix until blended. Add sausage. Fill greased muffin cups three-fourths full.

2 Bake at 350° for 20-25 minutes or until a toothpick inserted near the center comes out clean. Cool for 5 minutes before removing from pans to wire racks. Serve warm. **YIELD:** about 1-1/2 dozen.

I like to substitute these soft, oniony wedges for Italian bread when I serve spaghetti. They are also fantastic served with soup or salad.

Diane Hixon // Niceville, Florida

PARMESAN ONION WEDGES
Prep/Total Time: 25 min.

  2 cups biscuit/baking mix
2/3 cup milk
1/2 cup grated Parmesan cheese
  1 small onion, chopped
1/2 cup mayonnaise
  1 teaspoon Italian seasoning

1 In a small bowl, stir biscuit mix and milk just until moistened. Turn onto a floured surface; gently knead 6-8 times. Roll out to an 11-in. circle; transfer to a greased 12-in. pizza pan. Build up edges slightly.

2 Combine the cheese, onion and mayonnaise; spread over dough. Sprinkle with Italian seasoning. Bake at 400° for 15-20 minutes or until golden brown. Cut into wedges; serve warm. Refrigerate leftovers. **YIELD:** 8 servings.

HERB GARLIC LOAF
Prep: 5 min. **Bake:** 3 hours

Everyone who tastes this savory bread wants the recipe. With its mild garlic seasoning, slices of it are excellent with spaghetti, chili, stew or soup.

Juanita Patterson // Quartzsite, Arizona

  1 cup plus 2 tablespoons water (70° to 80°)
4-1/2 teaspoons butter, softened
1/2 teaspoon salt
  3 cups bread flour
  1 envelope savory herb with garlic soup mix
4-1/2 teaspoons nonfat dry milk powder
  1 tablespoon sugar
2-1/4 teaspoons active dry yeast

1 In a bread machine pan, place all ingredients in order suggested by manufacturer. Select basic bread setting. Choose crust color and loaf size if available.

2 Bake according to the bread machine directions (check dough after 5 minutes of mixing; add 1 to 2 tablespoons of water or flour if needed). **YIELD:** 1 loaf (16 slices).

MINI CHEDDAR LOAVES

Prep: 10 min. **Bake:** 35 min. + cooling

It's hard to believe you need only four ingredients to bake up a batch of these beautiful miniature loaves. Sliced warm from the oven, this golden, cheesy bread is simple and delicious.

Melody Rowland // Chattanooga, Tennessee

3-1/2 cups biscuit/baking mix
2-1/2 cups (10 ounces) shredded sharp
    cheddar cheese
   2 eggs
1-1/4 cups 2% milk

1 In a large bowl, combine biscuit mix and cheese. Beat the eggs and milk; stir into cheese mixture just until moistened. Pour into four greased and floured 5-3/4-in. x 3-in. x 2-in. loaf pans.

2 Bake at 350° for 35-40 minutes or until a toothpick inserted near the center comes out clean. Cool for 10 minutes. Remove from pans; slice and serve warm. **YIELD:** 4 mini loaves (4 slices each).

The mango adds a great tropical flavor to these scones. I love to serve these for tea or for breakfast.

**Cheryl Perry //
Hertford, North Carolina**

MANGO COLADA SCONES

Prep/Total Time: 25 min.

2-1/2 cups biscuit/baking mix
   2 tablespoons brown sugar
   3 tablespoons cold butter, *divided*
 1/2 cup frozen non-alcoholic pina colada mix, thawed
   1 cup chopped peeled mango
   3 tablespoons flaked coconut
 1/4 cup macadamia nuts, chopped

1 In a large bowl, combine biscuit mix and brown sugar. Cut in 2 tablespoons butter until mixture resembles coarse crumbs. Stir in pina colada mix just until moistened. Fold in mango.

2 Turn onto a floured surface; knead 10 times. Pat into a 9-in. x 7-in. rectangle. Cut into 10 rectangles; separate rectangles and place on a greased baking sheet. Melt remaining butter; brush over scones.

3 Bake at 400° for 12 minutes. Sprinkle with coconut and nuts; bake 2-4 minutes longer or until golden brown. Serve warm. **YIELD**: 10 scones.

PARMESAN HERB BREAD   PICTURED ON RIGHT

Prep/Total Time: 30 min.

Wedges of this delicious, cheese-topped bread go great with spaghetti and other Italian dishes. This loaf also tastes special when dressed up with one of the accompanying spreads.

Diane Hixon // Niceville, Florida

1-1/2 cups biscuit/baking mix
   1 egg, lightly beaten
 1/4 cup apple juice
 1/4 cup 2% milk
   1 tablespoon dried minced onion
   1 tablespoon sugar
 1/2 teaspoon dried oregano
 1/4 cup grated Parmesan cheese
HERB BUTTER:
 1/2 cup butter, softened
   1 garlic clove, minced
   2 tablespoons minced fresh parsley
    or 2 teaspoons dried parsley flakes
   1 teaspoon dried basil
TOMATO BUTTER:
 1/2 cup butter, softened
   4 teaspoons tomato paste
Dash cayenne pepper

1 In a large bowl, combine the first seven ingredients just until blended. Spoon into a greased 9-in. round baking pan. Sprinkle with cheese. Bake at 400° for 18-20 minutes or until golden brown.

2 In separate small bowls, combine herb butter and tomato butter ingredients; beat until smooth. Serve with warm bread. **YIELD**: 6-8 servings.

SQUASH CORN BREAD

Prep: 15 min. **Bake:** 20 min.

Enjoy the fresh flavor of summer squash with this moist and hearty cornbread. It's so tasty, you can forget the butter and enjoy a square by itself!
Marlene Huffstetler // Chapin, South Carolina

- 5 medium yellow summer squash (about 2 pounds), chopped
- 2 packages (8-1/2 ounces *each*) corn bread/muffin mix
- 4 eggs, lightly beaten
- 2/3 cup 4% cottage cheese
- 1/2 cup shredded cheddar cheese
- 1/2 cup chopped onion
- 1/4 teaspoon salt
- 1/4 teaspoon pepper

1 Place squash in a steamer basket; place in a large saucepan over 1 in. of water. Bring to a boil; cover and steam for 3-5 minutes or until tender. Drain and squeeze dry.

2 In a large bowl, combine mixes and eggs. Fold in squash, cheeses, onion, salt and pepper.

3 Pour into two 8-in. square baking pans coated with cooking spray. Bake at 400° for 20-25 minutes or until a toothpick inserted near the center comes out clean.

4 Serve warm or cool for 10 minutes before removing from pan to a wire rack to cool completely. Wrap in foil and freeze for up to 3 months.

5 TO USE THE FROZEN BREAD: Thaw at room temperature. Serve warm. **YIELD:** 2 dozen.

Cakes, Cookies & Bars

TRIPLE CHOCOLATE CAKE, PG. 161

CITRUS MINI CAKES

Prep: 15 min. **Bake:** 20 min.

"Melt-in-your mouth good" is how I would describe these bite-size muffins. With their appealing look and big-batch yield, it's the perfect recipe for large gatherings.

Linda Terrell // Palatka, Florida

   1 package (18-1/4 ounces) yellow cake mix
1-1/4 cups water
   3 eggs
 1/3 cup canola oil
3-1/2 cups confectioners' sugar
 1/2 cup orange juice
 1/4 cup lemon juice
Toasted chopped almonds

1 In a large bowl, combine the cake mix, water, eggs and oil; beat on low speed for 30 seconds. Beat on medium for 2 minutes.

2 Fill well-greased miniature muffin cups two-thirds full. Bake at 350° for 10-12 minutes or until a toothpick inserted near the center of the muffin comes out clean.

3 Meanwhile, in a large bowl, combine confectioners' sugar and juices until smooth. Cool cakes for 2 minutes; remove from pans. Immediately dip cakes into glaze, coating well. Place cakes top down on wire racks; sprinkle with chopped almonds. **YIELD:** about 6 dozen.

I've been bringing this cake to family get-togethers and church meetings for a very long time. The scrumptious standby, topped with cream cheese and nuts, can be prepared in a wink.

Doris Schloeman // Chicago, Illinois

RICH BUTTER CAKE

Prep: 15 min. **Bake:** 35 min.

- 1 package (16 ounces) pound cake mix
- 1/2 cup butter, melted
- 5 eggs
- 2 cups confectioners' sugar, *divided*
- 2 packages (one 8 ounces, one 3 ounces) cream cheese, softened
- 1/2 teaspoon vanilla extract
- 1 cup chopped walnuts

1 In a large bowl, combine the cake mix, butter and 3 eggs; beat until smooth. Spread into a greased 13-in. x 9-in. baking pan.

2 Set aside 2 tablespoons confectioners' sugar for topping. In a large bowl, beat the cream cheese, vanilla and remaining confectioners' sugar until smooth. Beat in remaining eggs. Pour over batter. Sprinkle with walnuts.

3 Bake at 350° for 35-40 minutes or until a toothpick inserted near the center comes out clean. Cool on a wire rack. Dust with reserved confectioners' sugar. Store in the refrigerator. **YIELD:** 12-15 servings.

TRIPLE CHOCOLATE CAKE

Prep: 15 min. **Bake:** 45 min. + cooling

This is a delicious way to perk up a cake mix. The whole family will love the chocolaty results.

Melissa Just // Minneapolis, Minnesota

- 1 package (18-1/4 ounces) white cake mix
- 1/3 cup sugar
- 4 eggs
- 1 cup (8 ounces) sour cream
- 2/3 cup canola oil
- 2 tablespoons baking cocoa
- 1/2 cup miniature semisweet chocolate chips
- 1 cup chocolate frosting
- 2 tablespoons 2% milk

1 In a large bowl, combine the cake mix, sugar, eggs, sour cream and oil. Beat on low for 1 minute; beat on medium for 2 minutes. Pour half of the batter into a large bowl. Stir in cocoa until blended. Fold chocolate chips into white cake batter.

2 Alternately spoon batters into a greased and floured 10-in. fluted tube pan. Bake at 350° for 45-50 minutes or until a toothpick inserted near the center comes out clean. Cool for 15 minutes before removing from pan to a wire rack to cool completely.

3 In a small bowl, combine frosting and milk. Spoon over top of cooled cake. **YIELD:** 12 servings.

This is a very festive dessert for Christmas. The angel food cake makes it less heavy than many traditional holiday recipes. My husband loves the flavor, and I love it because it's so convenient during a hectic season!

Holly Dicke // Plain City, Ohio

PEPPERMINT ANGEL ROLL

Prep: 30 min. **Bake:** 15 min. + freezing

        1 **package (16 ounces) angel food cake mix**
        1 **tablespoon confectioners' sugar**
    1/2 **gallon peppermint ice cream, softened**
        1 **jar (11-3/4 ounces) hot fudge ice cream topping, warmed**
Crushed peppermint candies and additional confectioners' sugar, optional

1 Prepare cake batter according to package directions. Line a greased 15-in. x 10-in. x 1-in. baking pan with waxed paper and grease the paper. Spread batter evenly into pan. Bake at 350°

for 15-20 minutes or until cake springs back when lightly touched.

2 Cool for 5 minutes. Turn cake onto a kitchen towel dusted with confectioners' sugar. Gently peel off waxed paper. Roll up cake in the towel jelly-roll style, starting with a short side. Cool completely on a wire rack.

3 Unroll cake and spread ice cream over cake to within 1/2 in. of edges. Roll up again. Cover and freeze until firm.

4 Cut into slices; drizzle with hot fudge topping. If desired, garnish with crushed candies and dust with confectioners' sugar. **YIELD:** 10 servings.

RHUBARB UPSIDE-DOWN CAKE

Prep: 15 min. **Bake:** 50 min. + cooling

I prepare this colorful dessert quite often in the summer when fresh rhubarb is abundant. When I take it to church potlucks, people really line up for a piece.

Bonnie Krogman // Thompson Falls, Montana

    5 **cups cut fresh or frozen rhubarb (1/2-inch pieces), thawed and drained**
    1 **package (6 ounces) strawberry gelatin**
1/2 **cup sugar**
    2 **cups miniature marshmallows**
    1 **package (18-1/4 ounces) white or yellow cake mix**
Whipped topping, optional

1 Place rhubarb in a greased 13-in. x 9-in. baking pan. Sprinkle with the gelatin, sugar and marshmallows. Prepare cake mix according to package directions; pour batter over marshmallows.

2 Bake at 350° for 50-55 minutes or until a toothpick carefully inserted near the center comes out clean. Cool for 10 minutes; invert cake onto a serving plate. Serve with whipped topping if desired. **YIELD:** 12-16 servings.

CHOCOLATE BUNDT CAKE

Prep: 15 min. **Bake:** 1 hour + cooling

Chocolate lovers will delight in this moist rich cake that uses handy mixes and canned frosting. I only make this dessert if I'm taking it somewhere. I don't want it sitting in my kitchen, where I might be tempted to eat it all!

Nancy Baker // Boonville, Missouri

- 1 package (18-1/4 ounces) yellow cake mix
- 1 package (3.4 ounces) instant vanilla pudding mix
- 1 cup (8 ounces) sour cream
- 3 eggs
- 1/2 cup canola oil
- 1/2 cup water
- 4 ounces German sweet chocolate, grated
- 1 cup (6 ounces) semisweet chocolate chips
- 1/2 cup chopped pecans
- 1/2 cup chocolate frosting, melted
- Pecan halves

1 In a large bowl, combine the cake and pudding mixes, sour cream, eggs, oil and water. Beat on low speed for 2 minutes. Fold in the grated chocolate, chocolate chips and pecans. Transfer to a greased and floured 10-in. fluted tube pan.

2 Bake at 350° for 60-65 minutes or until a toothpick inserted near the center comes out clean. Cool for 10 minutes before removing from pan to a wire rack. Drizzle with frosting; garnish with pecan halves. **YIELD:** 12-14 servings.

LIGHTER MOIST CAKE

Use any flavor cake mix and beat in a 12-ounce can of diet soda. Try diet lemon-lime soda with white or yellow cake mix and diet cola with a chocolate cake mix. Do not add any other ingredients. Just mix and pour the batter into a pan and bake as usual. Top each piece with 2 tablespoons of fat-free whipped topping instead of icing. —Debbie M., Owensboro, Kentucky

I bring these sensational treats to church meetings, potlucks and housewarming parties. I often make a double batch so we can enjoy some at home.

Kimberly Biel // Java, South Dakota

CAN'T LEAVE ALONE BARS

Prep: 20 min. **Bake:** 20 min. + cooling

  1 package (18-1/4 ounces) white cake mix
  2 eggs
1/3 cup canola oil
  1 can (14 ounces) sweetened condensed milk
  1 cup (6 ounces) semisweet chocolate chips
1/4 cup butter, cubed

1 In a large bowl, combine the cake mix, eggs and oil. Press two-thirds of the mixture into a greased 13-in. x 9-in. baking pan. Set remaining cake mixture aside.

2 In a microwave-safe bowl, combine the milk, chocolate chips and butter. Microwave, uncovered, until chips and butter are melted; stir until smooth. Pour over crust.

3 Drop teaspoonfuls of remaining cake mixture over top. Bake at 350° for 20-25 minutes or until lightly browned. Cool before cutting. **YIELD:** 3 dozen.

CARAMEL APPLE CUPCAKES PICTURED ON RIGHT

Bring these extra-special cupcakes to your next bake sale and watch how quickly they disappear! Kids will go for the fun appearance and tasty toppings, while adults will appreciate the moist spiced cake underneath.

Diane Halferty // Corpus Christi, Texas

  1 package (18-1/4 ounces) spice cake mix
    or 1 package (18 ounces) carrot cake mix
  2 cups chopped peeled tart apples
20 caramels
  3 tablespoons 2% milk
  1 cup finely chopped pecans, toasted
12 Popsicle sticks

1 Prepare cake batter according to package directions; fold in apples.

2 Fill 12 greased or paper-lined jumbo muffin cups three-fourths full. Bake at 350° for 20 minutes or until a toothpick inserted near the center comes out clean. Cool for 10 minutes before removing from pans to wire racks to cool completely.

3 In a small saucepan, cook the caramels and milk over low heat until smooth. Spread over cupcakes. Sprinkle with pecans. Insert a wooden stick into the center of each cupcake. **YIELD:** 1 dozen.

PECAN BUTTERSCOTCH COOKIES

Prep/Total Time: 25 min.

These are the quickest, tastiest cookies I've ever made. They can be varied endlessly, but I come back to this version time after time.

Trisha Kruse // Eagle, Idaho

- 1 cup complete buttermilk pancake mix
- 1 package (3.4 ounces) instant butterscotch pudding mix
- 1/3 cup butter, melted
- 1 egg
- 1/2 cup chopped pecans, toasted

1 In a large bowl, beat the pancake mix, dry pudding mix, butter and egg until blended. Stir in pecans.

2 Roll into 1-1/2-in. balls. Place 2 in. apart on greased baking sheets. Flatten with the bottom of a glass. Bake at 350° for 8-10 minutes or until edges begin to brown. Remove cookies to wire racks to cool.
YIELD: about 1-1/2 dozen.

My family often requests this delightful layer cake. They love the mocha flavor and extra chocolate surprise hidden beneath the taste-tempting frosting.

Terry Gilbert // Orlean, Virginia

MOCHA LAYER CAKE

Prep: 25 min. **Bake:** 30 min.

- 1 package (18-1/4 ounces) devil's food *or* chocolate cake mix
- 1-1/3 cups brewed coffee, room temperature
- 1/2 cup canola oil
- 3 eggs
- 1/2 cup semisweet chocolate chips

FROSTING:

- 1/2 cup butter, softened
- 1/2 cup shortening
- 4 cups confectioners' sugar
- 3/4 cup baking cocoa
- 1/4 teaspoon almond extract
- 7 tablespoons brewed coffee, room temperature, *divided*
- 1/2 cup semisweet chocolate chips

1 In a large bowl, combine the cake mix, coffee, oil and eggs; beat on low speed for 30 seconds. Beat on medium for 2 minutes. Pour into two greased and floured 8-in. round baking pans.

2 Bake at 350° for 30-35 minutes or until a toothpick inserted near the center comes out clean. Cool in pans for 5 minutes; invert onto a wire rack. Sprinkle each cake with 1/4 cup chocolate chips; when melted, gently spread chocolate over cakes. Place cakes in the freezer.

3 Meanwhile, for frosting, in a large bowl, cream the butter, shortening and confectioners' sugar until light and fluffy. Beat in cocoa and extract. Add 5 tablespoons coffee, 1 tablespoon at a time, beating until light and fluffy. Spread between layers and over the top and sides of cake.

4 In a microwave, melt chocolate chips and remaining coffee; stir until smooth. Pour over cake; carefully spread over the top, allowing it to drizzle down the sides. **YIELD:** 10-12 servings.

This moist cake had a delightful sweet and crunchy surprise sprinkled throughout it. Top with a dollop of whipped cream and you're ready to enjoy.

Margaret Wilson //
Sun City, California

CINNAMON NUT CAKE

Prep: 20 min. **Bake:** 35 min.

   1 package (18-1/4 ounces) yellow cake mix
   3 eggs
1-1/3 cups water
  1/4 cup canola oil
1-1/4 cups finely chopped walnuts
7-1/2 teaspoons sugar
4-1/2 teaspoons ground cinnamon

1 In a large bowl, combine the cake mix, eggs, water and oil. Beat on medium speed for 2 minutes. Combine walnuts, sugar and cinnamon.

2 Sprinkle a third of the nut mixture into a greased 10-in. fluted tube pan. Top with half of the batter and another third of the nut mixture. Repeat layers.

3 Bake at 350° for 35-40 minutes or until a toothpick inserted near the center comes out clean. Cool for 10 minutes before removing from pan to a wire rack to cool completely. **YIELD:** 12-14 servings.

EASY GERMAN CHOCOLATE CAKE

Prep: 15 min. **Bake:** 55 min. + cooling

There's no need to frost this yummy chocolate cake. After baking, just turn the cake upside down onto a pretty platter; the coconut and pecan topping is already in place.

Dawn Glenn // Johnson City, Tennessee

1-1/3 cups flaked coconut
   1 cup chopped pecans
   1 package (18-1/4 ounces) German chocolate cake mix
   1 package (8 ounces) cream cheese, softened
1/2 cup butter, softened
   1 egg
   4 cups confectioners' sugar

1 Sprinkle the coconut and pecans into a greased and floured 13-in. x 9-in. baking pan. Prepare cake mix according to package directions. Pour batter into prepared pan.

2 In a large bowl, beat cream cheese and butter until fluffy. Beat in egg and confectioners' sugar until smooth. Drop by tablespoonfuls over the batter. Carefully spread to within 1 in. of edges.

3 Bake at 325° for 55-60 minutes or until a toothpick inserted near the center comes out clean. Cool for 10 minutes; invert onto a serving plate. **YIELD:** 12-16 servings.

RASPBERRY OATMEAL BARS

Prep: 10 min. **Bake:** 35 min. + cooling

Cake mix hurries along the prep work for these yummy bars. Raspberry jam adds a pop of color and sweetness, and oats lend a homey touch.

Trish Bosman-Golata // Rock Hill, South Carolina

- 1 package (18-1/4 ounces) yellow cake mix
- 2-1/2 cups quick-cooking oats
- 3/4 cup butter, melted
- 1 jar (12 ounces) seedless raspberry preserves
- 1 tablespoon water

1 In a large bowl, combine the cake mix, oats and butter until crumbly. Press 3 cups of the crumb mixture into a greased 13-in. x 9-in. baking pan. Bake at 350° for 10 minutes. Cool on a wire rack for 5 minutes.

2 In a small bowl, stir preserves and water until blended. Spread over crust. Sprinkle with remaining crumb mixture. Bake for 25-28 minutes or until lightly browned. Cool on a wire rack. Cut into bars. **YIELD:** 2 dozen.

Baking mix makes these soft, moist cookies a snap to stir-up, yet they're pretty enough for parties. I'm often asked to bring them to wedding and baby showers, and they're popular around the holidays, too. I sometimes mix the dough the day before and chill it until I want to bake the cookies.

Stephanie DeLoach //
Magnolia, Arkansas

DIPPED PEANUT BUTTER COOKIES

Prep: 30 min. + chilling **Bake:** 15 min.

    1 cup peanut butter
    1 can (14 ounces) sweetened condensed milk
    1 egg
    1 teaspoon vanilla extract
    2 cups biscuit/baking mix
3/4 to 1 pound milk chocolate candy coating,
      coarsely chopped
    1 tablespoon shortening

1 In a large bowl, combine the peanut butter, milk, egg and vanilla; beat until smooth. Gradually stir in biscuit mix and mix well. Cover and refrigerate for 1 hour.

2 Shape into 1-in. balls and place 1 in. apart on ungreased baking sheets. Flatten each ball with the bottom of a glass. Bake at 350° for 8-10 minutes or until golden brown. Cool on wire racks.

3 In a microwave, melt candy coating and shortening; stir until smooth. Dip each cookie halfway into chocolate; allow excess to drip off. Place on waxed paper-lined baking sheets; let stand until set. **YIELD:** about 5 dozen.

APRICOT BARS   PICTURED ON RIGHT

Prep: 25 min. **Bake:** 25 min. + cooling

I created this recipe one winter's day and shared it with my friend. I've had many favorable comments from those who've sampled it. Great apricot flavor and a sprinkling of coconut make these bars special!

Barbara Rohlf // Spirit Lake, Iowa

    1 package (16 ounces) pound cake mix
    4 eggs
1/2 cup butter, melted
    2 teaspoons vanilla extract, *divided*
    1 cup chopped dried apricots
    1 package (8 ounces) cream cheese, softened
    2 cups confectioners' sugar
1/2 cup apricot preserves

3/4 cup flaked coconut
3/4 cup sliced almonds

1 In a bowl, combine the cake mix, 2 eggs, butter and 1 teaspoon vanilla; beat until well blended. Fold in dried apricots. Spread into a greased 15-in. x 10-in. x 1-in. baking pan; set aside.

2 In another bowl, beat the cream cheese, confectioners' sugar, preserves and remaining vanilla. Add remaining eggs; beat on low speed just until combined. Gently spread over cake batter. Sprinkle with coconut and almonds.

3 Bake at 350° for 25-30 minutes or until golden brown. Cool on a wire rack. Cut into bars. Refrigerate leftovers. **YIELD:** 2 dozen.

APPLE SNACK CAKE

Prep: 15 min. **Bake:** 35 min. + cooling

A quick-bread mix is the secret behind this speedy and versatile spice cake. The moist cake is flecked with bits of apple, and is fabulous for dessert or as a breakfast coffee cake.

Marilyn Terman // Columbus, Ohio

- 1/2 cup butter, softened
- 1/2 cup packed brown sugar
- 3 eggs
- 1 teaspoon vanilla extract
- 1 package (15.4 ounces) nut quick bread mix
- 1 teaspoon ground cinnamon
- 2 medium tart apples, peeled and finely chopped
- 1/2 cup raisins

ICING:
- 3/4 cup confectioners' sugar
- 1/4 teaspoon ground cinnamon
- 2 tablespoons butter, melted
- 1/4 teaspoon vanilla extract
- 3 to 5 tablespoons 2% milk

1 In a large bowl, cream butter and brown sugar until light and fluffy. Beat in eggs and vanilla. Add quick bread mix and cinnamon and mix well. Fold in apples and raisins.

2 Transfer to a greased 13-in. x 9-in. baking dish. Bake at 350° for 35-40 minutes or until a toothpick inserted near the center comes out clean. Cool on a wire rack.

3 In a small bowl, combine the confectioners' sugar, cinnamon, butter, vanilla and enough milk to achieve desired consistency. Drizzle over cake. **YIELD:** 12-15 servings.

These colorful kid-tested treats are great for bake sales, especially when you find out about the sale at eight the night before the kids need them.

Debbie Brunssen //
Randolph, Nebraska

FUN MARSHMALLOW BARS

Prep: 10 min. **Bake:** 25 min. + cooling

- 1 package (18-1/4 ounces) devil's food cake mix
- 1/4 cup water
- 1/4 cup butter, melted
- 1 egg
- 3 cups miniature marshmallows
- 1 cup milk chocolate M&M's
- 1/2 cup chopped peanuts

1 In a large bowl, combine the cake mix, water, butter and egg. Press into a greased 13-in. x 9-in. baking pan. Bake at 375° for 20-22 minutes or until a toothpick inserted near the center comes out clean.

2 Sprinkle with marshmallows, M&M's and peanuts. Bake 2-3 minutes longer or until the marshmallows begin to melt. Cool on a wire rack. Cut into bars. **YIELD:** 3-1/2 dozen.

QUICK LITTLE DEVILS

Prep/Total Time: 30 min.

Enjoy the classic combination of peanut butter and chocolate in these speedy squares. A short list of ingredients, including devil's food cake mix, yields chocolaty results that are sure to satisfy any sweet tooth.

Denise Smith // Lusk, Wyoming

- 1 package (18-1/4 ounces) devil's food cake mix
- 3/4 cup butter, melted
- 1/3 cup evaporated milk
- 1 jar (7 ounces) marshmallow creme
- 3/4 cup peanut butter

1 In a large bowl, combine the cake mix, butter and milk. Spread half the mixture into a greased 13-in. x 9-in. baking pan. In a small bowl, combine marshmallow creme and peanut butter; carefully spread over cake mixture to within 1 in. of edge.

2 Drop remaining cake mixture by teaspoonfuls over marshmallow mixture. Bake at 350° for 20-22 minutes or until edges are golden brown. Cool completely on a wire rack. Cut into squares. **YIELD:** about 2-1/2 dozen.

Brownies are an easy way to make any event better, and no one seems to tire of them. Served warm with ice cream, these coconutty delights are a favorite!

Barbara Carlucci //
Orange Park, Florida

COCONUT BROWNIES

Prep: 10 min. **Bake:** 30 min. + cooling

   1 **package fudge brownie mix**
     (13-inch x 9-inch pan size)
   1 **cup (8 ounces) sour cream**
   1 **cup coconut-pecan frosting**
   2 **eggs**
1/4 **cup water**
   1 **cup (6 ounces) semisweet chocolate chips**

1 In a large bowl, combine the brownie mix, sour cream, frosting, eggs and water just until moistened.

2 Pour into a 13-in. x 9-in. baking dish coated with cooking spray. Bake at 350° for 30-35 minutes or until center is set (do not overbake). Sprinkle with chocolate chips; let stand for 5 minutes. Spread chips over brownies. **YIELD:** 2 dozen.

PINEAPPLE UPSIDE-DOWN CAKE

Prep: 10 min. **Bake:** 25 min.

I like to dole out slices of this sunny-colored dessert while it's still warm from the oven. The delectable cake gets fruity flavor from crushed pineapple and lemon gelatin.

Anna Polhemus // North Merrick, New York

   1 **can (20 ounces) unsweetened**
     crushed pineapple
   1 **package (.3 ounce) sugar-free lemon gelatin**
1/2 **cup egg substitute**
   1 **egg white**
3/4 **cup sugar**
   1 **teaspoon vanilla extract**
3/4 **cup all-purpose flour**
   1 **teaspoon baking powder**

1 Drain pineapple, reserving 1/3 cup juice (discard or save remaining juice for another use). Line a 9-in. round baking pan with waxed paper; coat with cooking spray. Spread pineapple over waxed paper; sprinkle with gelatin.

2 In a large bowl, beat egg substitute and egg white. Beat in the sugar, reserved pineapple juice and vanilla. Combine flour and baking powder; add to egg mixture and mix well. Pour over gelatin.

3 Bake at 350° for 25-30 minutes or until a toothpick inserted near the center comes out clean. Cool for 5 minutes; invert onto a serving plate. Serve warm. **YIELD:** 10 servings.

BLACK FOREST CAKE

Prep: 10 min. **Bake:** 25 min. + chilling

When my daughter went to Germany, she said the streets were lined with pastry shops. This rich treat reminds her of that visit.

Patricia Rutherford // Winchester, Illinois

- 1 package (9 ounces) chocolate cake mix
- 1/2 cup water
- 1 egg
- 1 package (3 ounces) cream cheese, softened
- 2 tablespoons sugar
- 1 carton (8 ounces) frozen whipped topping, thawed
- 1 can (21 ounces) cherry pie filling

1 In a small bowl, beat the cake mix, water and egg on medium speed for 3-4 minutes. Pour into a greased 9-in. springform pan; place pan on a baking sheet.

2 Bake at 350° for 23-25 minutes or until cake springs back when lightly touched. Cool on a wire rack.

3 In a small bowl, beat cream cheese and sugar until fluffy; fold in whipped topping. Spread pie filling over cake; top with cream cheese mixture. Cover and refrigerate for 4 hours. Remove sides of pan. **YIELD:** 6-8 servings.

Chocolate chips and a convenient brownie mix provide the rich chocolate flavor in these sweet cookies. Rolling the dough in powdered sugar gives them their inviting crackled appearance.

Ellen Govertsen // Wheaton, Illinois

BROWNIE CRACKLES

Prep: 15 min. **Bake:** 10 min./batch

- 1 package fudge brownie mix
  (13-in. x 9-inch pan size)
- 1 cup all-purpose flour
- 1 egg
- 1/2 cup water
- 1/4 cup canola oil
- 1 cup (6 ounces) semisweet chocolate chips

Confectioners' sugar

1 In a bowl, beat the brownie mix, flour, egg, water and oil until well blended. Stir in chocolate chips.

2 Place confectioners' sugar in a shallow dish. Drop dough by tablespoonfuls into sugar; roll to coat. Place 2 in. apart on greased baking sheets. Bake at 350° for 8-10 minutes or until set. Remove from pans to wire racks to cool. **YIELD:** 4-1/2 dozen.

ALMOST A CANDY BAR PICTURED ON RIGHT

Prep: 15 min. **Bake:** 15 min. + chilling

Because I love candy bars and marshmallows, this recipe was a cinch to invent, and I've yet to find anyone who doesn't enjoy it! With all the different layers and flavors, they're sure to please just about everyone.

Barb Wyman // Hankinson, North Dakota

- 1 tube (16-1/2 ounces) refrigerated chocolate chip cookie dough
- 4 nutty s'mores trail mix bars
  (1.23 ounces *each*), chopped
- 1 package (10 to 11 ounces) butterscotch chips
- 2-1/2 cups miniature marshmallows
- 1 cup chopped walnuts
- 1-1/2 cups miniature pretzels
- 1 package (10 ounces) peanut butter chips
- 3/4 cup light corn syrup
- 1/4 cup butter, cubed
- 1 package (11-1/2 ounces) milk chocolate chips

1 Let dough stand at room temperature for 5-10 minutes to soften. In a large bowl, combine dough and trail mix bars. Press into an ungreased 13-in. x 9-in. baking pan. Bake, uncovered, at 350° for 10-12 minutes or until golden brown.

2 Sprinkle with butterscotch chips and marshmallows. Bake 3-4 minutes longer or until marshmallows begin to brown. Sprinkle with walnuts; arrange pretzels over the top. In a small saucepan, melt the peanut butter chips, corn syrup and butter; spoon over bars.

3 In a microwave, melt chocolate chips; stir until smooth. Spread or drizzle over bars. Refrigerate for 1 hour or until firm before cutting. **YIELD:** 3 dozen.

RASPBERRY CAKE

Prep: 10 min. + chilling **Bake:** 35 min. + cooling

Let raspberry gelatin and frozen berries turn a cake mix into a special dessert. Spread with a light, fruity whipped topping, the festive results make a cool and refreshing treat.

Marion Anderson // Dalton, Minnesota

- 1 package (18-1/4 ounces) white cake mix
- 1 package (3 ounces) raspberry gelatin
- 4 eggs
- 1/2 cup canola oil
- 1/4 cup hot water
- 1 package (10 ounces) frozen sweetened raspberries, thawed, undrained

FROSTING:

- 1 carton (12 ounces) frozen whipped topping, thawed
- 1 package (10 ounces) frozen sweetened raspberries, thawed, undrained

Fresh raspberries, optional

1 In a bowl, combine the cake mix, gelatin, eggs, oil and water; beat on low speed for 30 seconds. Beat on medium for 2 minutes. Stir in raspberries.

2 Pour into a greased 13-in. x 9-in. baking pan. Bake at 350° for 35-40 minutes or until a toothpick inserted near the center comes out clean. Cool.

3 For frosting, in a large bowl, fold whipped topping into raspberries. Spread over cake. Refrigerate for 2 hours before serving. Store in the refrigerator. Garnish with fresh raspberries if desired. **YIELD:** 12-16 servings.

SUNK IN THE CENTER

There are several factors that may cause a cake to sink in the center after baking. The most important one is oven temperature. An oven that is not hot enough can cause the cake to rise and then sink.
—Taste of Home Test Kitchen

Inside each of these cupcakes is a fruity surprise! Kids and adults will love them.

Bertille Cooper // California, Maryland

CHOCOLATE CHERRY CUPCAKES

Prep: 15 min. **Bake:** 20 min.

   1 package (18-1/4 ounces) chocolate cake mix
1-1/3 cups water
 1/2 cup canola oil
   3 eggs
   1 can (21 ounces) cherry pie filling
   1 can (16 ounces) vanilla frosting

1 In a large bowl, combine the cake mix, water, oil and eggs; beat on low speed for 30 seconds. Beat on medium for 2 minutes.

2 Spoon batter by 1/4 cupfuls into paper-lined muffin cups. Spoon a rounded teaspoon of pie filling onto the center of each cupcake. Set remaining pie filling aside.

3 Bake at 350° for 20-25 minutes or until a toothpick inserted near the center comes out clean. Remove from pans to wire racks to cool completely.

4 Frost cupcakes; top with one cherry from pie filling. Serve additional pie filling with cupcakes or refrigerate for another use. **YIELD:** 2 dozen.

CRUNCHY DESSERT BARS

Prep: 10 min. + freezing

My son-in-law is diabetic and loves these five-ingredient frozen dessert bars. With their nutty crunch from Grape Nuts cereal, we think they taste like the inside of a Snickers candy bar.

Shirley Reed // San Angelo, Texas

   1 pint fat-free no-sugar-added vanilla
     ice cream, softened
   1 cup reduced-fat whipped topping
 1/2 cup reduced-fat peanut butter
   1 package (1.0 ounce) sugar-free instant
     butterscotch pudding mix
   1 cup Grape-Nuts

1 In a large bowl, beat the first four ingredients until smooth. Stir in cereal.

2 Transfer to a foil-lined 8-in. square pan. Cover and freeze for 3-4 hours or until firm. Use foil to lift out of pan; discard foil. Cut into bars. **YIELD:** 2 dozen.

This awesome dessert is perfect to bake when unexpected guests stop by. A boxed cake mix and canned pie filling make the moist snack cake a cinch to put together while chocolate chips and nuts create the wonderful topping.

Shirley Weaver // Zeeland, Michigan

APPLE GERMAN CHOCOLATE CAKE

Prep: 15 min. **Bake:** 40 min.

   1 can (21 ounces) apple pie filling
   1 package (18-1/4 ounces) German chocolate cake mix
   3 eggs
3/4 cup coarsely chopped walnuts
1/2 cup miniature semisweet chocolate chips

1 Place pie filling in a blender; cover and process until the apples are in 1/4-in. chunks. Pour into a large bowl; add cake mix and eggs. Beat on medium speed for 5 minutes. Pour into a greased 13-in. x 9-in. baking pan. Sprinkle with nuts and chocolate chips.

2 Bake at 350° for 40-45 minutes or until a toothpick inserted near the center comes out clean. Cool completely on a wire rack before cutting. **YIELD:** 12-15 servings.

CREAMY CENTER CUPCAKES

Prep: 45 min. + cooling

My mother made these cupcakes from scratch when I was growing up. I simplified it with a cake mix. Sometimes Mom would replace the smooth filling with homemade whipped cream. These treats are good with either filling.

Caroline Anderson // Waupaca, Wisconsin

   1 package (18-1/4 ounces) devil's food cake mix
3/4 cup shortening
2/3 cup confectioners' sugar
   1 cup marshmallow creme
   1 teaspoon vanilla extract
   2 cans (16 ounces *each*) chocolate frosting

1 Prepare and bake cake according to package directions for cupcakes, using paper-lined muffin cups. Cool for 10 minutes before removing from pans to wire racks to cool completely.

2 Meanwhile in a large bowl, cream shortening and sugar until light and fluffy. Beat in marshmallow creme and vanilla.

3 Cut a small hole in the corner of a pastry or plastic bag; insert a very small tip. Fill with cream filling. Push the tip through the bottom of a paper liner to fill each cupcake. Frost with chocolate frosting. **YIELD:** 2 dozen.

POPPY SEED CITRUS CAKE

Prep: 15 min. **Bake:** 40 min. + cooling

My youngest daughter loves anything with lemon and this is her favorite cake. It's refreshing and easy to pack for picnics.

Charolette Westfall // Houston, Texas

> 1 package (18-1/4 ounces) lemon cake mix
> 3 eggs
> 1-1/3 cups orange juice
> 1/2 cup canola oil
> 1 to 2 tablespoons poppy seeds
> 1 teaspoon grated lemon peel
> 1 teaspoon grated orange peel

GLAZE:

> 2 cups confectioners' sugar
> 3 to 4 tablespoons orange juice
> 1/2 teaspoon grated lemon peel
> 1/2 teaspoon grated orange peel

1 In a large bowl, combine the cake mix, eggs, orange juice and oil; beat on low speed for 30 seconds. Beat on medium for 2 minutes. Fold in the poppy seeds, lemon and orange peel.

2 Pour into a well-greased and floured 10-in. fluted tube pan. Bake at 350° for 40-45 minutes or until a toothpick inserted near the center comes out clean. Cool for 10 minutes before removing from pan to a wire rack to cool completely.

3 In a small bowl, combine the confectioners' sugar and orange juice until smooth. Drizzle over warm cake. Sprinkle top with lemon and orange peel. **YIELD:** 12 servings.

S'MORES BARS

Prep: 10 min. **Bake:** 30 min. + cooling

  8 to 10 whole graham crackers
  1 package fudge brownie mix
    (13-inch x 9-inch pan size)
  2 cups miniature marshmallows
  1 cup (6 ounces) semisweet chocolate chips
2/3 cup chopped peanuts

1 Arrange graham crackers in a single layer in a greased 13-in. x 9-in. baking pan. Prepare the brownie batter according to package directions. Spread over crackers.

2 Bake at 350° for 25-30 minutes or until a toothpick inserted near the center comes out clean. Sprinkle with marshmallows, chocolate chips and peanuts. Bake 5 minutes longer or until marshmallows are slightly puffed and golden brown. Cool on a wire rack before cutting. **YIELD:** 2 dozen.

CHOCOLATE MINT CREAM CAKE   PICTURED ON RIGHT

Prep: 30 min. **Bake:** 20 min. + cooling

I had a lot of fun dreaming up and making this dessert. It's easy, but guests will be impressed when you serve it.

Patty Thompson // Jefferson, Iowa

  1 package (18-1/4 ounces) white cake mix
  1 cup water
1/2 cup canola oil
  3 eggs
1/2 teaspoon peppermint extract
  1 cup crushed mint cream-filled chocolate
    sandwich cookies

TOPPING:

  2 packages (3.9 ounces *each*) instant chocolate
    pudding mix
1/3 cup confectioners' sugar
1-1/2 cups cold whole milk
1/2 to 1 teaspoon peppermint extract
  1 carton (12 ounces) frozen whipped
    topping, thawed
1/2 cup crushed mint cream-filled chocolate
    sandwich cookies
 15 mint Andes candies

1 In a large bowl, combine the cake mix, water, oil, eggs and extract; beat on low speed for 30 seconds. Beat on medium speed for 2 minutes. Fold in crushed cookies.

2 Pour into three greased and floured 9-in. round baking pans. Bake at 350° for 18-24 minutes or until a toothpick inserted near the center comes out clean. Cool for 10 minutes before removing from pans to wire racks to cool completely.

3 For topping, combine the dry pudding mixes, confectioners' sugar, milk and extract until thickened. Fold in the whipped topping and crushed cookies.

4 Place one cake layer on a serving plate; spread with topping. Repeat layers twice. Frost sides of cake with remaining topping.

5 Chop eight Andes candies; sprinkle over center of cake. Cut remaining candies in half; garnish each serving with a half candy. Store in the refrigerator. **YIELD:** 14 servings.

RAISIN POUND CAKE

Prep: 10 min. **Bake:** 45 min.

Yellow cake mix, applesauce and raisins make this moist, spiced loaf a no-fuss favorite. I turn to this recipe when unexpected guests drop by because I usually have the ingredients in the pantry. For a special occasion, top slices with fresh fruit.

LuEllen Spaulding // Caro, Michigan

 1 package (18-1/4 ounces) yellow cake mix
 1 cup applesauce
1/2 cup water
1/4 cup canola oil
 3 eggs
1/2 teaspoon ground cinnamon
1/4 teaspoon ground nutmeg
1/4 teaspoon ground allspice
1/2 cup raisins

1 In a large bowl, combine cake mix, applesauce, water, oil, eggs, cinnamon, nutmeg and allspice. Beat on medium speed for 2 minutes. Stir in raisins. Pour into two greased 8-in. x 4-in. loaf pans.

2 Bake at 350° for 45-50 minutes or until a toothpick inserted near the center comes out clean. Cool for 5-10 minutes before removing from pans to wire racks. **YIELD:** 2 loaves.

I first tasted this cake over 15 years ago when a dear aunt brought it to a family reunion. I knew I had to have the recipe, and I was thrilled to discover how easy it is to make.

Donna Britsch //
Tega Cay, South Carolina

PEACH CAKE

Prep: 15 min. **Bake:** 30 min. + cooling

    3/4 cup cold butter, cubed
      1 package (18-1/4 ounces) yellow cake mix
      2 egg yolks
      2 cups (16 ounces) sour cream
      1 can (29 ounces) sliced peaches, drained
    1/2 teaspoon ground cinnamon
      1 carton (8 ounces) frozen whipped
         topping, thawed

1 In a large bowl, cut butter into cake mix until the mixture resembles coarse crumbs. Pat into a greased 13-in. x 9-in. baking pan.

2 In another bowl, beat egg yolks; add sour cream until smooth. Set aside 6-8 peach slices for garnish. Cut remaining peaches into 1-in. pieces; stir into the sour cream mixture. Spread over crust; sprinkle with cinnamon.

3 Bake at 350° for 25-30 minutes or until the edges begin to brown and a toothpick inserted near the center comes out clean. Cool on a wire rack. Spread with whipped topping; top with reserved peaches. Store in the refrigerator. **YIELD:** 12 servings.

LEMON BERRY CAKE

Prep: 15 min. **Bake:** 35 min.

Lemon gelatin and blueberries add a tangy taste to a plain yellow cake mix. Serve this dessert warm with a dollop of sweet whipped cream.

Karen Ehatt // Chester, Maryland

      1 package (18-1/4 ounces) yellow cake mix
      1 tablespoon grated lemon peel
      2 cups fresh *or* frozen blueberries
      1 package (6 ounces) lemon gelatin
    1-1/2 cups boiling water
    Confectioners' sugar
    Whipped cream *or* topping, optional

1 Prepare cake batter according to package directions. Stir in lemon peel. Pour into a lightly greased 13-in. x 9-in. baking dish. Sprinkle with blueberries. In a small bowl, whisk gelatin and water until gelatin is dissolved. Slowly pour over batter.

2 Bake at 350° for 33-38 minutes or until a toothpick carefully inserted near the center of cake layer comes out with moist crumbs (cake will set upon cooling). Cool slightly on a wire rack. Gently dust with confectioners' sugar. Serve warm with whipped cream if desired. Store in the refrigerator. **YIELD:** 12 servings.

This decadent dessert is a taste of heaven. The hot mixed berry topping seeps through the brownie layer into the cool vanilla ice cream for a zippy chilled cake.

Allene Bary-Cooper //
Wichita Falls, Texas

HOT BERRIES 'N' BROWNIE ICE CREAM CAKE

Prep: 20 min. **Bake:** 30 min. + freezing

1 package fudge brownie mix
  (13-inch x 9-inch pan size)
1/4 cup water
1/4 cup unsweetened applesauce
1/4 cup canola oil
2 eggs
1 carton (1-3/4 quarts) reduced-fat no-sugar-added vanilla ice cream, softened

BERRY SAUCE:
2 tablespoons butter
1/3 cup sugar
1/4 cup honey
2 tablespoons lime juice
1 tablespoon balsamic vinegar
1 teaspoon ground cinnamon
1/4 to 1/2 teaspoon cayenne pepper
1 quart fresh strawberries, hulled and sliced
2 cups fresh blueberries
2 cups fresh raspberries

1 Prepare brownie mix using water, applesauce, oil and eggs. Bake according to package directions; cool completely on a wire rack.

2 Crumble brownies into 1-in. pieces; sprinkle half into a 13-in. x 9-in. dish coated with cooking spray. Spread evenly with ice cream. Press remaining brownie pieces into ice cream. Cover and freeze for 1 hour or until firm.

3 Remove from the freezer 5 minutes before serving. For sauce, in a large skillet, melt butter over medium heat. Stir in the sugar, honey, lime juice, vinegar, cinnamon and cayenne. Add berries; cook for 3-5 minutes or until heated through, stirring occasionally. Cut cake into squares; top with hot berry sauce. **YIELD:** 24 servings.

CHOOSING BERRIES

Look for fresh blueberries that are firm, dry, plump and smooth-skinned and relatively free from leaves and stems. Berries should be deep purple-blue to blue-black; reddish berries aren't ripe, but may be used in cooking. —Taste of Home Test Kitchen

LIGHT LEMON CAKE

Prep: 15 min. **Bake:** 25 min.

I started with a recipe I saw in the newspaper and used my imagination to devise this lemony cake topped with a light and creamy frosting. You'll find that it is a real crowd-pleaser.

Edna Thomas // Warsaw, Indiana

- 1 package (18-1/4 ounces) yellow cake mix
- 1 package (3.4 ounces) instant lemon pudding mix
- 1-3/4 cups water
- 2 egg whites
- 3/4 cup cold fat-free milk
- 1/2 teaspoon lemon extract
- 1 package (1 ounce) instant sugar-free vanilla pudding mix
- 1 carton (8 ounces) frozen reduced-fat whipped topping, thawed

1 In a large bowl, combine cake mix, lemon pudding mix, water and egg whites. Beat on low spread for 30 seconds. Beat on medium for 2 minutes.

2 Pour into a 13-in. x 9-in. baking pan coated with cooking spray. Bake at 350° for 23-28 minutes or until a toothpick inserted near the center comes out clean. Cool on a wire rack.

3 Meanwhile, in a large bowl, whisk the milk, extract and vanilla pudding mix for 2 minutes. Let stand for 2 more minutes or until soft-set. Fold in whipped topping. Spread over cake. Store in the refrigerator. **YIELD:** 20 servings.

This unusual dessert came from a little book I bought at a flea market many years ago. The broiled orange-coconut topping really dresses up the gingerbread mix. When I bring it to potlucks and family get-togethers, it never lasts long!

Paula Hartlett // Mineola, New York

COCONUT GINGERBREAD CAKE

Prep: 15 min. **Bake:** 25 min.

    1 package (14-1/2 ounces) gingerbread cake/
      cookie mix
    1 large navel orange
1-1/3 cups flaked coconut
  1/2 cup packed brown sugar
    2 tablespoons orange juice

1 Prepare and bake cake according to package directions, using a greased 8-in. square baking pan. Cool slightly on a wire rack.

2 Grate 1 tablespoon of peel from the orange; set aside. Peel and section orange, removing white pith; dice the orange.

3 In a small bowl, combine the coconut, brown sugar, orange juice, diced orange and reserved peel; spread over warm cake. Broil 4 in. from the heat for 2-3 minutes or until the top is lightly browned. Cool on a wire rack. **YIELD:** 9 servings.

PEANUT BUTTER-FILLED BROWNIE CUPCAKES   PICTURED ON RIGHT

Prep: 15 min. **Bake:** 20 min. + cooling

I have made this outstandingly delicious recipe for years. These rich cupcakes are sure to delight everyone you share them with.

Carol Gillespie // Chambersburg, Pennsylvania

    1 package fudge brownie mix (8-inch square
      pan size)
1/2 cup miniature semisweet chocolate chips
1/3 cup creamy peanut butter
    3 tablespoons cream cheese, softened
    1 egg
1/4 cup sugar
1/2 teaspoon confectioners' sugar

1 Prepare brownie batter according to package directions; stir in chocolate chips. For filling, in a small bowl, beat peanut butter, cream cheese, egg and sugar until smooth.

2 Fill paper-lined muffin cups one-third full with batter. Drop filling by teaspoonfuls into the center of each cupcake. Cover with remaining batter.

3 Bake at 350° for 15-20 minutes or until a toothpick inserted in brownie portion comes out clean. Cool for 10 minutes before removing from pan to a wire rack to cool completely. Dust with confectioners' sugar. Store in the refrigerator. **YIELD:** 1 dozen.

BANANA-CHIP MINI CUPCAKES

Prep: 30 min. **Bake:** 15 min./batch + cooling

These adorable mini-muffins are packed with yummy banana flavor, chocolate chips and topped off with a creamy frosting. The decadent little bites make a great dessert addition to any appetizer buffet or potluck.

Beverly Coyde // Gasport, New York

- 1 package (14 ounces) banana quick bread and muffin mix
- 3/4 cup water
- 1/3 cup sour cream
- 1 egg
- 1 cup miniature semisweet chocolate chips, *divided*
- 1 tablespoon shortening

1 In a large bowl, combine the muffin mix, water, sour cream and egg; stir just until moistened. Fold in 1/2 cup chocolate chips.

2 Fill greased or paper-lined miniature muffin cups two-thirds full. Bake at 375° for 12-15 minutes or until a toothpick inserted near the center comes out clean. Cool for 5 minutes before removing from pans to wire racks to cool completely.

3 For frosting, in a microwave bowl, melt shortening and remaining chocolate chips; stir until smooth. Frost cupcakes. **YIELD:** 3-1/2 dozen.

It is hard to believe this spectacular dessert started with a cake mix. Cream cheese in the icing provides a luscious finishing touch.

Dorothy Monroe // Pocatello, Idaho

LAYERED CHOCOLATE CAKE

Prep: 30 min. **Bake:** 25 min. + cooling

1 package (18-1/4 ounces) German chocolate
  cake mix
1-1/3 cups water
3 eggs
1/3 cup canola oil
1 package (3 ounces) cook-and-serve vanilla
  pudding mix
1 teaspoon unflavored gelatin
2 cups 2% milk
1 package (8 ounces) cream cheese, softened
1/2 cup butter, softened
1-1/2 cups confectioners' sugar
3 tablespoons baking cocoa
1 teaspoon vanilla extract

1 In large bowl, combine the first four ingredients. Pour into a greased 15-in. x 10-in. x 1-in. baking pan. Bake at 350° for 23-25 minutes. Cool on a wire rack.

2 In a large saucepan, combine the dry pudding mix, gelatin and milk; cook according to package directions for pudding. Cool. Cut cake into three 10-in. x 5-in. rectangles. Place one on a serving platter. Spread with half of the pudding mixture; repeat layers. Top with third layer.

3 In a large bowl, beat cream cheese and butter until fluffy. Beat in the sugar and cocoa and vanilla until smooth. Frost top and sides of cake. Refrigerate until serving. **YIELD:** 10 servings.

CRISP WALNUT COOKIES

Prep/Total Time: 30 min.

This is a terrific way to bake fresh cookies without much fuss or bother. The easy one-bowl preparation results in yummy treats that are crisp and chewy at the same time.

Alice Walcher // Fairfield, Ohio

1 package (18-1/4 ounces) yellow cake mix
2 cups quick-cooking oats
1/2 cup sugar
1 cup canola oil
3 eggs
1-1/2 teaspoons vanilla extract
1 cup finely chopped walnuts

1 In a large bowl, combine the cake mix, oats and sugar. Beat in oil, eggs and vanilla. Stir in walnuts.

2 Drop by rounded teaspoonfuls 2 in. apart onto ungreased baking sheets. Bake at 350° for 12-14 minutes or until lightly browned. Remove to wire racks to cool. **YIELD:** 6 dozen.

Five kitchen staples are all that's needed to fix this light and lovely dessert. Tiny bits of pear provide sweetness to the moist slices.

Veronica Ross //
Columbia Heights, Minnesota

PEAR BUNDT CAKE

Prep: 15 min. **Bake:** 50 min.

- 1 can (15 ounces) reduced-sugar sliced pears
- 1 package (18-1/4 ounces) white cake mix
- 2 egg whites
- 1 egg
- 2 teaspoons confectioners' sugar

1 Drain pears, reserving the syrup; chop pears. Place pears and syrup in a large bowl; add the cake mix, egg whites and egg. Beat on low speed for about 30 seconds. Beat on high for 4 minutes.

2 Coat a 10-in. fluted tube pan with cooking spray and dust with flour. Add batter. Bake at 350° for 50-55 minutes or until a toothpick inserted near the center comes out clean. Cool for 10 minutes before removing from pan to a wire rack to cool completely. Dust with confectioners' sugar. **YIELD:** 16 servings.

COCONUT CHIP COOKIES

Prep/Total Time: 25 min.

Coconut, nuts and chocolate are combined with a cake mix to create a big batch of tasty cookies. They take only six ingredients, so you can mix up the batter in a jiffy.

Flora Alers // Clinton, Maryland

- 1 package (18-1/4 ounces) white cake mix
- 2 eggs
- 1/3 cup canola oil
- 1 cup flaked coconut
- 1/2 cup semisweet chocolate chips
- 1/4 cup chopped macadamia nuts *or* almonds

1 In a large bowl, beat cake mix, eggs and oil (batter will be very stiff). Stir in the coconut, chips and nuts. Roll into 1-in. balls. Place on lightly greased baking sheets.

2 Bake at 350° for 10 minutes or until a slight indentation remains when lightly touched. Cool for 2 minutes; remove to a wire rack to cool completely. **YIELD:** 3-1/2 dozen.

CHEWY DATE NUT BARS

Prep: 15 min. **Bake:** 35 min. + cooling

You'll need just six ingredients, including a convenient boxed cake mix, to bake up these chewy bars chock-full of walnuts and dates. They are my husband's favorite snack, and he loves to take them to work. I often whip up a batch for bake sales or to share with my coworkers.

Linda Hutmacher // Teutopolis, Illinois

- 1 package (18-1/4 ounces) yellow cake mix
- 3/4 cup packed brown sugar
- 3/4 cup butter, melted
- 2 eggs
- 2 cups chopped dates
- 2 cups chopped walnuts

1 In a large bowl, combine cake mix and brown sugar. Add butter and eggs; beat on low speed for 30 seconds. Beat on medium for 2 minutes. Combine dates and walnuts; stir into batter (batter will be stiff)

2 Spread into a greased 13-in. x 9-in. baking pan. Bake at 350° for 35-45 minutes or until edges are golden brown. Cool on a wire rack for 10 minutes. Run a knife around sides of pan to loosen; cool completely before cutting. **YIELD:** 3 dozen.

The recipe makes the most of a handy packaged brownie mix. If you don't have the mini M&Ms, use chocolate chips instead. Our kids love these rich fudgy squares with a scoop of ice cream.

Jennifer Trenhaile //
Emerson, Nebraska

OATMEAL BROWNIES

Prep: 15 min. **Bake:** 25 min. + cooling

1-1/2 cups quick-cooking oats
    1 cup M&M's miniature baking bits
  1/2 cup all-purpose flour
  1/2 cup packed brown sugar
  1/2 cup chopped walnuts
  1/2 teaspoon baking soda
  1/2 cup butter, melted
    1 package fudge brownie mix
      (13-inch x 9-inch pan size)

1 In a large bowl, combine the oats, baking bits, flour, sugar, walnuts, baking soda and butter. Set aside 1 cup for topping. Pat the remaining mixture into a greased 15-in. x 10-in. x 1-in. baking pan.

2 Prepare brownie batter according to package directions. Spread over the crust. Sprinkle with the reserved oat mixture.

3 Bake at 350° for 25-30 minutes or until a toothpick inserted near the center comes out clean. Cool on a wire rack. Cut into bars. **YIELD:** 5 dozen.

PUMPKIN PECAN BITES   PICTURED ON RIGHT

Prep: 20 min. **Bake:** 20 min. + cooling

Since this recipe makes a lot, these bite-size treats are ideal for potlucks. To easily frost them, try putting the frosting in a pastry bag and piping it on top of the cupcakes.

Carol Beyerl // East Wenatchee, Washington

    1 package (18-1/4 ounces) spice cake mix
    1 can (15 ounces) solid-pack pumpkin
    3 eggs
  1/2 cup canola oil
    1 tablespoon ground cinnamon
    1 teaspoon baking soda
  1/4 teaspoon ground cloves
  36 pecan halves
CREAM CHEESE FROSTING:
  1/2 cup butter, softened
    4 ounces cream cheese, softened
    1 teaspoon vanilla extract
3-3/4 cups confectioners' sugar
    2 to 3 tablespoons milk
Ground cinnamon

1 In a large bowl, combine the cake mix, pumpkin, eggs, oil, cinnamon, baking soda and cloves; beat on low speed for 30 seconds. Beat on medium for 2 minutes.

2 Fill paper-lined miniature muffin cups two-thirds full. Press a pecan piece into each. Bake at 350° for 17-20 minutes or until a toothpick inserted near the center comes out clean. Cool for 5 minutes before removing from pans to wire racks to cool completely.

3 In a small bowl, cream the butter, cream cheese and vanilla until light and fluffy. Gradually add confectioners' sugar and mix well. Add enough milk to achieve spreading consistency. Frost cupcakes. Sprinkle with cinnamon. **YIELD:** about 6 dozen.

MACADAMIA CHIP COOKIES

Prep/Total Time: 30 min.

If you like cookies with a crunch, you'll love these golden treats. Crushed peanut brittle adds an unexpected kick to the vanilla chips and brown sugar that flavor the dough. It's hard to believe something this easy to make tastes so terrific.

Dorothy Kollmeyer // Dupo, Illinois

- 1 cup butter, softened
- 3/4 cup packed brown sugar
- 1/4 cup sugar
- 2 eggs
- 1 teaspoon vanilla extract
- 2-1/4 cups all-purpose flour
- 1 package (3.4 ounces) instant vanilla pudding mix
- 1 teaspoon baking soda
- 1/4 teaspoon salt
- 1 package (10 to 12 ounces) white baking chips
- 2 jars (3-1/4 ounces *each*) macadamia nuts, chopped
- 1/2 cup finely crushed peanut brittle

1 In a large bowl, cream butter and sugars until light and fluffy. Add eggs, one at a time, beating well after each addition. Beat in vanilla. Combine the flour, dry pudding mix, baking soda and salt; gradually add to creamed mixture and mix well. Stir in the chips, nuts and peanut brittle.

2 Drop by rounded tablespoonfuls 2 in. apart onto greased baking sheets. Bake at 375° for 10-12 minutes or until golden brown. Remove to wire racks to cool. **YIELD:** 5-1/2 dozen.

No one will guess this stunning dessert with luscious cinnamon frosting started with a mix. It's a perfect treat year-round.

Linda Murray //
Allenstown, New Hampshire

PUMPKIN SPICE LAYER CAKE

Prep: 25 min. **Bake:** 25 min. + cooling

- 1 package (18-1/4 ounces) yellow cake mix
- 3 eggs
- 1 cup water
- 1 cup canned pumpkin
- 1-3/4 teaspoons ground cinnamon, *divided*
- 1/4 teaspoon ground ginger
- 1/4 teaspoon ground nutmeg
- 2-1/2 cups vanilla frosting
- 1-1/4 cups chopped walnuts

1 In a large bowl, combine the cake mix, eggs, water, pumpkin, 1 teaspoon cinnamon, ginger and nutmeg; beat on low speed for 30 seconds. Beat on medium for 2 minutes.

2 Pour into two well-greased and floured 9-in. round baking pans. Bake at 375° for 25-30 minutes or until a toothpick inserted near the center comes out clean. Cool for 10 minutes before removing from pans to wire racks to cool completely.

3 Combine frosting and remaining cinnamon; spread between layers and over top and sides of cake. Press walnuts lightly into frosting on sides of cake. **YIELD:** 10-12 servings.

BROWNIE DELIGHT

Prep: 20 min. **Bake:** 30 min. + cooling

Brownie mix and instant pudding hurry along the preparation of this scrumptious layered dessert. My family asks for this rich treat for birthdays instead of cake.

Opal Erickson // Branson, Missouri

- 1 package brownie mix (13-inch x 9-inch pan size)
- 2 packages (one 8 ounces, one 3 ounces) cream cheese, softened
- 2 cups confectioners' sugar
- 1 carton (16 ounces) frozen whipped topping, thawed, *divided*
- 2 cups cold 2% milk
- 1 package (3.9 ounces) instant chocolate pudding mix
- 1/2 cup chopped pecans

1 Prepare and bake brownies according to package directions. Cool completely on a wire rack.

2 In a large bowl, beat cream cheese and sugar until creamy. Fold in 2 cups whipped topping. Spread over brownies. In a small bowl, whisk milk and dry pudding mix for 2 minutes.

3 Refrigerate for 5 minutes; spread over the cream cheese layer. Spread with remaining whipped topping; sprinkle with pecans. Chill until serving. **YIELD:** 12-15 servings.

HUGS 'N' KISSES BROWNIE

Prep: 20 min. **Bake:** 35 min. + cooling

 1 package fudge brownie mix
  (8-inch square pan size)
 1 egg
 1/4 cup canola oil
 1/4 cup water
1-1/2 cups vanilla *or* white chips, *divided*
 14 to 16 milk chocolate kisses
 14 to 16 striped chocolate kisses
1-1/2 teaspoons shortening

1 In a large bowl, stir brownie mix, egg, oil and water until well blended. Fold in 1 cup vanilla chips. Pour into a greased 9-in. heart-shaped or round springform pan. Bake at 350° for 35-40 minutes or until a toothpick inserted 2 in. from edge of pan comes out clean.

2 Let stand for 10 minutes; alternate milk chocolate and striped kisses around edge of pan with points toward center. Melt shortening and remaining chips; stir until smooth. Drizzle over brownie. Cool completely. Remove sides of springform pan before cutting. **YIELD:** 12 servings.

CARROT-TOPPED CUPCAKES

Prep: 15 min. **Bake:** 20 min.

A handy spice cake mix is turned into fabulous carrot cupcakes with shredded carrots and chopped walnuts. The minicakes are eye-catching, too, when decorated with carrots piped on with prepared cream cheese frosting and parsley sprigs for the green tops.

Taste of Home Test Kitchen

 1 package (18-1/4 ounces) spice cake mix
1-1/2 cups shredded carrots
 1/2 cup chopped walnuts
 1 teaspoon ground cinnamon
 1 can (16 ounces) cream cheese frosting
Orange paste food coloring
Fresh parsley sprigs

1 Prepare cake batter according to package directions. Fold in carrots, walnuts and cinnamon.

2 Fill paper-lined muffin cups half full. Bake at 350° for 18-23 minutes or until a toothpick inserted near the center comes out clean. Remove from pans to wire racks to cool completely.

3 Frost cupcakes with 1-1/4 cups frosting. Place the remaining frosting in a small resealable bag; tint frosting with orange food coloring. Cut a small hole in the corner of bag; pipe a carrot on the top of each cupcake. Add a parsley sprig for greens. **YIELD:** 2 dozen.

HAWAIIAN CAKE

Prep: 25 min. **Bake:** 20 min.

Pineapple, coconut and a delightful blend of instant pudding, cream cheese and whipped topping turn a plain yellow cake mix into something sensational. This is a favorite dessert that suits any occasion.

Estella Traeger // Milwaukee, Wisconsin

- 1 package (18-1/4 ounces) yellow cake mix
- 2 cups cold 2% milk
- 2 packages (3.4 ounces *each*) instant vanilla pudding mix
- 1 package (8 ounces) cream cheese, softened
- 1 carton (8 ounces) frozen whipped topping, thawed
- 1 can (20 ounces) crushed pineapple, drained
- 1/2 cup chopped maraschino cherries, drained
- 1/2 cup flaked coconut
- 1/2 cup chopped walnuts

1 Prepare cake mix according to package directions. Pour into a greased 15-in. x 10-in. x 1-in. baking pan. Bake at 350° for 20-25 minutes or until cake tests done; cool completely.

2 In a large bowl, combine milk and pudding mixes; beat in cream cheese until smooth. Fold in whipped topping. Spread over cooled cake. Top with the pineapple, cherries, coconut and walnuts. Store in the refrigerator. **YIELD:** 16-20 servings.

PEANUT CRUNCH CAKE

Prep: 10 min. **Bake:** 40 min.

*Here's a recipe that takes a plain box of cake mix
and with the help of peanut butter and chocolate
chips makes something wonderful.*

Sue Smith // Norwalk, Connecticut

- 1 package (18-1/4 ounces) yellow cake mix
- 1 cup peanut butter
- 1/2 cup packed brown sugar
- 1 cup water
- 3 eggs
- 1/4 cup canola oil
- 1/2 to 3/4 cup semisweet chocolate chips, *divided*
- 1/2 to 3/4 cup peanut butter chips, *divided*
- 1/2 cup chopped peanuts

1 In a large bowl, beat the cake mix, peanut butter and brown sugar on low speed until crumbly. Set aside 1/2 cup. Add the water, eggs and oil to remaining crumb mixture; blend on low until moistened. Beat on high for 2 minutes. Stir in 1/4 cup each chocolate and peanut butter chips.

2 Pour into a greased 13-in. x 9-in. baking pan. Combine the peanuts, reserved crumb mixture and remaining chips; sprinkle over batter.

3 Bake at 350° for 40-45 minutes or until a toothpick inserted near the center comes out clean. Cool completely. **YIELD:** 12-16 servings.

More Sweet Treats

CHOCOLATE CHIP
COOKIE DELIGHT, PG. 203

CREAMY LEMON FUDGE

Prep: 15 min. + chilling

Fast-to-fix fudge is a fantastic way to try your hand at candy making. This version is a refreshing change from traditional chocolate varieties. It's a must at our house for the holidays.

Darlene Brenden // Salem, Oregon

1-1/2 teaspoons plus 1/2 cup butter, *divided*
   1 package (4.3 ounces) cook-and-serve lemon pudding mix
1/2 cup cold 2% milk
3-3/4 cups confectioners' sugar
   1 teaspoon lemon extract

1 Line a 9-in. square pan with foil. Grease the foil with 1-1/2 teaspoons butter; set aside.

2 In a large heavy saucepan, combine the pudding mix, milk and remaining butter. Cook and stir over medium heat until thickened. Remove from the heat. Beat in confectioners' sugar and extract. Pour into prepared pan; refrigerate until set.

3 Using foil, lift fudge out of pan. Discard foil; cut fudge into 1-in. squares. Store in the refrigerator. **YIELD**: about 1-1/2 pounds.

BANANA CREAM DESSERT
Prep: 20 min. + chilling

- 3 cups graham cracker crumbs
- 1/2 cup butter, melted
- 3-1/2 cups cold 2% milk
- 2 packages (3.4 ounces *each*) instant vanilla pudding mix
- 5 medium firm bananas, halved lengthwise and cut into 1/2-inch slices
- 1 can (20 ounces) crushed pineapple, drained
- 1 carton (20 ounces) frozen whipped topping, thawed
- 1/3 cup chopped pecans, optional
- 2 (1.55 ounces *each*) milk chocolate candy bar, broken into squares
- Maraschino cherries, optional

1 Combine cracker crumbs and butter. Press into an ungreased 13-in. x 9-in. dish. In a large bowl, beat milk and pudding mix on low speed for 2 minutes. Pour over crust; top with bananas and pineapple. Spread with whipped topping (dish will be full). Sprinkle with pecans if desired.

2 Chill for at least 4 hours before cutting. Garnish with candy bar pieces and cherries if desired. **YIELD:** 16-20 servings.

CHOCOLATE CHIP COOKIE DELIGHT
Prep: 35 min. + chilling

- 1 tube (16-1/2 ounces) refrigerated chocolate chip cookie dough
- 1 package (8 ounces) cream cheese, softened
- 1 cup confectioners' sugar
- 1 carton (12 ounces) frozen whipped topping, thawed, *divided*
- 3 cups cold 2% milk
- 1 package (3.9 ounces) instant chocolate pudding mix
- 1 package (3.4 ounces) instant vanilla pudding mix
- Chopped nuts and chocolate curls, optional

1 Let cookie dough stand at room temperature for 5-10 minutes to soften. Press into an ungreased 13-in. x 9-in. baking pan. Bake at 350° for 14-16 minutes or until golden brown. Cool on a wire rack.

2 In a bowl, beat cream cheese and confectioners' sugar until smooth. Fold in 1-3/4 cups whipped topping. Spread over crust.

3 In a large bowl, whisk milk and pudding mixes for 2 minutes; let stand for 2 minutes or until soft-set. Spread over cream cheese layer. Top with remaining whipped topping. Sprinkle with nuts and chocolate curls if desired.

4 Cover and refrigerate for 8 hours or overnight until firm. **YIELD:** 15 servings.

This family favorite has all the satisfaction of traditional strawberry shortcake with just a dash of distinction. It really showcases the beauty of the bright red strawberries.

Karen Ann Bland // Gove, Kansas

MAKE-AHEAD SHORTCAKE

Prep: 15 min. + chilling

 1 loaf loaf-shaped angel food cake
   (10-1/2 ounces), cut into 1/2-inch slices
 1/2 cup cold 2% milk
 1 package (5.1 ounces) instant vanilla
   pudding mix
 1 pint vanilla ice cream, softened
 1 package (6 ounces) strawberry gelatin
 1 cup boiling water
 2 packages (10 ounces *each*) frozen sweetened
   sliced strawberries
Sliced fresh strawberries, optional

1 Arrange cake slices in a single layer in an ungreased 13-in. x 9-in. dish. In a large bowl, beat milk and pudding mix for 2 minutes or until thickened; beat in ice cream. Pour over cake. Chill.

2 Meanwhile, in a large bowl, dissolve gelatin in boiling water; stir in frozen strawberries. Chill until partially set.

3 Spoon strawberries over pudding mixture. Chill until firm. Garnish with fresh strawberries if desired. **YIELD:** 12 servings.

CANDY BAR BROWNIE TRIFLE

Prep: 20 min. **Bake:** 30 min. + cooling

Even something as simple as a trifle can make an extraordinary ending to a any meal. You and your guests will love digging into layers of brownie, chocolate pudding, whipped topping, Snickers candy bars and caramel.

Adriane Louie // Jackson, Mississippi

 1 package fudge brownie mix
   (13-inch x 9-inch pan size)
 1 package (3.9 ounces) instant chocolate
   pudding mix
 1 package (11-1/2 ounces) miniature
   Snickers candy bars, refrigerated

 1 carton (8 ounces) frozen whipped
   topping, thawed
 1 jar (12 ounces) caramel ice cream topping

1 Prepare and bake brownies according to package directions. Cool on a wire rack. Prepare pudding according to package directions. Crush candy bars; set aside.

2 Cut brownies into 1-in. cubes; place half of the cubes in a 3-qt. trifle bowl or large glass serving bowl; press down lightly. Top with half of the whipped topping, pudding, caramel topping and crushed candy bars; repeat layers. Cover and refrigerate until serving. **YIELD:** 16 servings.

FLUFFY KEY LIME PIE

Prep: 20 min. + chilling

For a taste of paradise, try this light and creamy confection. It's low in fat, sugar and fuss. Dessert doesn't get any easier!

Frances VanFossan // Warren, Michigan

 1 package (.3 ounce) sugar-free lime gelatin
1/4 cup boiling water
 2 cartons (6 ounces *each*) key lime yogurt

 1 carton (8 ounces) frozen fat-free whipped topping, thawed
 1 reduced-fat graham cracker crust (8 inches)

1 In a large bowl, dissolve gelatin in boiling water. Whisk in yogurt. Fold in whipped topping. Pour into crust.

2 Cover and refrigerate for at least 2 hours or until set. **YIELD:** 8 servings.

These rich tarts are scrumptious but really no fuss, because they call for prepared tart shells, instant pudding and whipped topping.

Traci Maloney //
Toms River, New Jersey

WHITE CHOCOLATE TARTS

Prep/Total Time: 30 min.

- 1 can (14 ounces) sweetened condensed milk
- 1 cup cold water
- 1 package (3.4 ounces) instant white chocolate pudding mix
- 2 cups whipped topping
- 2 packages (6 count *each*) individual graham cracker tart shells

1 In a large bowl, whisk the milk, water and pudding mix for 2 minutes. Let set for 2 minutes or until soft-set. Cover and refrigerate for 10 minutes.

2 Fold in whipped topping. Spoon about 1/3 cup into each tart shell. Refrigerate tarts until serving. **YIELD:** 12 servings.

COUNTRY-STYLE VANILLA ICE CREAM   PICTURED ON RIGHT

Prep: 30 min. + chilling
Process: 20 min./batch + freezing

Store-bought ice cream just can't compare to the creamy texture of this old-fashioned favorite. It's a winner with everyone who tries it.

Cyndi Fynaardt // Oskaloosa, Iowa

- 6 cups cold 2% milk, *divided*
- 2 cups sugar
- 4 eggs, lightly beaten
- 1 teaspoon vanilla extract
- 2 packages (3.4 ounces *each*) instant vanilla pudding mix
- 1 carton (8 ounces) frozen whipped topping, thawed

1 In a large saucepan, heat 2-1/2 cups milk to 175°; stir in the sugar until dissolved. Whisk a small amount of hot mixture into the eggs. Return all to the pan, whisking constantly. Cook and stir over low heat until mixture reaches at least 160° and coats the back of a metal spoon. Remove from the heat. Cool quickly by placing pan in a bowl of ice water; stir for 2 minutes. Stir in vanilla.

2 Place remaining milk in a large bowl; whisk in pudding mixes for 2 minutes. Let stand for 2 minutes or until soft-set. Stir into egg mixture. Stir in whipped topping. Press waxed paper onto surface of custard. Refrigerate for several hours or overnight.

3 Fill cylinder of ice cream freezer two-thirds full; freeze according to the manufacturer's directions. Refrigerate remaining mixture until ready to freeze. Transfer to a freezer container; freeze for 2-4 hours before serving. **YIELD:** 2-1/2 quarts.

GELATIN PARFAITS

Prep: 15 min. + chilling

Here's a quick, airy treat that's so versatile you can whip it up for almost any season just by varying the colors of gelatin you use.

Joyce Thompson // Bellingham, Washington

1 package (3 ounces) lemon gelatin
1 package (3 ounces) orange gelatin
3 cups cubed pound cake (1-inch cubes)
2-1/4 cups whipped topping
2 tablespoons sugar
1/8 teaspoon ground cinnamon
6 maraschino cherries with stems

1 Prepare gelatins separately according to package directions. Pour into separate ungreased 9-in. x 5-in. pans. Refrigerate until set. Cut gelatin into 1-in. cubes.

2 In each of six 1-1/2-cup parfait glasses or dessert dishes, layer 1/4 cup cake cubes, 1/3 cup cubed orange gelatin, 3 tablespoons whipped topping, 1/3 cup cubed lemon gelatin, 1/4 cup cake cubes and 3 tablespoons whipped topping. Combine sugar and cinnamon; sprinkle over whipped topping. Top with a cherry. **YIELD:** 6 servings.

These sweet frozen treats are simple to prepare and guaranteed to bring out the kid in anyone. The creamy pops feature a special chocolate and peanut topping.

Karen Grant // Tulare, California

ROCKY ROAD FUDGE POPS

Prep: 10 min. + freezing
Cook: 10 min. + cooling

   1 package (3.4 ounces) cook-and-serve
      chocolate pudding mix
2-1/2 cups 2% milk
  1/2 cup chopped peanuts
  1/2 cup miniature semisweet chocolate chips
   12 disposable plastic cups (3 ounces *each*)
  1/2 cup marshmallow creme
   12 Popsicle sticks

1 In a large microwave-safe bowl, combine pudding mix and milk. Microwave, uncovered, on high for 4-6 minutes or until bubbly and slightly thickened, stirring every 2 minutes. Cool for 20 minutes, stirring several times.

2 Meanwhile, combine peanuts and chocolate chips; place about 2 tablespoons in each plastic cup. Stir marshmallow cream into pudding; spoon into cups. Insert Popsicle sticks; freeze. **YIELD:** 12 servings.

EDITOR'S NOTE: This recipe was tested in a 1,100-watt microwave.

APRICOT ANGEL DESSERT

Prep: 10 min. **Cook:** 10 min. + chilling

This light dessert is particularly good after a heavy meal. By simply topping fluffy angel food cake with canned apricot halves and a yummy sauce, you can assemble it in a snap.

Beverly King // Vulcan, Michigan

   1 prepared angel food cake (8 to 10 ounces),
      cubed
   1 can (15-1/4 ounces) apricot halves, drained
      and diced
Sugar substitute equivalent to 1/2 cup sugar
   3 tablespoons cornstarch
   3 cups apricot nectar
   1 package (.3 ounces) sugar-free orange gelatin
   1 carton (8 ounces) frozen reduced-fat whipped
      topping, thawed

1 Place the cake cubes in an ungreased 13-in. x 9-in. dish; top with apricots. In a large saucepan, combine the sugar substitute, cornstarch and apricot nectar until smooth. Bring to a boil; cook and stir for 2 minutes or until thickened. Remove from the heat. Stir in gelatin until dissolved.

2 Pour over cake and apricot. Cover and chill for 3 hours or until gelatin is set. Spread with whipped topping. Refrigerate leftovers. **YIELD:** 12 servings.

I use on-hand ingredients, including canned pie filling and a cake mix, to create this dazzling dessert. It's fast to fix, looks special and tastes absolutely amazing.

**Connie Raterink //
Caledonia, Michigan**

CHERRY ALMOND TART

Prep: 15 min. **Bake:** 15 min. + cooling

- 1 package (18-1/4 ounces) yellow cake mix
- 2/3 cup graham cracker crumbs (about 11 squares)
- 1/2 cup butter, softened
- 1 egg
- 1/2 cup chopped almonds
- 1 package (8 ounces) cream cheese, softened
- 1/4 cup confectioners' sugar
- 1 can (21 ounces) cherry pie filling
- 1/2 cup sliced almonds, toasted

1 In a large bowl, combine the cake mix, cracker crumbs and butter until crumbly. Beat in egg. Stir in chopped almonds.

2 Press onto the bottom and up the sides of a greased 14-in. pizza pan. Bake at 350° for 11-13 minutes or until lightly browned. Cool completely.

3 In a small bowl, beat cream cheese and sugar until smooth. Spread over crust. Top with pie filling. Sprinkle with sliced almonds. Store leftovers in the refrigerator. **YIELD:** 14-16 servings.

PISTACHIO COOKIE DESSERT

Prep: 20 min. + freezing

With its smooth pistachio filling, this cool treat is a favorite refreshment at summer 4-H meetings. It's best made and frozen a day in advance.
Audrey Phillips // Gambier, Ohio

- 1 package (20 ounces) chocolate cream-filled sandwich cookies
- 1/2 cup plus 2 tablespoons butter, melted
- 1-1/2 cups cold 2% milk
- 2 packages (3.4 ounces *each*) instant pistachio pudding mix
- 1 quart vanilla ice cream, softened
- 1 carton (16 ounces) frozen whipped topping, thawed

1 Place cookies in a blender; cover and process until fine crumbs form. Stir in butter. Set aside 1 cup for topping. Press remaining crumb mixture into an ungreased 13-in. x 9-in. dish.

2 In a large bowl, beat milk and pudding mix on low speed for 2 minutes. Gradually add ice cream. Fold in whipped topping.

3 Spread over crust. Sprinkle reserved crumb mixture over top, pressing down lightly. Cover and freeze for 4 hours or overnight. Remove from the freezer 20 minutes before cutting. **YIELD:** 12-15 servings.

STRAWBERRY LEMON TRIFLE

Prep: 20 min. + chilling

This summery, luscious treat is a favorite with my family. The time-saving secret is starting with a purchased angel food cake. It looks so beautiful layered in a glass bowl.

Lynn Marie Frucci // LaCenter, Washington

4 ounces fat-free cream cheese, softened
1 cup fat-free vanilla yogurt
2 cups fat-free milk
1 package (3.4 ounces) instant lemon pudding mix
2 teaspoons grated lemon peel
2-1/2 cups sliced fresh strawberries, *divided*
1 tablespoon white grape juice *or* water
1 prepared angel food cake (8 to 10 ounces)

1 In a large bowl, beat cream cheese and yogurt. Add the milk, dry pudding mix and lemon peel; beat until smooth. In a blender, process 1/2 cup strawberries and grape juice until blended.

2 Tear cake into 1-in. cubes; place a third in a trifle bowl or 3-qt. serving bowl. Top with a third of the pudding mixture and half of the remaining strawberries. Drizzle with half of the strawberry sauce. Repeat. Top with remaining cake and pudding mixture. Cover and refrigerate for at least 2 hours. **YIELD:** 14 servings.

The recipe for this frosty treat is more than 30 years old, and kids love it. You'd never guess that powdered soft drink mix provides the yummy flavor.

Elizabeth Stanton //
Mt. Vernon, Washington

KOOL-AID SHERBET

Prep: 10 min. + freezing

1 cup sugar
1 envelope unsweetened orange Kool-Aid mix *or* flavor of your choice
3 cups 2% milk

1 In a large bowl, combine the sugar, Kool-Aid mix and milk until sugar is dissolved. Pour into a shallow freezer container; cover and freeze for 1 hour or until slightly thickened.

2 Transfer to a large bowl, beat until smooth. Return to freezer container; cover and freeze until firm. Remove from the freezer 20 minutes before serving. **YIELD:** about 3 cups.

DREAMY CREAMY PEANUT BUTTER PIE   PICTURED ON RIGHT

Prep: 30 min. **Bake:** 10 min. + chilling

Peanut butter fans love both the crust and creamy filling of this popular pie. As a busy mom, a lot of my baking happens after bedtime. So I need the recipes to be quick and guaranteed good.

Dawn Moore // Warren, Pennsylvania

24 peanut butter cream-filled sandwich cookies, crushed
1/3 cup butter, melted
1 cup cold 2% milk
1 package (3.4 ounces) instant vanilla pudding mix
1 cup creamy peanut butter
4 ounces cream cheese, softened
1/2 cup sweetened condensed milk
1/4 cup hot fudge ice cream topping, warmed
1 cup heavy whipping cream
2 tablespoons sugar
Chocolate curls

1 Combine cookie crumbs and butter; press onto the bottom and up the sides of an ungreased 9-in. pie plate. Bake at 350° for 6-8 minutes or until crust is lightly browned. Cool on a wire rack.

2 In a small bowl, whisk milk and pudding mix for 2 minutes. Let stand for 2 minutes or until soft-set. Meanwhile, in a large bowl, beat the peanut butter, cream cheese and condensed milk until smooth; stir in pudding. Set aside.

3 Gently spread ice cream topping into crust. In a large bowl, beat cream until it begins to thicken. Add sugar; beat until stiff peaks form. Fold 1-1/2 cups into pudding mixture; pour into crust. Spread remaining whipped cream over top; garnish with chocolate curls. Refrigerate until ready to serve. **YIELD:** 8 servings.

RASPBERRY LEMONADE PIE

Prep: 10 min. + freezing

You can't beat this tangy freezer dessert as the finale for an outdoor summer meal. Combined with a chocolate crust and vanilla ice cream, the vibrant fruit flavors are to-die-for.

Sue Stewart // Hales Corners, Wisconsin

1/3 cup sweetened raspberry lemonade drink mix
1/2 cup water
  2 cups vanilla ice cream, softened
  1 carton (8 ounces) frozen whipped topping, thawed
  1 chocolate crumb crust (9 inches)
Chocolate syrup, optional

1 In a large bowl, combine drink mix and water. Add ice cream; beat on low speed for 2 minutes or until blended. Fold in whipped topping. Spoon into crust.

2 Freeze for 4 hours or until firm. Remove from the freezer 10 minutes before serving. Serve with chocolate syrup if desired. **YIELD:** 8 servings.

Our kids love banana splits, so I came up with this simple dessert. One bite of this quick-to-fix finale and you'll agree, it's to die for!

Sherry Lee // Shelby, Alabama

BANANA SPLIT PUDDING

Prep/Total Time: 10 min.

    3 cups cold 2% milk
    1 package (5.1 ounces) instant vanilla
      pudding mix
    1 medium firm banana, sliced
    1 cup sliced fresh strawberries
    1 can (8 ounces) crushed pineapple, drained
    1 carton (8 ounces) frozen whipped
      topping, thawed

    1/4 cup chocolate syrup
    1/4 cup chopped pecans
    Additional sliced strawberries and bananas, optional

1 In a large bowl, whisk milk and pudding mix for 2 minutes. Let set for two minutes or until soft-set. Add the banana, strawberries and pineapple.

2 Transfer to a serving bowl. Dollop with whipped topping. Drizzle with chocolate syrup; sprinkle with pecans. Top with additional strawberries and bananas if desired. **YIELD:** 6-8 servings.

EASY COCOA MOUSSE

Prep: 15 min. + chilling

This airy, melt-in-your-mouth mousse has a light cocoa flavor that's so tasty. It's simple to mix, then pop in the fridge while you're preparing the rest of your meal.

Donna Brooks // Jefferson, Maine

    1 envelope unflavored gelatin
    1/4 cup cold water
    1-1/4 cups fat-free milk
    Artificial sweetener equivalent to 1/3 cup sugar

    1/4 cup baking cocoa
      1 teaspoon vanilla extract
    1-3/4 cups reduced-fat whipped topping, *divided*

1 In a small saucepan, sprinkle gelatin over water; let stand for 5 minutes. Cook over low heat until gelatin is dissolved.

2 In a blender, combine the milk, sweetener, cocoa and vanilla. Slowly add gelatin mixture. Fold in 1-1/2 cups whipped topping. Spoon into serving dishes. Cover and chill for at least 1 hour. Garnish with remaining topping. **YIELD:** 6 servings.

Leftover crushed cookies create the yummy crust for this crowd-pleasing dessert. It's covered with a smooth cream cheese mixture, chocolate pudding and whipped topping for a lovely layered look.

Nancy Mueller //
Bloomington, Minnesota

PEANUT BUTTER ICEBOX DESSERT

Prep: 20 min. + chilling

2-1/4 cups crushed peanut butter cookies
    (about 11 cookies)
  1/4 cup sugar
  1/4 cup butter, melted
    2 packages (3 ounces *each*) cream
    cheese, softened
    1 cup confectioners' sugar
    1 carton (8 ounces) frozen whipped topping,
    thawed, *divided*
2-1/2 cups cold 2% milk
    2 packages (3.9 ounces *each*) instant chocolate
    pudding mix
Additional peanut butter cookies, broken into pieces

1 In a large bowl, combine crushed cookies, sugar and butter; press into an ungreased 13-in. x 9-in. baking dish. Bake at 350° for 6-8 minutes or until golden brown; cool on a wire rack.

2 In a large bowl, beat the cream cheese and the confectioners' sugar until smooth; fold in 1 cup whipped topping. Spread over cooled crust.

3 In another large bowl, beat milk and pudding mix on low speed for 2 minutes or until thickened. Spread over cream cheese layer. Top with remaining whipped topping; sprinkle with cookie pieces. Cover and refrigerate for at least 1 hour before serving. **YIELD:** 12-15 servings.

TROPICAL FRUIT CREAM PIE

Prep/Total Time: 10 min.

This sweet and fruity pie can be stirred up in a jiffy with pantry staples I like to keep on hand.

Carolyn Dixon // Wilmar, Arkansas

    2 cups cold 2% milk
  1/2 teaspoon coconut extract
    1 package (3.4 ounces) instant vanilla
    pudding mix

    1 can (15-1/4 ounces) mixed tropical
    fruit, drained
  1/2 cup flaked coconut, toasted
    1 graham cracker crust (9 inches)

1 In a large bowl, whisk the milk, extract and pudding mix for 2 minutes. Let stand for 2 minutes or until soft-set.

2 Fold in fruit and coconut. Pour into crust. Refrigerate until serving. **YIELD:** 6-8 servings.

BANANA CHEESECAKE PIE

Prep: 25 min. + chilling

I came up with this recipe when I needed to make something sweet for a family gathering. It's a quick combination of two classic desserts.

Kelly Haberny // West Carrollton, Ohio

- 1 package (11.1 ounces) no-bake home-style cheesecake mix
- 1/2 cup crushed vanilla wafers (about 15 wafers)
- 2 tablespoons sugar
- 1/2 cup cold butter, cubed
- 1 cup 2% milk plus 1-1/2 cups 2% milk, *divided*
- 1 package (3.4 ounces) instant banana cream pudding mix
- 2 medium bananas, cut into 1/4-in. slices
- 1 cup whipped topping
- 1/4 cup chopped pecans, toasted

1 In a large bowl, combine the contents of the crust mix, wafers and sugar; cut in butter until mixture resembles coarse crumbs. Press onto the bottom and up the sides of an ungreased 9-in. deep-dish pie plate.

2 In a large bowl, beat 1 cup milk and the contents of filling mix on low speed until blended. Beat on medium for 3 minutes or until smooth (filling will be thick). Spoon mixture into the crust. Chill for 30 minutes.

3 Meanwhile, in a small bowl, whisk remaining milk and pudding mix for 2 minutes. Let stand for 2 minutes or until soft-set (pudding will be stiff). Arrange banana slices over filling. Spread with pudding, then whipped topping. Sprinkle with pecans. Chill for at least 1 hour before serving. **YIELD:** 8 servings.

I love the flavor of peanut butter cups, so I dreamed up this creamy, no-fuss pie to serve to company. It always gets rave reviews.

Rosanne Marshall // Depew, New York

CHOCOLATE PEANUT DREAM PIE

Prep: 10 min. + chilling

  1 package (3.4 ounces) cook-and-serve
    chocolate pudding mix
1/2 cup creamy peanut butter
  1 cup whipped topping
  1 graham cracker crust (9 inches)
Peanuts and additional whipped topping, optional

1 Prepare pudding according to package directions. Remove from the heat; whisk in peanut butter. Place pan in a large bowl of ice water for 5 minutes, stirring occasionally. Fold in whipped topping.

2 Pour into the crust. Cover and refrigerate for 1 hour or until set. Garnish with peanuts and whipped topping if desired. **YIELD:** 6-8 servings.

BLACK FOREST DREAM DESSERT PICTURED ON RIGHT

Prep: 45 min. + chilling

This rich, chilled treat seems to hit the spot on a hot summer's day. The recipe makes a large dessert, but my family never complains if there happen to be leftovers!

Angela Leinenbach // Mechanicsvlle, Virginia

  1 cup all-purpose flour
  2 tablespoons sugar
1/2 cup cold butter, cubed
1/2 cup flaked coconut
1/2 cup chopped walnuts, toasted
  1 package (8 ounces) cream cheese, softened
  1 cup confectioners' sugar
  1 carton (8 ounces) frozen whipped topping,
    thawed, *divided*
  1 can (21 ounces) cherry pie filling
1-1/2 cups semisweet chocolate chips
2-1/2 cups cold milk
  2 packages (3.4 ounces *each*) instant vanilla
    pudding mix
Chocolate curls, optional

1 In a large bowl, combine flour and sugar; cut in butter until crumbly. Stir in coconut and walnuts. Press into an ungreased 13-in. x 9-in. baking dish. Bake at 350° for 15-18 minutes or until lightly browned. Cool on a wire rack.

2 In a small bowl, beat cream cheese and confectioners' sugar until smooth. Fold in 1 cup whipped topping. Spread over crust. Top with pie filling; cover and chill.

3 In a microwave, melt chocolate chips; stir until smooth. In a large bowl, whisk milk and pudding mixes for 2 minutes. Let stand for 2 minutes or until soft-set. Whisk a small amount of pudding into melted chocolate. Return all to the pudding, whisking constantly. Pour over cherry filling. Chill for 2 hours or until set.

4 Just before serving, spread remaining whipped topping over dessert. Garnish with chocolate curls if desired. **YIELD:** 12 servings.

AUNT RUTH'S FAMOUS BUTTERSCOTCH CHEESECAKE

Prep: 30 min. **Bake:** 65 min. + chilling

Aunt Ruth was our nanny when I was little and made this cheesecake often. It was torture when my sister and I had to wait until the next day to have a piece since it had to chill overnight.

Trisha Kruse // Eagle, Idaho

1-1/2 cups graham cracker crumbs
  1/3 cup packed brown sugar
  1/3 cup butter, melted
    1 can (14 ounces) sweetened condensed milk
  3/4 cup cold 2% milk
    1 package (3.4 ounces) instant butterscotch
      pudding mix
    3 packages (8 ounces *each*) cream
      cheese, softened
    1 teaspoon vanilla extract
    3 eggs, lightly beaten
Whipped cream and crushed butterscotch
    candies, optional

1 Place a greased 9-in. springform pan on a double thickness of heavy-duty foil (about 18 in. square). Securely wrap foil around pan. In a small bowl, combine cracker crumbs and sugar; stir in butter. Press onto the bottom of prepared pan. Place pan on a baking sheet. Bake at 325° for 10 minutes. Cool on a wire rack.

2 In a small bowl, whisk the milks and the pudding mix for 2 minutes. Let stand for 2 minutes or until soft-set.

3 Meanwhile, in a large bowl, beat cream cheese until smooth. Beat in pudding and vanilla. Add eggs; beat on low speed just until combined. Pour over crust. Place springform pan in a large baking pan; add 1 in. of hot water to larger pan.

4 Bake at 325° for 65-75 minutes or until center is almost set and top appears dull. Remove springform pan from water bath. Cool on a wire rack for 10 minutes.

5 Carefully run a knife around edge of pan to loosen; cool 1 hour longer. Refrigerate overnight. Garnish with whipped cream and butterscotch candies if desired. **YIELD:** 12 servings.

I rely on canned pumpkin and a yellow cake mix to fix this effortless alternative to pumpkin pie. It's a tried-and-true dessert that always elicits compliments and requests for the recipe.

Linda Guyot //
Fountain Valley, California

GREAT PUMPKIN DESSERT

Prep: 5 min. **Bake:** 1 hour

    1 can (15 ounces) solid-pack pumpkin
    1 can (12 ounces) evaporated milk
    3 eggs
    1 cup sugar
    4 teaspoons pumpkin pie spice
    1 package (18-1/4 ounces) yellow cake mix
 3/4 cup butter, melted
1-1/2 cups chopped walnuts
Vanilla ice cream *or* whipped cream

1 In a large bowl, beat pumpkin, evaporated milk, eggs, sugar and pumpkin pie spice until smooth.

2 Transfer to a greased 13-in. x 9-in. baking dish. Sprinkle with cake mix and drizzle with butter. Top with walnuts.

3 Bake at 350° for 1 hour or until a knife inserted near the center comes out clean. Serve with ice cream or whipped cream. **YIELD:** 12-16 servings.

EASY STRAWBERRY NAPOLEON

Prep: 10 min. + chilling

This rich pudding-like dessert is one of my family's absolute favorites. Fresh strawberries make a pretty topping, while convenient saltine crackers form a no-fuss crust.

Karen Sawatsky // Vineland, Ontario

    2 cups cold 2% milk
    1 package (3.4 ounces) instant vanilla
       pudding mix
    1 cup heavy whipping cream, whipped
 36 saltines
    1 pint fresh strawberries, sliced

1 In a large bowl, whisk milk and pudding mix for 2 minutes. Let stand for 2 minutes or until soft-set. Fold in the whipped cream.

2 Place a third of the crackers in an ungreased 8-in. square dish (break crackers to completely cover bottom of dish). Top with a third of the pudding mixture. Repeat the layers twice.

3 Cover; refrigerate for at least 6 hours. Top individual slices with fresh strawberries before serving. **YIELD:** 9-12 servings.

It may look fancy, but this heavenly cheesecake comes together without a fuss. A brownie crust is a yummy change of pace.

Taste of Home Test Kitchen

DECADENT BROWNIE SWIRL CHEESECAKE

Prep: 30 min. **Bake:** 1-1/2 hours + chilling

    1 package fudge brownie mix
      (13-inch x 9-inch pan size)
FILLING:
    4 packages (8 ounces *each*) cream
      cheese, softened
    1 cup sugar
    4 eggs, lightly beaten
    3 teaspoons vanilla extract *or* 1 teaspoon almond
      extract and 2 teaspoons vanilla extract
Fresh raspberries and chocolate curls, optional

1 Prepare the brownie mix according to package directions for chewy fudge brownies. Set aside 2/3 cup brownie batter; spread remaining batter into a greased 9-in. springform pan.

2 Place pan on a double thickness of heavy-duty foil (about 18 in. square). Securely wrap foil around pan. Bake at 350° for 25-28 minutes (brownies will barely test done). Cool 10 minutes on a wire rack.

3 In a large bowl, beat cream cheese and sugar until smooth. Beat in eggs and vanilla on low speed just until combined. Stir 1/3 cup into reserved brownie batter; set aside. Spoon half the cheesecake batter into crust; dollop with half of reserved chocolate cheesecake batter. Repeat layers. Cut through batter with a knife to swirl.

4 Place in a larger baking pan; add 1 in. of hot water to larger pan. Bake at 325° for 1-1/2 hours or until surface is no longer shiny and center is almost set. Remove pan from water bath and foil. Cool on a wire rack for 10 minutes. Carefully run a knife around the edge of pan to loosen; cool 1 hour longer. Refrigerate overnight. Remove sides of pan. Garnish with raspberries and chocolate curls if desired. **YIELD:** 16 servings.

BLACK FOREST MOUSSE

Prep/Total Time: 15 min.

If you like chocolate and cherries, you'll love this smooth, light dessert. Instant pudding and canned pie filling allow you to make it in minutes.

Deanna Richter // Elmore, Minnesota

    2 cups cold 2% milk
    1 package (3.9 ounces) instant chocolate
      pudding mix

    1 can (21 ounces) cherry pie filling
    2 cups whipped topping

1 In a large bowl, beat milk and pudding mix for about 2 minutes or until smooth. Let stand for 2 more minutes or until thickened. Stir in pie filling. Gently fold in whipped topping.

2 Spoon into individual dessert dishes; refrigerate until serving. **YIELD:** 8 servings.

BANANA PUDDING PARFAITS

Prep: 15 min. + chilling

With fresh bananas, vanilla wafers and a snappy pudding mix, these creamy after-dinner sweets are easy to assemble. You can also substitute your favorite fresh berries or other flavors of sugar-free instant pudding mix.

Margaret Allen // Abingdon, Virginia

3-1/3 cups cold fat-free milk
    2 packages (1 ounce *each*) sugar-free instant vanilla pudding mix
  2/3 cup fat-free sour cream
  1/4 teaspoon vanilla extract
    1 carton (8 ounces) frozen fat-free whipped topping, thawed, *divided*
  32 reduced-fat vanilla wafers
    3 medium ripe bananas, cut into 1/4-inch slices

1 In a large bowl, whisk milk and pudding mix for 2 minutes. Let stand for 2 minutes. Whisk in sour cream and vanilla. Fold in three-fourths of the whipped topping.

2 Set aside eight vanilla wafers. Place one wafer into each of eight parfait glasses; top with a third of the banana slices and pudding mixture. Repeat layers twice. Top with remaining whipped topping. Refrigerate for at least 1 hour. Garnish with reserved vanilla wafers. **YIELD:** 8 servings.

PUMPKIN PUDDING

To enjoy a bit of pumpkin at any time of year, I add several heaping tablespoons of canned pumpkin pie filling to a package of sugar-free instant vanilla pudding mix. —Ione K., West Bend, Wisconsin

S'MORE TARTS

Prep: 10 min. **Bake:** 25 min.

    1 package fudge brownie mix
      (13-inch x 9-inch pan size)
  12 individual graham cracker shells
1-1/2 cups miniature marshmallows
    1 cup milk chocolate chips

1 Prepare brownie batter according to package directions. Place graham cracker shells on a baking sheet and fill with brownie batter.

2 Bake at 350° for 20-25 minutes or until a toothpick inserted in the center comes out with moist crumbs. Immediately sprinkle with marshmallows and chocolate chips. Bake 3-5 minutes longer or until marshmallows are puffed and golden brown. **YIELD:** 1 dozen.

CHEDDAR-BISCUIT PEACH COBBLER   PICTURED ON RIGHT

Prep: 20 min. **Bake:** 35 min.

Celebrate the golden days of summer with fresh peaches bubbling in sweet juices. Tender, savory biscuits top this the dessert for a tasty twist.

Marie Oliphant // Homer, Michigan

    4 pounds fresh peaches, peeled and sliced
     or 8 cups frozen unsweetened sliced peaches
    2 tablespoons lemon juice
1/2 teaspoon almond extract
1-1/2 cups sugar
    2 tablespoons cornstarch
1/2 teaspoon salt
    3 tablespoons cold butter
CHEDDAR BISCUITS:
    2 cups biscuit/baking mix
    1 cup (4 ounces) shredded cheddar cheese
2/3 cup 2% milk
    1 tablespoon butter, melted

1 In a large bowl, combine the peaches, lemon juice and extract. Transfer to a greased 13-in. x 9-in. baking dish. Combine the sugar, cornstarch and salt; sprinkle over peaches. Dot with butter.

2 Bake cobbler uncovered, at 400° for 15 minutes. Meanwhile, in a large bowl, combine the biscuit mix and cheese. Combine milk and butter; stir into biscuit mixture just until blended. Drop by tablespoonfuls onto hot peach mixture.

3 Bake 20-25 minutes longer or until biscuits are golden brown. Serve warm. **YIELD:** 10-12 servings.

STREUSEL STRAWBERRY PIZZA

Prep: 15 min. **Bake:** 30 min.

This is the best dessert pizza I've ever tasted. The fast-to-fix fruity treat is great for parties where lots of children will be present.

Karen Ann Bland // Gove, Kansas

- 1 package (18-1/4 ounces) white cake mix
- 1-1/4 cups quick-cooking oats
- 1/3 cup butter, softened
- 1 egg
- 1 can (21 ounces) strawberry pie filling *or* flavor of your choice
- 1/2 cup chopped nuts
- 1/4 cup packed brown sugar
- 1/8 teaspoon ground cinnamon

1 In a large bowl, combine the cake mix, oats and butter until crumbly; set aside 3/4 cup for topping. Add egg to the remaining crumb mixture and mix well.

2 Press dough into a greased 12-in. pizza pan. Build up the edges and flute if desired. Bake at 350° for 12 minutes.

3 Spread pie filling over crust to within 1 in. of edges. Combine the nuts, brown sugar, cinnamon and reserved crumb mixture; sprinkle over filling.

4 Bake for 15-20 minutes or until lightly browned. Cool on a wire rack. Refrigerate leftovers. **YIELD:** 8-10 servings.

Let these delightful watermelon wannabes add a bit of fun to your next picnic spread. Limes are halved and hollowed to hold pretty pink gelatin while mini chocolate chips serve as seeds in the cute cups.

Taste of Home Test Kitchen

WATERMELON GELATIN CUPS

Prep: 15 min. + chilling

   1 package (3 ounces) watermelon gelatin
   1 cup boiling water
   1 cup cold water
   4 large limes
 1/4 cup miniature chocolate chips

1 In a small bowl, dissolve gelatin in boiling water. Stir in cold water. Refrigerate for 1 hour or until slightly thickened.

2 Meanwhile, slice limes in half lengthwise. With a small scissors or sharp knife, cut the membrane at each end to loosen pulp from shell. Using fingertips, pull membrane and pulp away from shell (discard pulp or save for another use).

3 Fold chocolate chips into gelatin; spoon into lime shells. Refrigerate for 2 hours or until completely set. **YIELD:** 8 servings.

PEANUT BUTTER SNACK CUPS

Prep: 10 min. + freezing

When our kids were little, they loved this cool and creamy summertime treat. We'd keep several batches in the freezer so there were plenty when their neighborhood friends came over to play.

Nancy Clark // Cochranton, Pennsylvania

 12 vanilla wafer
  1 carton (8 ounces) frozen whipped topping, thawed, *divided*
  1 cup cold 2% milk
 1/2 cup peanut butter
  1 package (3.9 ounces) instant chocolate pudding mix

1 Place wafers in paper or foil-lined muffin cups. Top each with 1 tablespoon whipped topping.

2 In a large bowl, combine milk and peanut butter. Add chocolate pudding mix; beat on low speed for 2 minutes. Fold in remaining whipped topping. Spoon into prepared cups.

3 Cover and freeze. Remove from the freezer 10 minutes before serving. **YIELD:** 12 servings.

VANILLA FRUIT DESSERT

Prep/Total Time: 5 min.

- 1/2 cup cold 2% milk
- 1 package (3.4 ounces) instant vanilla pudding mix
- 1 cup (8 ounces) vanilla yogurt
- 1/2 cup thawed orange juice concentrate
- 4 to 6 cups assorted fruit (apples, grapes, mandarin oranges, etc.)

1 In a bowl, combine the milk, pudding mix, yogurt and orange juice concentrate. Beat on low speed for 2 minutes. Serve over fruit. Refrigerate any leftover topping. **YIELD:** 4-6 servings (1-3/4 cups topping).

TROPICAL AMBROSIA

Prep/Total Time: 10 min.

I add whipped topping to everyday pantry items to create this light and fluffy dessert. Toasted coconut and sweet pineapple give the creamy combination its tropical taste.

Marguerite Widrick // Adams, New York

- 1 can (20 ounces) pineapple tidbits
- 1/2 teaspoon coconut extract
- 1 package (3.4 ounces) instant vanilla pudding mix
- 1 carton (8 ounces) frozen whipped topping, thawed
- 4 tablespoons flaked coconut, toasted, *divided*
- Maraschino cherries, optional
- 1 teaspoon maraschino cherry juice, optional

1 Drain pineapple, reserving juice; set pineapple aside. In a large bowl, combine the pineapple juice, extract and pudding mix; whisk for 2 minutes. Let stand for 2 minutes or until soft-set. Fold in whipped topping. Stir in pineapple and 3 tablespoons coconut.

2 Transfer to a serving bowl. Garnish with remaining coconut, cherries and cherry juice if desired. Chill until serving. **YIELD:** 6 servings.

SHREDDED COCONUT

To soften shredded coconut that's turned hard, soak it in milk 30 minutes to soften it. Drain it and pat it dry on paper towels before using. The leftover coconut-flavored milk can be used within 5 days in baked goods or blended with fresh fruit for a tasty beverage. —Taste of Home Test Kitchen

CARAMEL FUDGE CHEESECAKE

Prep: 30 min. + cooling
Bake: 35 min. + chilling

I combined several recipes to create this dessert that satisfies both the chocolate lovers and the cheesecake lovers in my family. With a fudgy crust, crunchy pecans and a gooey layer of caramel, it's hard to resist.

Brenda Ruse // Truro, Nova Scotia

- 1 package fudge brownie mix
  (8-inch square pan size)
- 1 package (14 ounces) caramels
- 1/4 cup evaporated milk
- 1-1/4 cups coarsely chopped pecans
- 2 packages (8 ounces *each*) cream cheese, softened
- 1/2 cup sugar
- 2 eggs, lightly beaten
- 2 ounces unsweetened chocolate, melted and cooled

1 Prepare brownie batter according to package directions. Spread into a greased 9-in. springform pan. Place on a baking sheet. Bake at 350° for 20 minutes. Place pan on a wire rack for 10 minutes (leave oven on).

2 Meanwhile, in a microwave-safe bowl, melt the caramels with milk. Pour over brownie crust; sprinkle with pecans. In a large bowl, beat cream cheese and sugar. Add eggs; beat on low speed just until combined. Stir in melted chocolate. Pour over pecans. Return pan to baking sheet.

3 Bake for 35-40 minutes or until center is almost set. Cool on a wire rack for 10 minutes. Run a knife around edge of pan to loosen; cool 1 hour longer. Refrigerate overnight. Remove sides of pan. Refrigerate leftovers. **YIELD:** 12 servings.

This fluffy and refreshing four-ingredient pie is a breeze to make because it takes advantage of a prepared graham cracker crust.

Rhonda Olivieri //
East Earl, Pennsylvania

LIME YOGURT PIE

Prep/Total Time: 30 min.

    1 package (3 ounces) lime gelatin
1-1/2 cups (12 ounces) key lime pie yogurt
    1 carton (8 ounces) frozen whipped
      topping, thawed
    1 graham cracker crust (9 inches)

1 In a large bowl, combine the gelatin powder and yogurt. Fold in whipped topping.

2 Spread into crust. Refrigerate for at least 20 minutes before serving. **YIELD:** 6-8 servings.

CHOCOLATE BERRY PARFAITS PICTURED ON RIGHT

Prep/Total Time: 15 min.

Instant chocolate pudding is layered with a mixture of pureed strawberries and whipped cream to create yummy parfaits. For quicker results, use whipped topping rather than whipping cream or serve the dessert in a single bowl.

Lynn McAllister // Mt. Ulla, North Carolina

    2 cups cold 2% milk
    1 package (3.9 ounces) instant chocolate
      pudding mix
    1 package (10 ounces) frozen sweetened
      strawberries, thawed
    1 cup heavy whipping cream
1/4 cup confectioners' sugar
Sliced fresh strawberries, optional

1 In a large bowl, whisk milk and pudding mix for 2 minutes. Let stand for 2 minutes or until soft-set; set aside. Drain strawberries (discard the juice or save for another use); place berries in a blender. Cover and process until smooth; set aside.

2 In a large bowl, beat cream and sugar until stiff peaks form. Gently fold in strawberry puree. Divide half of the chocolate pudding among four or six parfait glasses. Top with half of the strawberry mixture. Repeat layers. Garnish with a strawberry slice if desired. **YIELD:** 4-6 servings.

EDITOR'S NOTE: 2 cups of whipped topping may be substituted for the whipping cream and sugar.

CHOCOLATE RASPBERRY DESSERT

Prep: 10 min. + freezing

Guests are sure to find wedges of this fruity and chocolaty frozen pie irresistible. The crustless concoction has a creamy mousse-like consistency that's melt-in-your-mouth good.

Judy Schut // Grand Rapids, Michigan

1 cup 1% cottage cheese
3/4 cup fat-free milk
1/3 cup raspberry spreadable fruit
1 package (1.4 ounces) sugar-free instant chocolate pudding mix
1 carton (8 ounces) frozen reduced-fat whipped topping, thawed

1 ounce semisweet chocolate, melted
1/2 cup frozen unsweetened raspberries, thawed

1 In a blender, combine the cottage cheese, milk and spreadable fruit; cover and process until smooth. Add dry pudding mix; cover and process until smooth.

2 Pour into a large bowl; fold in whipped topping. Spoon into a 9-in. pie plate. Drizzle with chocolate. Cover and freeze for 8 hours or overnight.

3 Let stand at room temperature for 20 minutes before serving. Garnish dessert with raspberries. **YIELD:** 8 servings.

I start with a basic brownie mix to create this luscious treat that's sure to impress company. Sometimes I will add mandarin oranges for a touch of added color.

Nancy Johnson // Laverne, Oklahoma

FRUITY BROWNIE PIZZA

Prep: 20 min. + chilling
Bake: 15 min. + cooling

> 1 package fudge brownie mix
> (8-inch square pan size)
> 1 package (8 ounces) cream cheese, softened
> 1/3 cup sugar
> 3/4 cup pineapple tidbits with juice
> 1 small firm banana, sliced
> 1 medium kiwifruit, peeled and sliced
> 1 cup sliced fresh strawberries
> 1/4 cup chopped pecans
> 1 ounce semisweet chocolate
> 1 tablespoon butter

1 Prepare brownie batter according to package directions. Spread onto a greased 12-in. pizza pan. Bake at 375° for 15-20 minutes or until a toothpick inserted near the center comes out clean. Cool crust completely.

2 In a large bowl, beat cream cheese and sugar until smooth. Spread over brownie crust. Drain pineapple, reserving juice. Toss banana slices with juice; drain well. Arrange the banana, kiwi, strawberries and pineapple over cream cheese layer; sprinkle with pecans.

3 In a small microwave, melt chocolate and butter; stir until smooth. Drizzle over fruit. Cover and refrigerate for 1 hour. **YIELD:** 12-14 servings.

ORANGE CREAM DESSERT

Prep: 15 min. + chilling

For a light and refreshing ending to a meal, I fill a cookie crumb crust with a combination of orange gelatin and ice cream and then top slices with a dollop of whipped cream.

Peggy Detjen // Lakeville, Minnesota

> 2 cups cream-filled chocolate sandwich
> cookie crumbs
> 1/3 cup butter, melted
> 1 package (6 ounces) orange *or* lime gelatin
> 2 cups boiling water
> 1 quart vanilla ice cream, softened

1 In a large bowl, combine cookie crumbs and butter; set aside 1/4 cup for topping. Press remaining crumb mixture into a greased 13-in. x 9-in. dish. In another bowl, dissolve gelatin in water; cover and refrigerate for 10 minutes.

2 Stir in ice cream until smooth. Pour over crust. Sprinkle with reserved crumb mixture. Chill until firm. **YIELD:** 12-15 servings.

This make-ahead recipe was given to me by an aunt many years ago. It called for lemon gelatin, but my family likes the light, fluffy squares best with lime instead.

Joyce Key // Snellville, Georgia

LIME CHIFFON DESSERT

Prep: 20 min. + chilling

1-1/2 cups crushed graham crackers
    (about 24 squares)
  1/3 cup sugar
  1/2 cup butter, melted
FILLING:
    1 package (3 ounces) lime gelatin
    1 cup boiling water
    2 packages (one 8 ounces, one 3 ounces)
    cream cheese, softened
    1 cup sugar
    1 teaspoon vanilla extract
    1 carton (16 ounces) frozen whipped
    topping, thawed

1 Combine the first three ingredients; set aside 2 tablespoons for topping. Press remaining crumbs onto the bottom of an ungreased 13-in. x 9-in. dish; set aside. In a small bowl, dissolve gelatin in boiling water; cool.

2 In a large bowl, beat cream cheese and sugar until smooth. Beat in vanilla. Slowly add gelatin until combined. Fold in whipped topping. Carefully spoon over crust; sprinkle with reserved crumbs. Cover and refrigerate for 3 hours or until set. **YIELD:** 12-15 servings.

FRUITY TAPIOCA

Prep: 15 min. + cooling

Folks who like tapioca will enjoy this fruity variation. Canned peaches and mandarin oranges give refreshing flavor to a traditional dessert.

Louise Martin // Mohnton, Pennsylvania

  4 cups water
  1 cup sugar
1/3 cup quick-cooking tapioca
  1 can (6 ounces) frozen orange juice
    concentrate, thawed

  1 can (29 ounces) sliced peaches, drained
    and diced
  1 can (11 ounces) mandarin oranges, drained

1 In a large saucepan, combine the water, sugar and tapioca; let stand for 5 minutes. Bring to a full rolling boil. Remove from the heat; stir in orange juice concentrate. Cool for 20 minutes.

2 Stir in the peaches and oranges. Transfer to a serving bowl. Cover and refrigerate until serving. **YIELD:** 10 servings.

COCONUT RHUBARB DESSERT

Prep: 25 min. **Bake:** 25 min.

Tart rhubarb is sweetened with crunchy pecans and flaked coconut, while a cake mix proves a tender base. What a delicious treat!

Connie Korger // Green Bay, Wisconsin

    4 cups sliced fresh *or* frozen rhubarb
1-1/2 cups sugar
1-1/2 cups water
  1/8 teaspoon red food coloring, optional
    1 package (18-1/4 ounces) butter pecan cake mix
    1 cup flaked coconut
  1/2 cup chopped pecans
  1/2 cup butter, melted
Vanilla ice cream, optional

1 In a large saucepan, combine the rhubarb, sugar, water and food coloring if desired. Cook over medium heat for 8-10 minutes or until rhubarb is tender; cool slightly. Transfer to a greased 13-in. x 9-in. baking dish; sprinkle with cake mix. Top with coconut and pecans. Drizzle with butter.

2 Bake at 350° for 25-30 minutes or until a toothpick inserted near the center comes out clean. Serve with ice cream if desired. **YIELD:** 12 servings.

EASY CHOPPED NUTS

To chop nuts easily—and without a mess—put them in a plastic bag and roll them with a rolling pin to the desired fineness. It's quick, plus I save even more time since there's no chopper to clean.
—Linda T., Crivitz, Wisconsin

BUTTER CRUNCH PUDDING

Prep/Total Time: 30 min.

  1 cup all-purpose flour
  1/2 cup flaked coconut
  1/4 cup packed brown sugar
  1/2 cup cold butter, cubed
  2 cups cold milk
  1 package (3.4 ounces) instant lemon pudding mix *or* flavor of your choice

1 In a large bowl, combine flour, coconut and brown sugar; cut in butter until crumbly. Spread the crumb mixture on a 15-in. x 10-in. x 1-in. baking pan. Bake at 375° for 15 minutes, stirring once. Cool slightly.

2 Meanwhile, in a another large bowl, whisk milk and pudding mix for 2 minutes. Let stand for 2 minutes or until soft-set; chill for 5 minutes.

3 Spoon half of the crumbs into each of four dessert bowls. Top with pudding and remaining crumb mixture. **YIELD**: 4 servings.

COCONUT PISTACHIO PIE   PICTURED ON RIGHT

Prep: 20 min. + chilling

The lightly toasted coconut in the crust pairs so well with the pale green pistachio pudding in this velvety smooth pie. It's convenient, too—you can make it ahead of time and chill until serving.
Taste of Home Test Kitchen

2-1/2 cups flaked coconut, lightly toasted
  1/3 cup butter, melted
  2 cups cold 2% milk
  2 packages (3.4 ounces *each*) instant pistachio pudding mix
  1 cup whipped topping
  2 tablespoons chopped pistachios, optional

1 In a small bowl, combine coconut and butter. Press onto the bottom and up the sides of a greased 9-in. pie plate. Refrigerate for at least 30 minutes or until firm.

2 In a small bowl, whisk milk and pudding mixes for 2 minutes. Let stand for 2 minutes or until soft-set. Spread 1-1/2 cups over crust.

3 Fold whipped topping into remaining pudding; spread over pie. Sprinkle with chopped pistachios if desired. Cover; refrigerate for at least 2 hours. **YIELD**: 8 servings.

RASPBERRY-GLAZED PIE

Prep: 15 min. **Bake:** 15 min. + chilling

Everyone raves about this quick and easy summer pie. It's always a bit hit with all ages at parties, picnics and get-togethers.

Kathy Voss // Jackson, Michigan

- 1 cup biscuit/baking mix
- 1/4 cup cold butter, cubed
- 3 tablespoons cold water

FILLING:

- 1 cup sugar
- 3 tablespoons plus 1-1/2 teaspoons cornstarch
- 1 cup water
- 2 teaspoons corn syrup
- 1 package (3 ounces) raspberry gelatin

3-1/2 cups fresh raspberries
Whipped topping, optional

1 Place baking mix in a small bowl; cut in butter until crumbly. Gradually add water, tossing with a fork until dough forms a ball. Press onto the bottom and up the sides of a 9-in. pie plate coated with cooking spray.

2 Line unpricked pastry shell with a double thickness of heavy-duty foil. Bake at 450° for 8 minutes. Remove foil; bake 5 minutes longer. Cool on a wire rack.

3 In a small saucepan, combine sugar and cornstarch. Stir in water and corn syrup until smooth. Bring to a boil, stirring constantly. Cook and stir for 2-3 minutes or until thickened. Remove from the heat; stir in gelatin until dissolved.

4 Place raspberries in pie crust; pour gelatin mixture over top. Cover and refrigerate for at least 4 hours or until set. Serve with whipped topping if desired. **YIELD:** 8 servings.

This luscious trifle will wow everyone who sees it, let alone tries it. Apricot preserves add a fruity touch to the pleasing pairing of chocolate and toasted coconut.

Donna Cline // Pensacola, Florida

COCONUT CHOCOLATE TRIFLE

Prep: 15 min. + chilling

  1 loaf (10-3/4 ounces) frozen pound cake, thawed
1/3 cup apricot preserves
1/3 cup plus 2 tablespoons orange juice, *divided*
  4 ounces German sweet chocolate
1-1/4 cups flaked coconut, toasted, *divided*
1-3/4 cups cold 2% milk
  1 cup half-and-half cream
  1 package (5.9 ounces) instant chocolate pudding mix

1 Trim crust from top, sides and bottom of cake. Cut cake into 16 slices. Spread preserves over eight slices; top with remaining cake. Cut into 1-in. cubes.

2 Place in a 2-qt. serving bowl; drizzle with 1/3 cup orange juice. Chop chocolate; set aside 2 tablespoons for garnish. Sprinkle remaining chocolate and 1 cup coconut over cake.

3 In a large bowl, combine the milk, cream, dry pudding mix and remaining orange juice; beat on low for 2 minutes. Spoon over cake. Sprinkle with remaining coconut and reserved chocolate. Refrigerate for at least 4 hours before serving. **YIELD:** 10-14 servings.

FESTIVE FRUIT PIE

Prep: 30 min. + chilling

Fresh banana slices, canned pineapple tidbits and chopped pecans dress up the cherry filling in this fuss-free pie. For quicker results, you can substitute a prepared graham cracker crust for the baked pastry shell.

Dorothy Smith // El Dorado, Arkansas

  1 cup sugar
1/4 cup all-purpose flour
  1 can (21 ounces) cherry pie filling
  1 can (14 ounces) pineapple tidbits, drained
  1 package (3 ounces) orange gelatin
  3 to 4 medium firm bananas, sliced
  1 cup chopped pecans
  2 pastry shells, baked (9 inches)
Whipped topping, optional

1 In a large saucepan, combine sugar and flour. Stir in pie filling and pineapple. Bring to a boil over medium heat; cook and stir for 2 minutes or until thickened. Remove from the heat; stir in gelatin. Cool. Stir in bananas and pecans.

2 Carefully pour into pie shells. Refrigerate for about 3 hours. Garnish with whipped topping if desired. **YIELD:** 2 pies (6-8 servings each).

BANANA BASICS

Look for plump bananas that are evenly yellow-colored. Green bananas are under-ripe, while a flecking of brown flecks indicates ripeness. If bananas are too green, place in a paper bag until ripe.
—Taste of Home Test Kitchen

This unique summer dessert is low in fat and a creative way to use cantaloupe. It's best when made with very ripe melon—it adds the sweetest flavor.
Sandy McKenzie // Braham, Minnesota

MELON MOUSSE

Prep: 15 min. + chilling

2 envelopes unflavored gelatin
3 tablespoons lemon juice
4 cups cubed ripe cantaloupe
1 tablespoon sugar
1 cup (8 ounces) fat-free lemon yogurt
Fresh raspberries, optional

1 In a small saucepan, sprinkle gelatin over lemon juice; let stand for 1 minute. Heat over low heat, stirring until gelatin is completely dissolved.

2 In a blender, combine gelatin mixture, cantaloupe and sugar. Cover; process until smooth.

3 Transfer to a bowl; stir in yogurt. Spoon into individual dishes; chill until firm. Garnish with raspberries if desired. **YIELD:** 6 servings.

CHOCOLATE DREAM DESSERT

Prep: 15 min. **Bake:** 20 min. + cooling

I quickly make a crowd-pleasing dessert with cake cubes, instant pudding, whipped topping, chocolate syrup and nuts. It's a surefire way to satisfy chocolate lovers.
Kathleen Gordon // Treadway, Tennessee

1 package (18-1/4 ounces) chocolate cake mix
1 package (3.4 ounces) instant vanilla pudding mix
1 cup chocolate syrup, *divided*
1 carton (12 ounces) frozen whipped topping, thawed
1/2 cup chopped pecans

1 Prepare and bake the cake according to package directions, using a greased 13-in. x 9-in. baking pan. Cool on wire rack.

2 Meanwhile, prepare pudding according to package directions; pour into a 13-in. x 9-in. dish.

3 Tear cake into small pieces and gently push down into the pudding. Drizzle with 3/4 cup of chocolate syrup. Spread with whipped topping. Drizzle with remaining chocolate syrup. Sprinkle with pecans. Refrigerate until serving. **YIELD:** 16-20 servings.

LEMON CHEESECAKE PIES

Prep: 30 min. + chilling

I've been making these scrumptious pies for at least 50 years. There's little cleanup, and kids and adults alike love the lemony, fluffy filling.

Lorraine Foss // Puyallup, Washington

1 can (12 ounces) evaporated milk
2 packages (3 ounces *each*) lemon gelatin
2 cups boiling water
1 package (8 ounces) cream cheese, cubed
1 tablespoon lemon juice
1 cup sugar
4 graham cracker crusts (9 inches)

TOPPING:
1 cup graham cracker crumbs
1/4 cup butter, melted
2 tablespoons sugar

1 Pour milk into a large metal bowl; cover and refrigerate for at least 2 hours.

2 In a large bowl, dissolve gelatin in boiling water. Cool for 10 minutes. Add cream cheese and lemon juice; beat until blended. Set aside.

3 Beat chilled milk until soft peaks form. Gradually add sugar. Beat in gelatin mixture. Pour into crusts.

4 Combine topping ingredients; sprinkle over pies. Refrigerate for 4 hours or until set. **YIELD:** 4 pies (8 slices each).

This pie was inspired by my husband, who loves coffee ice cream, and his mom, who makes a cool, creamy dessert using pudding mix. It's the best of both worlds!

April Timboe //
Siloam Springs, Arkansas

FROSTY COFFEE PIE

Prep: 15 min. + freezing

- 1/4 cup hot fudge ice cream topping, warmed
- 1 chocolate crumb crust (9 inches)
- 3 cups coffee ice cream, softened
- 1 package (5.9 ounces) instant chocolate pudding mix
- 1/2 cup cold strong brewed coffee
- 1/4 cup cold 2% milk
- 1-3/4 cups whipped topping
- 1 cup marshmallow creme
- 1/4 cup miniature semisweet chocolate chips

1 Spread the ice cream topping into crust. In a large bowl, beat the ice cream, dry pudding mix, coffee and milk until blended; spoon into crust.

2 In another bowl, combine the whipped topping and marshmallow creme; spread over top. Sprinkle with chocolate chips. Cover and freeze until firm. **YIELD:** 8 servings.

DIRT DESSERT PICTURED ON RIGHT

Prep: 30 min. + chilling

Here is a dessert that is so good, you're going to want to put a spoon in each hand and go to town. It's just that good!

Kristi Linton // Bay City, Michigan

- 1 package (8 ounces) cream cheese, softened
- 1/4 cup butter, softened
- 1 cup confectioners' sugar
- 3-1/2 cups cold 2% milk
- 2 packages (3.4 ounces *each*) instant vanilla pudding mix
- 1 carton (12 ounces) frozen whipped topping, thawed
- 1 package (16.6 ounces) cream-filled chocolate sandwich cookies
- Shaved white chocolate, optional

1 In a large bowl, beat the cream cheese, butter and confectioners' sugar until smooth. In a large bowl, whisk milk and pudding mixes for 2 minutes; let stand for 2 minutes or until soft-set. Gradually stir pudding mixture into cream cheese mixture. Fold in whipped topping.

2 Spread 1-1/3 cups of crushed cookies into an ungreased 13-in. x 9-in. dish. Layer with half of the pudding mixture and half of the remaining cookies. Repeat layers.

3 Refrigerate for at least 1 hour before serving. Serve with shaved white chocolate if desired. **YIELD:** 20 servings.

QUICK COCONUT CREAM PIE

Prep: 15 min. + chilling

I've found a way to make coconut cream pie without a lot of fuss and still get terrific flavor. Using a convenient purchased crust, instant pudding and frozen whipped topping, I can enjoy an old-time dessert even when time is short.

Betty Claycomb // Alverton, Pennsylvania

1-1/2 cups cold 2% milk
1 package (5.1 ounces) instant vanilla
    pudding mix

1 carton (8 ounces) frozen whipped topping,
    thawed, *divided*
3/4 to 1 cup flaked coconut, toasted, *divided*
1 pastry shell, baked *or* graham cracker crust
    (8 *or* 9 inches)

1 In a large bowl, beat milk and pudding on low speed for 2 minutes. Fold in half of the whipped topping and 1/2 to 3/4 cup of coconut.

2 Pour into crust. Spread with remaining whipped topping; sprinkle with remaining coconut. Chill. **YIELD:** 6-8 servings.

To complete a meal, I often serve this not-too-sweet pie. The rich and creamy dessert is so easy to assemble thanks to a short list of ingredients.

Glenda Parsonage //
Maple Creek, Saskatchewan

CHOCOLATE MALLOW PIE

Prep/Total Time: 20 min.

- 1 package (8 ounces) cream cheese, softened
- 2 cups cold 2% milk, *divided*
- 1 package (3.9 ounces) instant chocolate pudding mix
- 1-1/2 cups miniature marshmallows
- 1 graham cracker crust (9 inches)

1 In a large bowl, beat cream cheese and 1/2 cup milk until smooth. Beat in dry pudding mix and remaining milk. Carefully fold in the marshmallows.

2 Pour into the crust. Refrigerate until serving. **YIELD:** 6-8 servings.

BLUEBERRY DELIGHT

Prep/Total Time: 15 min.

I enjoy turning to a prepared angel food cake to create this impressive yet easy dessert. As an added bonus, it can be put together ahead, so there's no last-minute fuss.

Christine Halandras // Meeker, Colorado

- 1 package (8 ounces) cream cheese, softened
- 1/2 cup confectioners' sugar
- 1 can (14 ounces) sweetened condensed milk
- 1 package (3.4 ounces) instant vanilla pudding mix
- 1 carton (12 ounces) frozen whipped topping, thawed, *divided*
- 1 prepared angel food cake (8 to 10 ounces), cut into 1-inch cubes
- 1 quart fresh *or* frozen blueberries, thawed
Additional blueberries, optional

1 In a large bowl, beat the cream cheese and confectioners' sugar until smooth. Beat in the milk and dry pudding mix. Fold in 1-1/2 cups of whipped topping.

2 Place half of the cake cubes in a 3-qt. glass bowl. Layer with half of the berries and pudding mixture. Cover with remaining cake cubes. Layer with remaining berries and pudding mixture.

3 Spread remaining whipped topping over top. Garnish with additional berries if desired. Store leftovers in the refrigerator. **YIELD:** 12-14 servings.

BLUEBERRIES

Frozen blueberries have more juice than fresh berries. So be sure to reduce the liquid before tossing them into a dessert that isn't baked and calls for fresh blueberries.
—Taste of Home Test Kitchen

Raspberry or cherry pie filling gives a festive appearance to this rich no-bake cheesecake. Be ready to share the recipe!

Irene Pitzer // Madison, Tennessee

LADYFINGER CHEESECAKE

Prep: 30 min. + chilling

- 2 packages (11.1 ounces *each*) no-bake cheesecake mix
- 2/3 cup butter, melted
- 1/4 cup sugar
- 1 package (3 ounces) ladyfingers (25 cookies)
- 1 package (8 ounces) cream cheese, softened
- 3 cups cold 2% milk, *divided*
- 1 carton (12 ounces) frozen whipped topping, thawed
- 1 can (21 ounces) raspberry pie filling *or* flavor of your choice

1 In a large bowl, combine the contents of crust mix from both packages, butter and sugar. Press onto the bottom of an ungreased 10-in. springform pan. Arrange ladyfingers around edge of pan.

2 In a large bowl, beat cream cheese and 1/2 cup milk until smooth. Gradually beat in remaining milk. Add contents of filling mix from both packages; beat until smooth. Beat on medium for 3 minutes. Fold in whipped topping.

3 Pour over crust. Cover and refrigerate for at least 1 hour. Top with pie filling. Remove sides of pan before serving. **YIELD:** 12 servings.

BROWNIE CARAMEL PARFAITS

Prep: 25 min. **Bake:** 25 min. + cooling

Easily transform brownies, ice cream and caramel topping into a tempting treat. Layers of toasted coconut and nuts add nice crunch and make this in-a-dash dessert seem fancy.

Taste of Home Test Kitchen

- 1/2 cup chopped pecans
- 1/2 cup flaked coconut
- 1 package fudge brownie mix (8-inch square pan size)
- 1 pint vanilla ice cream
- 1 jar (12-1/4 ounces) caramel ice cream topping

1 Place pecans and coconut in an ungreased baking pan. Bake at 350° for 10-12 minutes or until toasted, stirring frequently.

2 Meanwhile, prepare the brownie batter and bake according to package directions. Cool on a wire rack; cut into small squares.

3 When ready to serve, in six parfait or dessert glasses, layer with brownies, ice cream, caramel topping and pecan mixture; repeat layers one or two times. **YIELD:** 6 servings.

INDEXES

GENERAL INDEX

This index lists each recipe by major ingredients and mixes or convenience items used.

BISCUIT/BAKING MIX
(continued)

Raspberry-Glazed Pie, 238
Round Cheese Bread, 147
Sausage Brunch Muffins, 27
Sausage Cheese Puffs, 24
Smoky Onion Biscuit Squares, 150
Sweet Raspberry Muffins, 31
Taco Casserole, 80
Taco Quiche, 20
Tex-Mex Biscuits, 152
Turkey Burger Pie, 110
Zucchini Cheddar Biscuits, 148
Zucchini Pancakes, 44

BLUEBERRIES
Baked Blueberry Pancake, 32
Blueberry Delight, 245
Hot Berries 'n' Brownie Ice Cream
    Cake, 186
Lemon Berry Cake, 185
Lemon Blueberry Muffins, 144

BREADS *(Also see Biscuit/Baking Mix; Corn Bread/Muffin Mix; Frozen & Refrigerated Doughs; Hot Roll Mix; Quick Bread Mix)*
Cinnamon Rolls, 22
Herb Garlic Loaf, 154
Italian Seasoned Bread, 141
Mexican Sunset Bread, 144
Onion Sandwich Rolls, 143

BREAKFAST & BRUNCH
(See Breads; Coffee Cakes; Eggs; Pancakes, Waffles & Pancake Mix)

BROCCOLI
Broccoli Wild Rice Soup, 131

BROWNIES & BROWNIE MIX
Brownie Caramel Parfaits, 246
Brownie Crackles, 176
Brownie Delight, 197
Candy Bar Brownie Trifle, 204
Caramel Fudge Cheesecake, 229
Coconut Brownies, 174
Decadent Brownie Swirl
    Cheesecake, 222
Fruity Brownie Pizza, 233
Hot Berries 'n' Brownie Ice Cream
    Cake, 186
Hugs 'n' Kisses Brownie, 198

Oatmeal Brownies, 194
Peanut Butter-Filled Brownie
    Cupcakes, 188
S'more Tarts, 224
S'mores Bars, 182

CABBAGE
Meat Bun Bake, 100
Pork and Cabbage Dinner, 71

CAKES & CAKE MIX
Apple German Chocolate Cake, 180
Apricot Bars, 170
Black Forest Cake, 175
Can't Leave Alone Bars, 164
Caramel Apple Cupcakes, 164
Carrot-Topped Cupcakes, 198
Cherry Almond Tart, 210
Chewy Date Nut Bars, 193
Chocolate Bundt Cake, 163
Chocolate Cherry Cupcakes, 179
Chocolate Dream Dessert, 240
Chocolate Mint Cream Cake, 182
Cinnamon Nut Cake, 168
Cinnamon Rolls, 22
Citrus Mini Cakes, 160
Coconut Chip Cookies, 192
Coconut Gingerbread Cake, 188
Coconut Rhubarb Dessert, 235
Creamy Center Cupcakes, 180
Crisp Walnut Cookies, 191
Easy German Chocolate Cake, 168
Fun Marshmallow Bars, 173
Great Pumpkin Dessert, 221
Green Chili Corn Muffins, 140
Hawaiian Cake, 199
Layered Chocolate Cake, 191
Lemon Berry Cake, 185
Light Lemon Cake, 187
Mocha Layer Cake, 167
Peach Cake, 185
Peanut Crunch Cake, 200
Pear Bundt Cake, 192
Peppermint Angel Roll, 162
Pineapple Upside-Down Cake, 174
Poppy Seed Citrus Cake, 181
Pumpkin Pecan Bites, 194
Pumpkin Spice Layer Cake, 197
Quick Little Devils, 173
Raisin Pound Cake, 184
Raspberry Cake, 178
Raspberry Oatmeal Bars, 169
Rhubarb Berry Coffee Cake, 36
Rhubarb Upside-Down Cake, 162
Rich Butter Cake, 161

Streusel Strawberry Pizza, 226
Sunshine Muffins, 149
Triple Chocolate Cake, 161

CANDY
Candy Bar Brownie Trifle, 204
Chocolate Mint Cream Cake, 182
Creamy Lemon Fudge, 202
Gumdrop Bread, 153
Hugs 'n' Kisses Brownie, 198
Peppermint Angel Roll, 162

CARAMEL
Brownie Caramel Parfaits, 246
Caramel Apple Cupcakes, 164
Caramel Fudge Cheesecake, 229

CARROTS
Carrot-Topped Cupcakes, 198
Glazed Carrots, 46

CEREALS
Crunchy Dessert Bars, 179
No-Bake Party Mix, 14
Oatmeal Brownies, 194
Raspberry Oatmeal Bars, 169

CHEESE
Bacon and Cheese Waffles, 23
Bacon Cheddar Muffins, 146
Cheddar-Biscuit Peach Cobbler, 224
Cheddar Sausage Muffins, 153
Cheddar Zucchini Wedges, 141
Cheesy Chicken Subs, 78
Cheesy Potato Beef Bake, 116
Cheesy Wild Rice, 124
Mini Cheddar Loaves, 155
Parmesan Herb Bread, 156
Parmesan Onion Wedges, 154
Round Cheese Bread, 147
Sausage Cheese Puffs, 24
Tuna Melt on Corn Bread, 62
Zucchini Cheddar Biscuits, 148

CHEESECAKE & CHEESECAKE MIX
Aunt Ruth's Famous Butterscotch
    Cheesecake, 220
Banana Cheesecake Pie, 217
Caramel Fudge Cheesecake, 229
Decadent Brownie Swirl Cheesecake, 222
Ladyfinger Cheesecake, 246
Lemon Cheesecake Pies, 241

PUDDINGS & PUDDING MIX (continued)

Butter Crunch Pudding, 236
Candy Bar Brownie Trifle, 204
Chocolate Berry Parfaits, 230
Chocolate Bundt Cake, 163
Chocolate Chip Cookie Delight, 203
Chocolate Dream Dessert, 240
Chocolate Mallow Pie, 245
Chocolate Mint Cream Cake, 182
Chocolate Peanut Dream Pie, 218
Chocolate Raspberry Dessert, 232
Coconut Chocolate Trifle, 239
Coconut Pistachio Pie, 236
Corn Bread Pudding, 55
Country-Style Vanilla Ice Cream, 206
Creamy Lemon Fudge, 202
Creamy Vanilla Coffee, 18
Crunchy Dessert Bars, 179
Dirt Dessert, 242
Dreamy Creamy Peanut Butter Pie, 212
Easy Strawberry Napoleon, 221
Frosty Coffee Pie, 242
Fruity Tapioca, 234
Hawaiian Cake, 199
Hot Cocoa Mix, 17
Layered Chocolate Cake, 191
Light Lemon Cake, 187
Macadamia Chip Cookies, 196
Make-Ahead Shortcake, 204
Peanut Butter Icebox Dessert, 216
Peanut Butter Snack Cups, 227
Pecan Butterscotch Cookies, 166
Pistachio Cookie Dessert, 210
Quick Coconut Cream Pie, 244
Raspberry Coffee Cake, 29
Rocky Road Fudge Pops, 209
Strawberry Lemon Trifle, 211
Tropical Ambrosia, 228
Tropical Fruit Cream Pie, 216
Vanilla Fruit Dessert, 228
White Chocolate Tarts, 206

PUMPKIN

Great Pumpkin Dessert, 221
Pumpkin Pancakes, 28
Pumpkin Pecan Bites, 194
Pumpkin Spice Layer Cake, 197

QUICK BREAD MIX

Apple Snack Cake, 172
Banana-Chip Mini Cupcakes, 190

RAMEN NOODLES

Beef Noodle Soup, 138
Crunchy Coleslaw, 52
Tasty Turkey Soup, 136
Veggie Noodle Side Dish, 38

RASPBERRIES

Chocolate Raspberry Dessert, 232
Fruit-Filled Raspberry Ring, 45
Hot Berries 'n' Brownie Ice Cream Cake, 186
Raspberry Cake, 178
Raspberry Coffee Cake, 29
Raspberry-Glazed Pie, 238
Raspberry Lemonade Pie, 214
Raspberry Oatmeal Bars, 169
Sweet Raspberry Muffins, 31

RHUBARB

Coconut Rhubarb Dessert, 235
Rhubarb Berry Coffee Cake, 36
Rhubarb Upside-Down Cake, 162

RICE & RICE MIX

Beefy Rice Dinner, 62
Broccoli Wild Rice Soup, 131
Cheesy Wild Rice, 124
Chicken and Rice, 95
Chicken Artichoke Bake, 71
Chicken Fried Rice, 116
Chicken Ham Casserole, 77
Chicken Wild Rice Soup, 126
Creole Shrimp & Rice, 64
Fiesta Fry Pan Dinner, 87
Herbed Chicken with Wild Rice, 100
Italian Chicken and Rice, 84
Lamb Ratatouille, 72
Lemon Garlic Shrimp, 93
Spanish Sausage Supper, 85
Special Wild Rice Salad, 56
Spicy Jambalaya, 119
Vegetable Rice Medley, 42
Vegetable Rice Salad, 45
Vegetable Wild Rice, 39
Veggie Rice Bowl, 47
Wild Rice Mushroom Chicken, 90
Zippy Spanish Rice Soup, 128

SALAD DRESSING MIX

Balsamic Vegetable Salad, 46
Cheesy Chicken Subs, 78
Chicken with Mushroom Gravy, 120

Club Roll-Ups, 104
Creamy Italian Noodles, 56
Crispy Cajun Potato Wedges, 58
Crumb-Coated Cod, 88
Cucumber Sandwiches, 17
Glazed Carrots, 46
Hash Brown Bake, 50
Hearty Taco Chili, 125
Herbed Tossed Salad, 54
Honey Mustard Chicken, 108
Hot Hoagies, 102
Italian Orange Roughy, 98
Italian Seasoned Bread, 141
Open-Faced Tuna Burgers, 84
Oregano Chicken, 115
Out to Sea Pasta Shell Salad, 52
Pull-Apart Bacon Bread, 35
Ranch Pretzels, 8
Simple Taco Soup, 135
Slow Cooker Mashed Potatoes, 48
Vegetable Rice Salad, 45

SALADS (Also see Gelatin; Slaw Mix)

Balsamic Vegetable Salad, 46
Ham Macaroni Salad, 90
Herbed Tossed Salad, 54
Out to Sea Pasta Shell Salad, 52
Shrimp Taco Salad, 115
Special Wild Rice Salad, 56
Vegetable Rice Salad, 45

SANDWICHES

Cheesy Chicken Subs, 78
Club Roll-Ups, 104
Corn Bread Sloppy Joes, 120
Cucumber Sandwiches, 17
Hot Hoagies, 102
Italian Beef Sandwiches, 60
Lasagna in a Bun, 94
Open-Faced Tuna Burgers, 84
Slow Cooker Sloppy Joes, 72
Tex-Mex Pitas, 99

SAUCE MIX

Cavatini Pasta, 82
Chicken-Pesto Pan Pizza, 110
Eggs Benedict Cups, 21
Eggs Benedict with Jalapeno Hollandaise, 27
Lasagna Pizza, 7
Puffed Pizza Casserole, 88
Salmon Pasta Primavera, 96

ALPHABETICAL INDEX

Refer to this index for a complete alphabetical listing of all the recipes in this book.